G000162573

THE GRIZZLY IN THE DRIVEWAY

THE GRIZZLY IN
THE DRIVEWAY

THE RETURN OF BEARS TO
A CROWDED AMERICAN WEST

Robert Chaney

UNIVERSITY OF WASHINGTON PRESS

Seattle

The Grizzly in the Driveway is published with the assistance of a grant from the Ruth Kirk Book Fund, which supports publications that inform the general public on the history, natural history, archaeology, and Native cultures of the Pacific Northwest.

Design by Katrina Noble
Composed in Adobe Caslon Pro, typeface designed by Carol Twombly
Frontispiece: Courtesy Montana Fish, Wildlife and Parks Department

24 23 22 21 20   5 4 3 2 1

Printed and bound in the United States of America

UNIVERSITY OF WASHINGTON PRESS
uwapress.uw.edu

LIBRARY OF CONGRESS CATALOGING-IN-PUBLICATION DATA

Names: Chaney, Robert (Environment reporter), author.
Title: The grizzly in the driveway : the return of bears to a crowded American west / Robert Chaney.
Description: 1st. | Seattle : University of Washington Press, [2020] | Includes bibliographical references and index.
Identifiers: LCCN 2020013482 (print) | LCCN 2020013483 (ebook) | ISBN 9780295747934 (hardcover) | ISBN 9780295747941 (ebook)
Subjects: LCSH: Grizzly bear—Conservation—West (U.S.) | Endangered species—Conservation—West (U.S.) | Wildlife conservation—West (U.S.)
Classification: LCC QL737.C27 C444 2020 (print) | LCC QL737.C27 (ebook) | DDC 599.7840978—dc23
LC record available at https://lccn.loc.gov/2020013482
LC ebook record available at https://lccn.loc.gov/2020013483

To Magda, who does not like grizzly bears,
and to Ania, who read every word

CONTENTS

PREFACE

Fear the Bear

Two kinds of grizzly bears roam the world.

One came with creation, a creature scientifically designated as *Ursus arctos*. It is one of the most dominant predator mammals on the planet, in the class with lions and tigers and orcas. It grows twice as big as the more timid and widespread black bear (*Ursus americanus*). While that larger species is commonly called the brown bear across its Northern Hemisphere habitat in North America, Europe, and Asia, the grizzly bear denotes a particular population of what is known as *Ursus arctos horribilis* living in Montana, Idaho, Wyoming, Washington, and Alaska, along with British Columbia, Alberta, and the Northwest Territories of Canada. It can live for thirty years and weigh up to a thousand pounds; it raises and teaches its cubs for multiple years and possesses a physical strength unmatched by any other animal currently native to this continent.

The second grizzly bear is a creation of human imagination. It lives in dreams and nightmares and legends. It also inhabits law books and policy manuals: an impressionistic collection of behaviors and demographics and recovery criteria defining a living organism for the purposes of human management. Both grizzly bears, the real and the imagined, form the focus of this book.

I have spent most of my thirty years in journalism covering the Rocky Mountain West. I am not a scientist by training, but I'm just a phone call and a cup of coffee away from a trove of researchers and policy advocates who've spent their careers working on grizzly bears. It's a remarkably small group. And their fascination with grizzlies is infectious.

One thing I've learned as a reporter is humans follow stories better than they follow statistics. So to frame my place in this story, let's start with the fact that my name is on the map of Glacier National Park.

To be honest, I have no known relation to L. W. Chaney, the Carleton College geology professor memorialized by Chaney Glacier. But growing up near and eventually working in Glacier Park, and having a personal landmark, a namesake icon to boot, is about as romantic a connection as one can get with a place.

To see *my* Chaney Glacier, you have to spend a lot of time in the presence of grizzly bears. And you do so in a landscape at once ancient beyond imagination and yet changing before your eyes.

Glacier National Park was named for the Pleistocene ice fields that carved the massive lake basins and melted away, not the elusive spots of white that currently decorate the surrounding peaks. Those remaining pocket glaciers will disappear too, within the lifetime of my children. Between the first time I trekked to Chaney Glacier as a college student in 1984 and a third time as newspaper reporter in 2007, the park's glacial inventory shrank from about fifty to about twenty-five. In the same geological instant, Glacier's population of grizzly bears grew from about two hundred to almost five hundred.

I picked my route to Chaney Glacier following the advice of J. Gordon Edwards, who wrote his first edition of *A Climber's Guide to Glacier National Park* in 1966. In it he described Chaney Notch as a clever shortcut from Fifty Mountain campsite over the Garden Wall and into the Belly River drainage, saving miles of roundabout over Stony Indian Pass. All you had to do, Edwards wrote decades before the invention of handheld Global Positioning System satellite receivers, was step off the notch onto Chaney Glacier and glissade to the bottom.

Looking over the notch twenty-five years later, that first step took a two-hundred-foot plunge to the ice below. Historical photos of Chaney Glacier depict it filling its basin in 1911. Images from the same vantage points in 2005 show it lost more than three-quarters of its mass. Edwards's shortcut now works only for an angel, or those intent on becoming one.

A friend who loves the outdoors but can't overcome his fear of grizzly bears asked me how I can sleep in such spots. For me, it's a balance of risks. My chances of a gruesome death getting hit by a car when walking from my newspaper office across the street to my favorite pizzeria rank several orders of magnitude greater than ever getting eaten by a grizzly bear. And I want to see a glacier with my name on it far more than I want to eat a slice of pizza. It's an acceptable risk.

Yet social scientists and stock brokers know the human species doesn't do rational choice well. The last time I backpacked to Chaney Glacier, I took a midday nap about fifty yards from where another ranger had found the body of nineteen-year-old Julie Helgeson after a grizzly pulled her from her sleeping bag on the infamous "Night of the Grizzlies" in 1967. She was the first person killed by a grizzly in the park since it opened in 1910. The odds against that happening were estimated at fifteen million to one.

And the potential of such a grizzly killing happening twice in the same night fall under what mathematicians refer to as a "black swan event." That August 13 was a black swan night. A second bear killed and ate a second backpacker, nineteen-year-old Michele Koons, just eight air-miles away from where Helgeson was attacked.

I share a sort-of connection with Koons and Helgeson: We all spent summers working in Glacier National Park. Helgeson was employed at the East Glacier Lodge, Koons had a job at McDonald Lake Lodge; and I spent two formative seasons as captain of the DeSmet tour boat on Lake McDonald. My boss, a local high school science teacher named Bill Schustrom, remembered meeting the rangers on the chaotic morning of August 14, and the confusion of sorting out how two different grizzly bears had killed two hotel workers in two campgrounds on the same night. A master storyteller himself, Schustrom inspired me to soak up and share the wonders of the place we both loved.

Bill Schustrom also taught and coached Ryan Zinke, who grew up to become secretary of the interior and preside over the 2017 attempt to remove the grizzly bear from Endangered Species Act protection. That brings up another reason why I'm writing this book. My life as a resident and journalist in Montana overlaps most of the key players in grizzly recovery. From listening to friends read the first edition of Jack Olsen's *Night of the Grizzlies* around a Halloween campfire to interviewing the tight-knit community of scientists and policy makers overseeing grizzly recovery for the *Missoulian* newspaper, the great bear and its impact on people has been an enduring fascination for me.

Early in my career, I got to spend a lot of time with an Episcopalian priest who'd honed his storytelling skill in the Oxford offices of J. R. R. Tolkien and C. S. Lewis. On a tour of Montana's first capitol city, now the ghost town of Bannack, the Reverend Donald Guthrie told me that when he was ordained in Scotland, he signed his name in a church registry next to the name of every previous priest dating back to 1520. Observing that Bannack's gold-rush heyday started in 1862 and lasted less than a decade, Guthrie gently observed that Montanans like myself didn't have history; we had current events.

Studying history can give the illusion of the world as a static place. We look back, at leisure, on events preserved between the covers of books. But the history of grizzly bear preservation, and the history of human relations with the environment outside our society, is evolving as we study it. And like parents on their first night home with a newborn, we're realizing that our old lives will never usefully inform the problems we confront now.

Historians refer to the last half of the twentieth century as "The Information Age." As the pace of change exponentially increased, they started calling the early twenty-first century "The Age of Acceleration." In kindergarten, I watched the entire focused will of American society allow Neil Armstrong take one small step for a man and a giant leap for mankind. As this book goes to press, I've got a gizmo in my pocket with more computing power than all of NASA needed to get Armstrong to the moon. It also maps every step I take, like the radio collars pioneered on grizzly bears. The one thing that smartphone can't tell me is if human powers of decision-making and cooperation have matured at the same pace. Nor has it slowed the avalanche of choices demanding to be made.

During the same period, we've packed an additional three billion people onto the planet. Bill Schustrom's school district today has more students than there are grizzly bears in the entire Northern Continental Divide Ecosystem. All those people want a place to live and play.

One of the most frequently cited benefits of wilderness is its respite from all that technology. There you can hear the wind in the trees as it sounded at the dawn of creation and see the stars in their milky majesty. Spend enough time and your atrophied sense of smell may alert you to the approach of a grizzly bear. Only a handful of animals have the capability of transforming life just by their presence. I count the grizzly on one of those fingers.

Few people have encountered a grizzly bear outside the safety of a zoo enclosure or a car window. But you know every one of your friends and acquaintances who has done so, because at some point, they've bragged about it to you.

This is what I mean about meetings with grizzly bears being transformative. It's not just seeing a priest but the Pope: not just a painting but the Mona Lisa. Your heroism, cowardice, dumb luck, or obliviousness in that moment becomes a defining mark on your timeline.

And if you want to be scared of something, why not a grizzly bear? We may watch them on YouTube videos, but we still see them by the light of cave campfires, fearing or revering the monster outside in the dark. How do you put a price on either the terror or the reverence a grizzly bear inspires?

The word *fear* has two meanings. The most common is "an unpleasant often strong emotion caused by anticipation or awareness of danger." The second, known to religious thinkers, is "profound reverence and awe." As in "I fear God."

I was once obstinate enough to debate this definition with the Reverend Guthrie. Being commanded in the Episcopalian Book of Common Prayer "to love and fear the Lord" sounded like an abusive relationship, I supposed. Rather than excommunicate me, or even make me polish the silver, Guthrie sent me to the dictionary for further confounding. Part of the etymology of *fear* comes from the Latin *periculum*: to attempt or risk.

The illustration for all those terms could be the grizzly bear.

Civilization celebrates human accomplishment. Nature absorbs it. Mountains and rivers and grizzly bears don't care about your credit score or your zip code. When they beat you, there is no complaint form to file, no bouncer at the door to bribe, no judge to persuade. When you win, you feel alive.

I fear the bear.

THE GRIZZLY IN THE DRIVEWAY

1

Entering Grizzly Country

WHEN CHUCK JONKEL DIED ON APRIL 12, 2016, FEW PEOPLE REAL-
ized the white-bearded old guy selling hand-woven flower leis at the
farmer's market had revolutionized the world of grizzly bears.

Jonkel wasn't the first biologist to make a career studying *Ursus arctos
horribilis*. But he found his passion just at the time when North America's
most fearsome native predator was about to vanish from the Lower 48
United States. He taught, researched, and sometimes fought with almost
every grizzly bear expert now working in the Pacific Northwest, where
federal government designated grizzly bears a threatened species under
the Endangered Species Act in 1975. Along the way, he founded an International Wildlife Film Festival that demolished the "nature-faker" style
of outdoor documentary movies in favor of presentations with scientific
rigor and ethical backbone. He even helped organize the farmer's market
where he sold his flower necklaces.

"Chuck knew as much or more about the natural history of bears in
general than probably anybody in the world at that time," recalled Dan
Pletscher, who went on to lead the University of Montana wildlife biology
department that Jonkel did so much to popularize. "And he acted in a lot

of ways like a grizzly bear. He knew what plants were edible. He would scratch his back on a tree like a bear when talking to a class in the field. He was a consummate naturalist."

When Jonkel started his grizzly research in 1969, finding one meant spending long summers along the Canadian border in some of the most remote bits of the Lower 48 states. As this book was going to press, those grizzly bears have become much more visible to the humans who have come to dominate that habitat in a very different way than the prehistoric apex predator.

Jonkel also spent years giving workshops for the bear-fascinated public. I date much of my interest in grizzly bears to a weekend class he taught on the edge of Glacier National Park.

Hearing about the man for years didn't lessen the oddity of meeting him. He wore a blue cotton shirt and jeans that looked like they'd been laundered alongside a creek with rocks. A tuft of chest hair poked out of the collar, as white as the unruly mass of his head and beard. He didn't look scary, but definitely bear-like. His high, wispy voice knocked all that grizzly aura askew. It missed the *Mutual of Omaha Wild Kingdom* gravitas like an opera singer on helium. It wasn't actually a helium quack—just an incongruously breathy tenor emanating from a basso reputation.

Because Chuck Jonkel was *the guy* about grizzly bears. And in class that morning, he laid claim to his experience with a grizzly bear skull. Grizzly people have all the best show-and-tell stuff. They bring the huge hides and the claws and the plaster-cast paw prints bigger than your head and the skulls with the teeth. Then they get to explain how those flying cheekbones scaffold the muscles that allow a grizzly to snap a cow's neck. And then Chuck pointed out the little hole in the eye socket.

This skull belonged to a grizzly Jonkel had accidentally caught in a black-bear trap. The leg-hold trap was attached to a chain with a grappling hook, and the bear ran until it snagged on a tree it couldn't pull over. Jonkel and a fellow biologist caught up with it, and he moved in to subdue it with a tranquilizer dart.

Before he could fire, the grizzly broke free of the drag and charged. The backup man with the shotgun fell over. Jonkel was standing in front, packing a .22-caliber Colt Woodsman pistol in addition to the dart gun. This is a great handgun, highly prized at gun shows for holding collectible value. It's perfect for plinking beer cans and the occasional grouse.

Jonkel pulled his .22 and shot the grizzly bear in the head. The bullet hit the bear between the eyes and bounced right off, barely breaking the skin. It did, however, halt the bear's charge—for about a second.

For whatever reason, Jonkel didn't get out of the way to give his partner a clear field with the shotgun. The grizzly gathered its wits and lunged again. Jonkel shot it again in the head. Same result.

A Colt Woodsman .22 pistol has a magazine with ten rounds. Jonkel said he was pretty sure he shot all ten. One bullet hit the grizzly in the eye, pierced the much thinner occipital lobe bone and entered the brain. The forehead bone showed only light scratching from the other impacts.

Jonkel delivered this lesson with neither a mountain man's tall-tale twinkle nor a braggart's bravado. Rather, it was a matter-of-fact lesson in grizzly behavior and occupational safety, albeit of extreme nature. Not that it mattered. Every student in the room was baptized as a grizzly bear disciple from the moment they held that skull and looked at the tiny hole in the eye socket, barely bigger than a BB.

I'm willing to wager my journalistic credibility on this version of the Jonkel .22 story, allowing for memory in lieu of notes. I've double-checked the details with Jonkel's son, Jamie Jonkel. But the story also has a viral life of its own. One version turned up on a sportsman's internet chat room discussing the "best pistol to pack in bear country." The advice rocked back and forth on .357 Magnum revolvers for reliability and .45 automatics for the hail of lead. Until some commenter chimed in about that time Chuck Jonkel killed a bear with a .22. Only in this version of the story, Jonkel was teaching a class on polar bears.

I can't tell a polar bear skull from a grizzly bear skull with any professional acumen. But I remember that morning, just as I remember the taste of wild onion that Jonkel shared fresh-plucked from the meadow alongside the Going-to-the-Sun Road, and the amazement of crawling into paths as wide and hard-packed as the Highline Trail tunneled through otherwise impenetrable alder thickets, blazed by generations of grizzlies.

Does knowing a story like this make me a grizzly bear expert? Ever since humans realized they competed with other predators for survival, they've argued over how to answer that question. We've worshiped those animals as gods, attacked them as enemies, and adopted them as servants. In the span of Chuck Jonkel's professional career, Americans have gone from nearly eradicating grizzly bears from their last redoubts in the mountains of Montana, Idaho, Washington, and Wyoming to nearly restoring them as a permanent part of the landscape. How will we know if we succeeded? That depends on who we acknowledge as a grizzly bear expert and what standards we agree to use. And by "we" I mean the people of the United States who claim legal ownership and ethical responsibility for this species of animal.

Some people justify their grizzly expertise by the amount of time they've spent in grizzly country, observing the bears and their world. Others experience the grizzly indirectly through radio signals and test-tubes of genetic material, or stacks of statistics and incident reports. Still others—the vast majority of Americans—know what they know about bears through virtual reality. Whether they recall a cartoon Yogi Bear or a National Geographic documentary, a social media meme or an anecdote printed on the pages of a paper book; those stories become the evidence we present as we debate the fate of grizzly bears. Those stories serve as doorstops, holding mental doors open or blocking them closed.

◄ ◄ ◄ · ► ► ►

In the summer of 2019, two separate grizzly bears showed up in the driveways of two communities on either side of the Continental Divide in Montana. The one near Browning, on the east side of the Rocky Mountains, prompted so much fear and anger from local ranchers that they demanded, and got, a visit from the United States Secretary of the Interior to plead their case for the prompt removal of dangerous predators from their midst. The grizzly, known as Marsha, had never been known to attack livestock or pilfer human food, but was still labeled a lethal threat. One rancher claimed the sound of her baby's crying "brought in a grizzly ten feet from my house."

Eighty air miles to the west in Condon, Montana, the second driveway-prowling grizzly bear earned so much local affection that residents named her Windfall. They shot video of the sow and her cubs in their yards and shared the images by cell phone. They also did *not* report her increasingly brazen raids on chicken coops, unsecured garbage, and pet food bowls to the state bear managers. When the grizzly finally became so habituated to human food sources that biologists had to kill her and relocate her cubs for public safety, twenty-nine people cosigned a letter to the editor apologizing "because this gracious and now grieving community had failed her."

Both of these grizzly bears belong to a population that's been under federal protection since 1975. Both possess a sense of smell capable of pinpointing food from miles away, and a memory to catalog those food sources across hundreds of square miles with more intimacy than most people know their own refrigerators. Both have five-inch-long claws and massive jaws that can bite through a cow's neck. Both have distinctive humps of muscle between their shoulders providing enough strength to lift that cow off the ground, or to outsprint a galloping horse, or to dig up meadows of wild onions more effectively than a motorized garden tiller. They share similar biological and legal facts of size, behavior, and management status.

Those same grizzly bears also evoke primeval memories. Just knowing such creatures exist keeps many people from feeling safe visiting public lands like Glacier National Park. Yet the presence of grizzlies draws many other people to the same landscape in hopes of experiencing some dream of authentic Nature.

And that crystallizes the great conundrum of life with grizzly bears. We three hundred and thirty million Americans hold total power over the fate of about two thousand animals that, in order to endure, must have the right to eat us alive.

I frame that in deliberately stark terms because the grizzly bear presents a unique and wicked problem. For Americans, no other creature sinks such deep barbs into our history, our culture, our image of ourselves as a dominant species and our vision of ourselves as good stewards of the planet.

Recovering the grizzly bear fits the classic definition of a "wicked problem"—a social or cultural challenge that is difficult or impossible to solve due to incomplete or contradictory knowledge, the number of people and opinions involved, the large economic burden, and the interconnected nature of the problem with other problems. The *Harvard Business Review* declares "wicked problems can't be solved, but they can be tamed." That verb choice when connected to grizzly bears makes wildlife biologists and natural philosophers snigger.

By 2020, many Americans believed the federal government had brought *Ursus arctos horribilis* to recovery and should remove it from Endangered Species Act protection. But does recovering grizzly bears "save" an endangered species or revive a romantic notion of what we think it means to be "natural"? More importantly, how do grizzly bears of Montana, Idaho, and Wyoming stack up against the grizzlies of our imagination?

In talking to hundreds of people about this "charismatic megafauna" over the past forty years, I've been struck by the radically different stories they use to frame their beliefs about the grizzly. Grizzly bears inspire fear in some, reverence in others, and fascination in all. I've never met anyone who, if they know that grizzly bears exist, doesn't also know a lot more about them. Imagine a bronze bear statue on Wall Street, or a grizzly wearing a tutu in a circus. You know what the animal signifies and when it's out of place. Financially, it symbolizes destructive power. Riding a bicycle under the Big Top, it testifies to the human ringmaster's taming of the wild. Can you say the same for a marmot? It has long brownish-silver fur and claws, lives in the mountains, hibernates and can look comically cute in the right circumstances. But it's not a grizzly bear. Emblazon a marmot on the side of a box of protein pancakes and nobody presumes it stands for strength.

Like a kind of ecological symphony, the saga of the grizzly bear has gone through movements that build to loud crescendos and then halt or fade, only to resume with a new tempo or theme. Americans spent the first century of their national existence deliberately removing the grizzly bear from landscapes they had better use for. Few felt they were doing wrong when they shot, trapped, and poisoned 99 percent of the grizzly bears south of Canada. They considered it a predatory pest, a quarter-ton mosquito that sucked the lifeblood out of their agricultural revolution. Period accounts refer to the grizzly as a disreputable scavenger, good for nothing but a test of manhood and a rug on the cabin floor.

Before the War of 1812, North American grizzlies dominated the food pyramid from the one hundredth meridian west of North Dakota to the California coast and deep into Mexico. By World War I, only the mountain ranges surrounding Glacier and Yellowstone National Parks sheltered the last breeding populations in the Lower 48 states.

Starting in the 1960s, Americans as a nation concluded they were wrecking the planet and directed the combined force of their government to fix things. They passed laws to clean the air and water, created an agency to protect the environment, and set about rescuing the plants and animals they'd nearly extirpated—a word biologists use to mean "remove completely or destroy."

The Wilderness Act of 1964 imposed strict barriers to protect "opportunities for solitude" in America's last wild country. But its writers never imagined deep-powder snowmobiles, ultralight pack rafts, drone cameras, and the human ambition to challenge the landscape with those tools in the twenty-first century. Nor did they acknowledge the extensive human influence predating European notions of wilderness as an Edenic place without people. The result is a law commanding preservation of places never well understood for relatively undefined purposes.

The Endangered Species Act of 1973 declared Americans have the power, and responsibility, to heal the harm they had done to other plants and animals. The law presumes we can essentially admit these victims of our actions into a sort of ecological hospital, restore them to health, and return them to their natural environment. Grizzly bears fell under the law's protection in 1975.

Some wild animals, like the bald eagle, needed rescuing from ignorance. Americans didn't account for the fact their effort to kill insect pests through widespread use of DDT would have collateral damage—the pesticide weakened egg shells and nearly wiped out *Haliaeetus leucocephalus*, their national symbol.

Those same Americans can't claim any such "Oops" factor with *Ursus arctos horribilis*, the grizzly bear. In the contiguous United States, the National Park Service led one of the bloodiest persecutions of grizzlies on record just three years before passage of the Endangered Species Act of 1973. At the time, federal biologists estimated about six hundred grizzly bears still survived in pockets of Montana, Wyoming, and Idaho, out of the presumed fifty thousand "great white bears" Lewis and Clark fought their way past in 1805. Both numbers were guesses—no one had systematically recorded the continent's grizzly population before we tried to either eliminate or recover them.

Grizzly populations in those three states had quadrupled since they received federal protection in 1975. By 2020, the Greater Yellowstone Ecosystem alone was habitat to at least seven hundred grizzlies. Another thousand lived in the Northern Continental Divide Ecosystem extending north from my home in Missoula, Montana, to Glacier National Park. Tens of thousands more *Ursus arctos* bears inhabit northwestern Canada and Alaska, as well as other landscapes around the planet. Defining *what* we can do for *which* bears has bedeviled wildlife management debates since we noticed some populations were more popular or fragile than others.

As the national legislative effort to undo environmental damage got underway, suspicions grew that the opportunity had been missed. Industries and communities dependent on old, polluting ways resisted change, even as environmentalists started writing about the end of nature (Bill McKibben made that the title of his 1989 book, in all capital letters). The environmentalist community itself split, as a powerful movement of social justice for people sickened and injured by ecological damage got separated from a parallel vigorous effort to preserve the nation's remaining wild landscapes—places hard for people to visit, especially when they were burdened by the economic affliction of living next to a toxic wasteland.

Meanwhile, the story of our relationship with grizzly bears takes place as the human species progressed into the single most disruptive half-century in its existence.

When the grizzly was placed on the Endangered Species List, the Cray 1 Supercomputer set world records with an internal memory of eight megabytes. In 2019, *National Geographic* reported each person generates about 1.7 megabytes of data per second. That stacks up to 2.5 quintillion bytes of data a day in Facebook posts, emails, and satellite tracking locations of radio-collared grizzly bears. Human standards of performance have never moved that fast in a single lifetime in any other era of our history.

A grizzly bear known as Kobuk the Destroyer attempts to break into a prototype resistant trash can at the Grizzly Discovery Center in West Yellowstone. The Interagency Grizzly Bear Committee requires container manufacturers to test their products with the captive grizzlies to earn a "bear resistant" certification. Photograph by Michael Gallacher. Courtesy *Missoulian* newspaper.

Chuck Jonkel was renowned for his ability to perform differential calculus on population trends with a pencil and paper in the 1980s. Today, his son, equally influential Montana bear management specialist Jamie Jonkel, tracks grizzlies by satellite through his smartphone.

Here I must warn you that the saga of grizzly bear recovery spends much more time in committee sessions, courtrooms, and computer labs than it does around actual grizzly bears. The fact is there are 165,000 Americans for every grizzly bear in the contiguous US, and the debate over who gets to decide what to do with them forms the heart of this book.

Much of that beats through the Interagency Grizzly Bear Committee, or IGBC, which as its name declares is a committee of committees. It brings together federal wildlife and land managers, state versions of the same, Indian tribal governments, Canadian provincial representatives, county commissioners, nongovernmental organizations, and scientists. They all meet twice a year, observed by an audience full of critical and litigious grizzly bear lovers and grizzly bear haters. The grizzlies themselves take little notice or regard of the proceedings. And that's the crux of the IGBC's task: Creating rules to manage an organism that doesn't follow rules.

Chris Servheen spent his entire career building those rules. He was also a student of Jonkel's, although the two eventually grew bitterly apart. Both were scientists advising politicians while appealing to the general public. Starting in 1981, Servheen coordinated grizzly bear recovery for the US Fish and Wildlife Service (FWS).

"I thought I would preside over the demise of the bears," Servheen told me. "I was given an impossible task. Grizzlies are big, dangerous animals that require a lot of space and solitude. They compete with humans for prey. They attack livestock. They reproduce very slowly. We don't really want them. There were all these conflicting feelings. And none of them were positive. I figured I'm going to be lucky to save maybe Yellowstone as a captive population."

Then in 1982, National Park Service deputy director Roland Wauer released a memo describing dire predictions for Yellowstone's grizzly population.

"He wrote the bears will be gone," Servheen said. "The assumption was we would lose the Yellowstone bears in the near future. That was a real sobering thought. And nobody knew anything about the other populations. That memo was the instigator of the Interagency Grizzly Bear Committee."

Servheen was summoned to Washington. He remembered a FWS assistant secretary turning to him and demanding "What the hell do you want?" Servheen essentially asked for a magic wand.

Nobody wanted to work together on the recovery plan. The Forest Service dealt with national forests, not wildlife. And it reported to the secretary of agriculture. The National Park Service didn't want to deal with anything outside park boundaries. It and FWS reported to the secretary of the interior. State wildlife agencies didn't like the feds telling them how to manage wildlife, and they reported to state governors.

"The FWS assistant secretary got together with the assistant secretary of agriculture, and they signed an agreement to work together on grizzly recovery," Servheen said. "It was just three pages long—really simple. It said to form a committee, implement the plan and create the IGBC. That meant the Forest Service, National Park Service, FWS, and the states. The feds all signed it, and then sent it to the governors of Montana, Idaho, Washington, and Wyoming. And the governors all signed it. It wasn't sent to the state fish-and-game directors."

That may have been the magic tweak. With the governors in line, the state wildlife managers had to follow. And nobody wanted to see the grizzly bear disappear on their watch.

"That Wauer memo laid out the dire straits," Servheen said. "There were sheep grazing everywhere, logging, garbage dumps, road-building. Yellowstone had cleaned up their dumps, but there still were big ones just across the border in Gardiner and Cooke City and West Yellowstone."

For the next thirty-five years, Servheen drove the research and policy efforts of the IGBC like a team of willful draft horses harnessed to a wagon full of grizzly bears. He led it through the administrations of Ronald Reagan, George H. W. Bush, Bill Clinton, George W. Bush, and Barack Obama. The complexity of that challenge went on display between that first recovery plan in 1986 and its 1993 revision. 1988 saw wildfires that blackened nearly half of Yellowstone National Park's two million acres as well as a remarkable fire that burned one hundred and eighty thousand acres of the Bob Marshall Wilderness Complex in sixteen hours. In 1989, Yellowstone biologists reported nearly a quarter of the whitebark pine trees in the park were dying from beetle infestations. In 1990, Yellowstone Lake's native cutthroat trout population started crashing due to predation by illegally introduced lake trout. Both fish and tree were considered crucial food sources for grizzlies.

"When you become coordinator like that, it's not all running around catching bears all the time," Servheen said. "There are a lot of people involved in grizzly recovery. You've got to get everyone to work together toward that common goal. It's sanitation and secure habitat and motorized route density, and outreach and education, and what to do with nuisance bears and limiting mortality, and getting good science so we have a good foundation to make decisions. That's all the things I do."

To save the wild grizzly bear, the IGBC proposed saving the places it lives: what the law calls critical habitat. The first grizzly recovery strategy in 1986 proposed three primary core areas, or ecosystems: the Greater Yellowstone Ecosystem around the intersection of Montana, Idaho, and Wyoming; the Northern Continental Divide Ecosystem containing Montana's northern Rocky Mountains and Glacier National Park; and the Cabinet-Yaak-Selkirk mountains of northern Montana and Idaho. The plan also contemplated a recovery zone in Colorado's San Juan Mountains. All four places had evidence of grizzly habitation, although the San Juans were in the process of losing their last known bears.

In 1991, the Interagency Grizzly Bear Committee revised its strategy to six places. Colorado fell off the list (although in a touch of bureaucratic inertia, from 1983 to 1998 the committee only met in Denver). Washington's North Cascades Ecosystem joined thanks to a tiny population of trans-border bears from Canada. The Selkirks of Washington and Idaho and Cabinet-Yaak region of Idaho and Montana got split into separate recovery areas. And the Bitterroot Ecosystem encompassing millions of wilderness acres along the Montana-Idaho border got included, despite having no remaining grizzlies. All six areas got both boundaries on a map and subcommittees of federal, state, local, academic, and affiliated stakeholders.

For readers not accustomed to the scale of the Rocky Mountain West, some comparisons may be in order. The Greater Yellowstone Ecosystem includes all of Yellowstone National Park and Grand Teton National Park, as well as surrounding chunks of Montana, Wyoming, and Idaho. That encloses about 9,200 square miles, a space roughly as big as the state of New Hampshire. The Northern Continental Divide Ecosystem spreads south from the Canadian border almost to Missoula, Montana, and includes both the Blackfeet and Flathead Indian reservations. It encompasses about 8,900 square miles—equivalent to the state of New Jersey. Together those two ecosystems host around 1,800 grizzly bears.

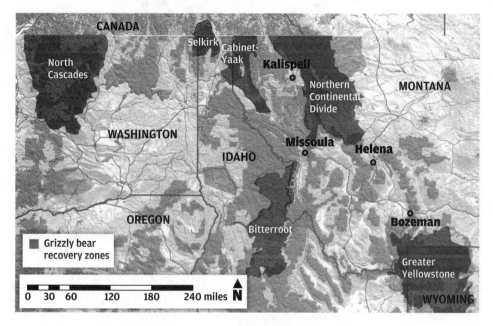

Interagency Grizzly Bear Committee grizzly recovery areas

The Selkirk, Cabinet-Yaak, and North Cascades ecosystems combined cover about fourteen thousand square miles, but struggle to preserve about one hundred and twenty-five grizzlies.

The Bitterroot Ecosystem has no resident bears in its official 5,800-square-mile recovery zone. However, surrounding wilderness areas and remote national forests bring the effective undeveloped country to about 25,000 square miles along the border of Idaho and Montana.

Inside 25,000 square miles, you can fit the whole state of West Virginia.

Greater Yellowstone's primary core area could contain the combined urban sprawl of the New York/Newark, Greater Los Angeles, Chicago, and Dallas metropolitan areas (which house about thirty-four million humans according to the 2010 census). I'm not sure which end of that comparison I find more mind boggling.

Yet in a half-century of monitoring, no wild grizzly has opted to emigrate from one core area to another, although a few have visited and biologists have translocated a few more by truck. Meanwhile, humans have built ever-higher fences to keep bears out of towns and ranches while at the same time demanding more access to the places designated for the grizzly.

Environmental historian Michael Dax chronicled an attempt to transplant a grizzly population into the Bitterroot Ecosystem in the 1990s. He saw the effort as less about the bear and more the heart of a struggle between what he called the Old West and the New West. The New West considered restoring grizzly bears, putting wildlife ahead of human needs, "a defining masculine and authentic experience." The Old West "believed that subduing and conquering nature was necessary to lay claim to masculinity and ward off modernity's corrupting influence." That time, the Old West won when Republican president George W. Bush's administration shelved a grizzly bear reintroduction project developed in the '90s during Democratic president Bill Clinton's administration. Claims of female experience or "femininity" were not considered.

⊰ ⊰ ⊰ · ⊱ ⊱ ⊱

In putting this book together, I started noticing a repeating pattern in the grizzly world. Little things drive big things. Compared to the balanced polarization of American presidential politics, the grizzly debate teeters like an upside-down pyramid suspended above its apex. Nine out of ten Americans do not hunt, yet the nation's public wildlife is managed by the 10 percent who do. Four-fifths of American citizens live in concentrated urban cityscapes far from the 1 percent of the contiguous United States considered occupied grizzly bear habitat. The tiny places crucial to grizzly survival tend to be dominated by an equally tiny number of wealthy individuals and institutions, whether cattle ranchers in linkage zones, or extractive industries seeking access to federal wilderness, or philanthropic organizations funding land trusts and animal-rights action. In 2016, the one hundred largest private landowning families in the United States held title to forty million acres—a landscape bigger than the state of Florida.

All of this feeds into a coming constitutional crisis in American public land management affecting far more than a handful of grizzlies in the

Northern Rocky Mountains. The Founders gave Congress an asymmetrical structure that has locked in rural power over mass population. No matter how many people live in New York, Los Angeles, and Chicago, their Supreme Court justices, the federal budget, and changes to the Endangered Species Act depend on the whims of senators from Montana, Idaho, and Wyoming, where the combined population barely exceeds that of Houston.

This isn't a Republican/Democratic political observation, despite the fact that in 2020 that split defined most of those asymmetries I just listed. It swings between that New West and Old West, between progressive and regressive instincts. Political values change with time. The structure of Congress requires constitutional amendment. Wyoming gave its female citizens the right to vote in 1869. It took fifty-one more years for the nation to ratify the 19th Amendment granting women's suffrage, four years after Montanans sent Jeannette Rankin to be the first female member of the House of Representatives. At the same time, miners in grizzly bear habitat were forming some of the nation's first labor unions to fight corporate dominance. By the end of the twentieth century, some of their children were leading the Sagebrush Rebellion rejecting federal oversight of private industry.

A grizzly bear follows a biological imperative to stay alive, and its evolutionary tactic is to physically overwhelm any opponent. Humans have developed a technological response against every threat on the planet. We also credit ourselves with a state of self-awareness that we doubt exists in lesser animals. Philosopher René Descartes, after declaring our cognitive existence in 1637, added that reason and knowledge enable us "to render ourselves the lords and possessors of nature." So we're the boss, and to paraphrase Harry Truman, the bear stops here.

Does nature get a voice or a vote? Many environmental philosophers take the precarious legal position that nature has rights beyond human value: The bear stops us.

But nature is scary. It's full of grizzly bears. And humans tend to kill whatever scares them.

When the northern spotted owl made the Endangered Species List in 1994, it got accused of killing an entire timber industry in Oregon and

California. But not by snatching loggers off the forest floor in its talons and feeding its young with their flesh. The owl biologically depended on specific places to survive; places covered in old-growth timber coveted by another species.

The grizzly bear also occupies places sought for timber, mining, and agriculture. Chuck Jonkel's initial work on the species was titled the Border Grizzly Project, and its findings threatened the timber industry in northwest Montana so greatly the US Forest Service worked actively to shut it down five years into the project's ten-year run. And unlike the spotted owl, grizzly bears do occasionally snatch humans off the forest floor and eat them. More commonly in these rare attacks they maul people, whacking them upside the head so hard their scalps dangle off the other side. That's scary.

The grizzly bear needs space: Hundreds of square miles per animal. It needs food: Forty thousand calories a day. It needs tolerance, for the days it decides to take what we think rightfully belongs to us. It needs to be left alone. So what if all those presumptions of protecting wilderness and endangered species prove unfounded? What if there's no sufficient natural environment to return to, and all we're doing is moving the patient from the hospital to a hospice ward? Are we prepared, or interested, in managing our planet like a global zoo? If so, do we want to live inside that zoo with a creature as chaotic and threatening as the grizzly bear?

The original wording of the Endangered Species Act reads "various species of fish, wildlife and plants in the United States have been rendered extinct as a consequence of economic growth and development untampered by adequate concern and conservation (and) the United States has pledged itself as a sovereign state in the international community to conserve to the extent practical the various species of fish or wildlife or plants facing extinction." Yet when I walk into the conference rooms where grizzly bear management gets legislated, the participants are so far beyond settled agreement on a shared language it's no wonder resolution seems reduced to a simple struggle over who has the most ability to command the power of the state. Can the Congressional and social will embodied by the ESA overcome those residents who claim the needs of undomesticated wildlife come second to their right to pursue happiness on private property through economic growth and development?

That matters, because grizzly bear management depends as much on concepts of social tolerance—what people will put up with—as it does on biological research or legal principle. And those social tolerances grow in importance as our technological prowess trespasses across virtually every other limit before us. In my lifetime, we've gone from identifying grizzly bears by colored ear tags to charting their entire family trees through DNA analysis. Are we socially tolerant of using those same innovations to investigate our own personal privacy? In the twenty-first century some governments are using the same DNA tracking methods to find and imprison millions of people and enforce political loyalty. When we add the scientific breakthroughs of the past generation into the mix, our ethics of right and wrong, good and bad, haven't kept up with our capabilities. I think that matters both in how we rule society and how we try to rule the world.

◄ ◄ ◄ · ► ► ►

Writer Wallace Stegner observed that "lawlessness, like wilderness, is attractive, and we conceive the last remaining home of both to be in the West." Grizzly bears, both lawless and wild, also claim that home. They're more than willing to fight humans for it. The people who displaced them stand equally willing.

The vast majority of their fellow citizens live in cities, and have much more welcoming opinions about the grizzly's future. This typifies the hard choices Americans face as they wrestle with their responsibility to guide a rapidly changing world. Will they relinquish some of their control desires and let a competitor species have its way, or will they rely on their tendency to impose a technological "fix" that created many of their current problems? As human-triggered climate disruption erodes notions of a "normal" world, how might their relationship with the "natural" world evolve? And do they still want to live up to the environmental ideals set into law a generation ago? This book ponders all three of these questions through the prism of grizzly bear recovery in the United States, and how that challenges some of our most basic beliefs of who we are as Americans, as masters of the Earth and even as a species. The coming chapters will explore many of the challenges that living with grizzly bears present. I will start by examining some of the ways Americans think about grizzlies, by exploring modern technological culture, the gruesome historical record of grizzly management, and some contrasting Indigenous and ethical perspectives. Next, I'll look at how science and society have shaped the way humans live with grizzly bears and the environment they depend on. Finally I'll consider some of the tools and options available to shape what's to come. How we choose to resolve those challenges may have irrevocable effect on the bear's world. Some challenges will resolve whether we choose a course of action or not as the world grows more crowded. Our decision space shrinks daily.

In that way, the grizzly bear becomes the ideal test of how each of us relates to the world around us. If we want to preserve the grizzly, we must preserve what it needs to survive. If we want wild bears, we must preserve wild country. If we want something less than that, either more controllable grizzlies or more control over their habitat, we must take responsibility for those choices.

Chuck Jonkel died in 2016, aged 85. Servheen retired as FWS grizzly bear recovery coordinator in that same year. He told me he wanted to spend more time with real bears.

Also in 2016, the US Fish and Wildlife Service and its daughter agencies in Montana, Wyoming, and Idaho all declared the grizzly legally and biologically recovered—no longer needing federal protection. Both the Obama and Trump administrations pleaded in court for the delisting to prove the Endangered Species Act can successfully recover something. They also proposed resumption of grizzly hunting seasons to reassure those living in grizzly country they could control a menace to their livelihoods. An Endangered Species Act victory was at hand, like the restoration of the bald eagle.

Then it didn't happen. As this book reached first-draft stage in 2018, a federal judge a mile from my house in Missoula ruled that grizzly bears weren't ready to come off the Endangered Species List. Days after that ruling, a grizzly bear killed a Wyoming hunter the day before Wyoming's first grizzly hunting season in forty years was to start.

Those legal and physical actions will have much influence on the future of the grizzly bear in the continental United States. But perhaps not so much as the visceral, emotional reactions people have to the idea of grizzly bears. Because the grizzlies of our imagination are far more powerful and prevalent than the real thing.

2

Ursus horribilis Facebookii

ONE AUGUST THURSDAY IN 2015, A GRIZZLY BEAR KILLED A MAN named Lance Crosby a few miles from the Lake Hotel in Yellowstone National Park. Yellowstone bear manager Kerry Gunther learned of the incident at 9:01 a.m. Friday. A search team saw an adult bear scramble away from the scene where they found Crosby's partially consumed remains. His body had been covered with dirt and debris, the way a grizzly caches a kill for later consumption.

The rangers set two culvert traps thirty feet from the incident scene. As counterintuitive as they are effective, culvert traps are big steel tubes with sliding gates mounted on a trailer. Bears apparently like the idea of exploring bait in a confined, tunnel-like space, even if it's obviously an uncamouflaged, metal anomaly. A two-hundred-sixty-pound grizzly sow trapped herself inside one shortly after midnight.

The bear's teeth shape and size matched the bite marks on Crosby's body. An air-freighted sample of the suspect bear's DNA matched the traces found on his skin. Gunther approved killing the captured sow on Saturday. He sent out a press release detailing the circumstances.

Two years previously, another Yellowstone grizzly had killed another hiker and the national news media barely noticed. This time however, somebody in the social media world jumped into the investigation, suggesting that the suspect bear had a name: Blaze, one of the best-known grizzlies in the Greater Yellowstone Ecosystem.

"Very quickly, my email and voicemail overloaded," Gunther recalled. "We got letters from all over the world. We got hate mail. Death threats. One person threatened my children. We had law enforcement patrolling our houses."

The incident took on a dual nature, as the Yellowstone Park officials competed with a digital community of grizzly bear fans, all trying to tell what had happened and what it meant. Gunther and his colleagues moved through a standardized process of investigation, collecting evidence from the scene and trying to recreate the sequence of events. Almost simultaneously the much larger digital community searched for clues in the cloud of social media flotsam. Today, the future of grizzly bears in North America now depends on how these two worlds, the animals on the ground and the people in cyberspace, come to some sort of shared reality.

The named bear, Blaze, was a photographer-tolerant grizzly with a namesake patch of white fur under her chin. She'd often been seen with her two cubs of the year in the early summer of 2015 cruising through Grand Teton National Park, fifty-five miles south of Yellowstone's border. She also had her own hashtag, #Blaze, broadening her audience in Instagram and Facebook circles.

At the time at least eight female grizzlies with cubs cruised the forests around Elephant Back Trail. At least four of those bears had twin cubs. Rangers showed pictures of the suspect bear to a network of professional and serious amateur photographers who prowl the area: None identified it as Blaze. But that had no effect on the online accusations that rangers had killed a photo-famous grizzly.

Gunther, who feigns to barely comprehend email, let alone Twitter and Facebook, learned an online petition was gathering signatures condemning him for killing a beloved grizzly. He set an alert to notify him every time another five hundred names were added. It eventually gathered more than fifty thousand signers.

The compact scene offered no evidence that Lance Crosby attempted to flee. He had facial wounds and bites on his arms, indicating a defensive struggle. Crosby wasn't carrying bear spray, but neither did nearly two of every three hikers in Yellowstone that year, according to trailhead surveys. Elephant Back Trail had gone forty-three days without a bear incident before Crosby's death.

The incident report stated Crosby was wearing leather boots, canvas pants, and a button-down shirt. He had a sprained ankle. His body was found a mile away from the employee housing complex at Yellowstone Lake Hotel, where he'd worked for five seasons. Investigators reported his backpack was torn open in a way showing he was using it to shield himself.

Those details didn't slow the "true crime" free-for-all on the internet. Many posters inferred that Crosby was at fault. Commenters claimed he triggered the grizzly's predatory chase instinct by jogging, although there was no evidence that he ran. One anonymous writer surmised Crosby punched Blaze in the nose, provoking the encounter. Another wrote it wasn't Blaze at all, but another frequently photographed bear known as Lightning who had torn into Crosby's daypack looking for food. Gunther soon learned about a whole constellation of grizzlies with their own Web-based fan clubs: Raspberry, Hobo, Snowball, Blondie, 399.

Online detectives kept posting more scenarios. One claimed it was really a big male that fed on the body, not a female. However, there were no male-sized tracks at the scene and the toothmarks matched the female. All of the DNA tests implicated the specific sow with cubs the rangers had caught and killed.

Ignoring decades of Yellowstone policy calling for lethal removal of bears that commit serious injury or loss of life to humans, posters concocted conspiracy theories accusing Yellowstone officials of violating their own guidelines to cover up a botched investigation.

"They claimed fear of litigation was the reason we removed the bear," Gunther said. "We wanted to make sure this bear wouldn't do this again to another hiker. We weren't worried about litigation. The bear was seen running away from the body. It was trapped 9.4 meters away from the body. From an evidence point of view, it was a slam-dunk."

Then came the fate of the two cubs. Rangers attempted to place them in zoos, only to find the online commenting world was already on the task. Some pretended to represent an association of zoos or aquariums, or even Yellowstone National Park itself, pleading with zoo authorities to adopt the cubs. A few went the other direction, pressuring institutions to refuse the donation. Gunther quickly learned many zoos around the nation didn't want to deal with the backlash of taking in an internet martyr's orphaned offspring. Neither did wild animal sanctuaries or the Canadian government. The cubs eventually got placed in the Toledo Zoo in Ohio.

◄ ◄ ◄ · ► ► ►

As social media has created new headaches for bear managers, it also appears to have created a new type of bear with a remarkable relationship to humans. I'll name it *Ursus horribilis Facebookii*.

In the early 1990s, rangers in Grand Teton and Yellowstone National Parks started noticing certain grizzlies adapted extremely well to roadside living. As long as they didn't attack people, get into picnic baskets, or otherwise cross some human tolerance line, they could graze the dandelions and dig for roots without hassle. The sows could also raise their cubs with less fear that a mature boar would attack (boars occasionally use infanticide to trigger a sow's reproductive receptivity). Older grizzlies usually dislike proximity to people, so they tend to stay in the backcountry.

Growing up alongside roads and tourists puts some odd kinks in a young grizzly's education. Its tolerance of humans weakens its future survival chances. Bear managers learned this when a few of the young roadside bears did break the rules and get aggressive with people. Such incidents earned the suspect a ride deep into the backcountry of relocation. But once let out of the culvert trap, the *Facebookiis* faced two threats.

The first, obviously, was exposure to those dominant, mature males. The relocated bears woke up in somebody else's territory, and predictable battles began. Unfamiliar with the antisocial, hyper-aggressive style of backcountry boars, the transplants tended to go down quick.

The second problem was downright perverse. The *Facebookii* grizzlies had grown up learning to maneuver around campgrounds and townsites and garbage cans without succumbing to temptation. In turn, they'd earned a level of comfort and disinterest from the surrounding humans. But human residents in the remote locations where the transplants were sent didn't have that same *sangfroid*. When they saw a grizzly moseying between their cabin and their shed, they called the game wardens and demanded action. The *Facebookii* bear's good-behavior medal apparently didn't transfer. And so the grizzly would get trapped again, relocated, and more often than not, end the year in the mortality listings.

That's exactly what happened to Grizzly Bear 760 in 2014. It was a child of royalty, one of Sow 399's three cubs born in 2011. The *Washington Post* called 399 "the most famous mother bruin on earth" for her tolerance of tourists along Grand Teton's main roadway. She was also prolific, birthing at least eighteen cubs. Grizzly reproductive rates are slow compared to other mammals. Females usually have about six years of productive motherhood, and typically give birth only two or three times in that period. Of the litters of one to four cubs, about two-thirds never reach reproductive adulthood. Mothers as successful as 399 are thus extremely rare and important to the species' survival.

Bear 760 left his mother in his third year and gained his own celebrity hanging around Grand Teton's Moose-Wilson Road. He also frequently prowled through a Jackson Hole subdivision on the park's southern tip. There he sufficiently frightened a man walking his dog that Wyoming State Game and Fish wardens decided to trap and relocate 760.

The grizzly bear woke up one hundred and twenty-six air miles away from home near Clark, Wyoming, east of Yellowstone's northeast corner. Within days, he claimed a hunter's deer carcass hanging outside a house and refused to give it back, even when the man tried to shoo him off with a pickup truck. Wyoming game wardens caught him in a leg snare. They determined he was a habituated bear and a menace, and killed him by lethal injection.

We know much of this because of the online web built around Sow 399 and her offspring. *Facebookii* grizzly families frequent road corridors. Tourists see them and post photos and news clips to Instagram, Twitter, and Facebook. Media-savvy wildlife watchers scan the interwebs for tips where to find roadside grizzlies. And the feedback loop spirals.

The traffic hazards known as "bear jams" have been a hassle for park rangers since there were national parks. But the pre-digital-age versions at least had an element of randomness, bears being where you find them. While some locations held more promise for a grizzly bear photo shoot than others, nobody knew if a photogenic mother and cubs was out there unless they got in the car and looked.

With the popularity and ease of social media, that question could be answered from the comfort of an Old Faithful Inn lobby chair. Any place with cell service or Wi-Fi could provide real-time tips for bear seekers.

The result was hundreds, even thousands of visitors getting the chance to see a grizzly in the wild, from the presumptive safety of a car window. It also meant regular bear jams on park roadways as tourists congregated around the latest sighting. That drains rangers' time spent untangling traffic and lecturing foolhardy visitors who leave their cars for a better look.

‹ ‹ ‹ · › › ›

In my research for this book, I tried an experiment. Could I use social media posts to nab my own grizzly photo? Could I catch a bear without resorting to any biological science or woodcraft—just by employing digital savvy?

After we took some out-of-state relatives for an extended tour of Yellowstone's postcard sites in mid-July 2018, my daughter Ania and I added an extra day for a bear chase. We searched Instagram and Facebook for hashtags indicating the latest posting of grizzly photos. We parsed their comments and metadata for clues hinting where the bears might be found. One 24-hour-old video post showed a grizzly walking past some logs obviously cut by a chainsaw—indicating nearness to a road. One hashtag the photographer included was "Tower," probably Tower Junction east of the Mammoth Gateway hotel lobby where we were browsing with our smartphones. We got in the car.

On the way, we saw the sign for the Blacktail Plateau—a one-way gravel road that felt promising. We turned right and followed the road into a grove of pines and willows. Within ten minutes, we saw another car pulled over. As I scanned for hints of what had stopped my fellow tourist, Ania noticed out her driver's-side window something moving on the hill. It looked like a black wolf in the tall grass. But through the viewfinder of my five-hundred-millimeter lens, it turned out to be a black bear sporting a radio collar. *Ursus americanus*, despite its common name, comes in a wide range of fur colors from blonde to brown to black. A really big black bear might weigh four hundred to six hundred pounds, while grizzlies at maturity can be almost twice that, weighing between five hundred and a thousand pounds. On the landscape, black bears rank below grizzlies as coyotes do to wolves, or hyenas to lions. Black bears lack the big muscles and aggressive attitude of grizzlies. They also inhabit virtually all of North and South America. Confusingly, while *Ursus arctos* is called a grizzly bear in the Lower 48 states it is called a brown bear in northern Canada, Alaska, and Eurasia.

At one point around the turn of the twentieth century, taxonomists proposed eighty-six subspecies of *Ursus arctos*, based on different skull shape, fur color, and body size. That sprawl has been compressed back to a handful of designations, primarily distinguishing what part of the planet the "brown bear" inhabits. *Ursus arctos horribilis* means the grizzly bears of North America.

I shot a few frames before our black bear scooted over the hilltop and out of sight. We motored on. Five minutes later, another line of cars signaled another sighting. I got out to join a clump of tourists excitedly pointing to a grove of trees. "A grizzly was right there," a man from North Carolina told me.

Movement. A very small bear was sitting in the shade of some big fir trees. I took a few more pictures, noticing how it looked particularly fuzzy and grizzly-like in the frame. Grizzlies compared to black bears have smaller ears, flatter muzzles, and a distinct shoulder hump on the adult bears. Their fur also tends to be two-toned with silver-gray tips: hence the nicknames "grizzly" and "silvertip." Without memory for scale, the cub might be possible to mistake it for a plump silvertip—except I know it was no bigger than a cocker spaniel. Plus, a grizzly would likely chase any black bears far out of the territory. Nevertheless, two bears in fifteen minutes. Not bad.

We rolled on, using fellow travelers as stalking horses. And about half an hour later, another clot appeared in the gravel artery. This time, we were high on a hillside where the road descended to a hairpin turn around a gully. We could look across the gap to a traffic jam below us. Not fifteen feet off the side of the road was a huge black blot. This time, I had the luxury to set up my tripod and focus carefully. A big bear munched red berries while tourists poked out of their car windows and filmed with abandon.

After documenting the bear jam from above, we joined it and waited our turn for the closeup. The bear obliged, ignoring everyone as it stripped the buffalo berries one car-length off the roadside. But on close inspection, it also turned out to be the wrong species. It looked to weigh at least two hundred and fifty pounds, but it wasn't a grizzly.

Three bears on the memory card before lunch. What else might the day hold? We rejoined the main road and continued on toward the Lamar Valley. About eight miles past the intersection, we saw another group of cars pulled over. A few buffalo were grazing the huge meadows, along with a small herd of pronghorn. But one clump of tourists looked promisingly excited, facing away from the obvious ungulates. I walked over to inquire.

Sure enough, they were certain they'd seen a grizzly two minutes before I arrived. It had just wandered around the crown of a low rocky hill about four hundred yards off the north side of the road. "Biggest bear I've ever seen," the father of the group told me, scrolling through fuzzy images on his point-and-shoot camera. They wouldn't qualify for printing in next month's *National Geographic*, but the bear had a distinctive hump looming above the sagebrush. Close enough to be a *Facebookii*. Like dozens of other satisfied tourists that morning, Ania and I declared victory and went in search of ice cream.

◄ ◄ ◄ · ► ► ►

Social media doesn't only direct you to where to find the bear, it brings it back to your living room if you're too lazy to go looking.

A video that gained popularity on Facebook in 2017 captured a curious grizzly climbing on, and sliding off, an interpretative sign along a road in Yellowstone. At one point it gets all four feet on the angled sign, looking for all the world like it was trying to read the caption upside down.

That says something about the confounding nature of dealing with grizzly bears, no?

The following spring, a black bear rose to fame when it chose to den in the bole of a cottonwood tree near the Glacier National Park headquarters. A sharp-eyed staffer saw it and set up a live-feed video camera. For almost two weeks, the bear sucked up the nation's desktop bandwidth by sleepily looking out of its hole, licking itself, and occasionally climbing out to add some new cottonwood buds to its nest.

"My retired father is pushing 80, and I'd get a text: 'The bear is climbing up the tree,'" Glacier Park chief bear biologist John Waller said. "It got to be where I'd look out my office window and see people sneaking through the woods, going where the webcam was to view the bear. It was getting out of control, so we took the camera down."

Then the bear climbed down and allegedly killed a couple of llamas on a nearby ranch. Nobody had got a DNA test from the cottonwood den, although circumstantial evidence fingered everyone's favorite screen saver.

"But how do you remove a bear with seven hundred and fifty thousand Facebook followers?" Waller asked. "It's sleepy and really cute, but it is a predator and predators eat meat. That's sometimes hard for people to accept."

Flathead National Forest supervisor Chip Weber called the internet situation a kind of "Bambi biology."

"People wind up with unrealistic expectations about the behavior of bears," Weber said. "In the long term, we could be doing a disservice for conservation of the species itself. We use the idea of attractive megafauna as a way to raise money to help with conservation of bears. As ecologists, we know there's as much importance in a snail as a bear, but you can raise a lot more money with a bear. You end up with the Hollywood version of ecology and wildlife, compared to what we know as scientists."

Thinking back on the "Blaze" controversy, Gunther had a similar thought: "There was a petition against me. It got more than fifty thousand people signing. Just think if every one of them donated twenty-five dollars to habitat conservation. What if they funneled all that hatred and aggression into conservation? Because this bear had an individual name, people started jumping on board. But their cause didn't do anything positive for the bears. Twenty-five bears a year die, but this one had a name."

Stylized concrete grizzly bear statues guard the entrance to Yellowstone National Park's administration building in Mammoth, on the park's northern border. Park managers started leaving garbage to attract grizzlies for tourist viewing as early as 1895. Photograph by the author.

The camera may be the grizzly's best friend. A century before social media sharing became common parlance, photos of Yellowstone grizzly bears generated tourist popularity that spared them from the National Park Service's otherwise systematic elimination of predators like wolves and mountain lions (which were seen as depleting the more desirable elk and deer).

In 1909, William Wright wrote about his conversion from grizzly hunter to grizzly photographer: "If one really wishes to study an animal, let him go without a gun." Even then, Wright worried the beast that his grandfather never knew existed was vanishing so fast that his grandson might only see one in a zoo.

By the turn of the twentieth century, Wright suspected grizzlies in the Pacific Northwest were so scarce and hunt-shy, they only traveled between dusk and dawn. That made photographing one with his bulky box camera and slow film a nearly impossible challenge. He recounted several comic examples of his attempts to rig the first remote camera in Yellowstone National Park.

This involved tripods and trip-wires strung across bear paths leading to the park's already notorious garbage dumps, and enormous batteries firing primitive flashbulbs. He presumed the bears' habituation to garbage-feeding would make them unwary subjects. He was wrong. Grizzlies consistently sniffed out his triggers and either retreated from them or moved around them.

As he watched on one occasion, a memorable family group trooped up to his wire and investigated:

> The one in front pushed out his nose and sniffed gingerly the suspicious object. Those in the rear also stopped, but being curious to learn what was causing the trouble, the second one placed his forefeet on the rump of the one in front, in order to see ahead, while the third one straightened up on his hind legs and looked over the other two. They made a beautiful group, and just as they had posed themselves, the one in front must have touched the string a little harder than he had intended to, for there was a sudden flash that lit up the surroundings, and I expected to see the bears go tearing off through the timber, but to my utter surprise, nothing of the kind happened. They all three stood up on their hind legs, and looked at each other as much as to say, 'Now what do you think of that?' And then they took up their investigation where it had been interrupted, followed the thread to where it was fastened to the stick, clawed up the spool, which I had buried in the ground, sniffed at it, and then went back to the trail, where they had first found the thread.

The trio walked away the way they came, and Wright discovered the classic photographer's mistake—not enough flash to expose his film.

A National Park Service visitors guide advises "Leave only footprints, take only photographs." Photographers from William Wright to Thomas Mangelson claim it takes more skill and chill to bag a bear with a camera than a rifle. But their trophies can be just as open to interpretation and controversy as any taxidermy mount.

Take the cover of *Large Carnivore Conservation: Integrating Science and Policy in the North American West.* A hardbound compendium of eleven scholarly articles about wildlife management, it appears destined for academic bookshelves only. Its cover features an ears-to-neck portrait of a grizzly bear.

So what? So what if you notice the photo credit goes to Mangelson, who donates many of his photos to causes protesting Wyoming's grizzly management policy? So what if you notice the grizzly is Blondie; one of the suspect bears mentioned in Lance Crosby's killing? If you know those things, does that color your impression of the book's intentions?

To me, that illustrates the complexity of the grizzly's meaning in our lives. The researchers who pioneered the use of radio collars for grizzly population monitoring lost trust with Yellowstone National Park officials in part because they tagged their study bears' ears with colored streamers for identification. Park administrators said that violated Yellowstone's "natural image" and tarnished the visitor experience. Many present-day photographers grouse when they encounter a grizzly with an "unnatural" radio collar.

Another sure way to get a photo of a grizzly is to accompany someone like Stacy Courville on one of his problem-bear management forays. Courville leads the Confederated Salish and Kootenai Tribe's grizzly biology efforts, and spends a busy eight months a year responding to the problems they cause on the Flathead Indian Reservation. The ringtone on his cellphone plays "The Bear Necessities" from Walt Disney's *The Jungle Book*. On an adventure with Courville, my reporting colleague Perry Backus got a great picture of a female grizzly in a culvert trap, again depicting the bear's conflict with a dominant species.

Is that too literal a photographic metaphor? Any image of a grizzly comes freighted with meaning. Cuddly grizzly cub or snarling mature boar? Female with cubs? Bear digging roots, or dripping with gore while excavating an elk's thoracic cavity? Even the background of the photo matters. A grizzly bear seen in the mountains peaceably inhabits its recovery zone, enjoying the sanctuary developed by fifty years of Wilderness Act protection. A grizzly seen on the prairie is a menace, threatening ranchers' livestock and school children as it explores the post-Lewis-and-Clark territory where it evolved as the apex predator of the grasslands.

Wildlife photographers often progress through stages of skill and interest, starting with an effort to capture an animal's mug shot. That usually means investment in super-telephoto lenses and heavy tripods. Once the shutterbugs can regularly fill the frame with a bear's tack-sharp eyelashes, they start to back out and catch moments of behavior—action shots. This tends to descend into a macho cul-de-sac of nature porn, where if some prey species isn't either joining or narrowly escaping the bloody circle of life, the photo lands in the trash.

Still other photographers pursue a third theme: the animal in its environment. They apply the rules of classic art, balancing composition and color and light in ways that make the subject species more a highlight than a spotlight feature. In his paintings of the Rocky Mountain West, nineteenth-century artist Albert Bierstadt offset some of his grandiose peaks and sunsets with a tiny animal. Look closely in the shadows of his "Lander's Peak" in Harvard University's Fogg Museum, and you'll spot a grizzly sitting by a dead deer, looking slightly like he killed one of the wrong flavor.

That brings us to anthropomorphic content—the attribution of human characteristics to animals. An uncounted number of presenters at the Interagency Grizzly Bear Committee's biannual meetings end their PowerPoint presentations with the same stock photo of a standing grizzly bear holding up a paw, as if waving bye-bye. Advocates of continued ESA protection for grizzlies put the same waving bear on billboards, indicating the potential departure of the species.

Missoulian photographer Michael Gallacher and I once visited a museum exhibit of Ansel Adams photographs. Gallacher had trained with photographers who were one degree of separation removed from Adams. He had mastered black-and-white news photography, knew the idiosyncrasies of Kodachrome shadow detail, and evolved into the fast-evolving world of digital cameras. But an exhibit of Adams's iconic prints of Half Dome and Denali remained a pilgrimage of devotion. And for Gallacher, a point of frustration.

Along with his coffee-table collections of art, Adams wrote three books on photography itself: One for the image, one for the negative, and one for the print. The first broke down how to take an eyeball's imagination of a scene and translate it through the frame of a shutter and aperture setting, using a technique Adams named the Zone System. The second explored the chemistry of photographic emoluments and developing tricks that ensured what was seen with the camera got captured on film. The third reversed the first two, unspooling light and negative to release an image that reproduced what the photographer saw before the shutter snapped.

For Gallacher, the fading of those old techniques hurts in two ways. First, an old *National Geographic* photo adage advises "F8 and be there." It meant set your camera at the ideal aperture for deep focus and have it with you when the incredible moment arrives.

Twenty-first-century cameras don't even have aperture rings anymore. Their computer brains have swallowed Adams's three books whole and reduced his Zone method to the flick of a thumb. Even highly esoteric tricks of using colored filters to change the intensities of sky or vegetation in a black-and-white print have been condensed to a slider on an Instagram control panel.

And second, with several billion digital cameras and their owners roaming every nook of the planet, "being there" is no longer an accomplishment. Smartphone cameras have flooded the photographic market with free versions of the images Gallacher used to earn a living shooting. Somebody's always there.

Ansel Adams himself faced a generational shift in technology. The establishment community of scenic painters mocked photographers as monkeys who pushed buttons and called it art. Adams changed his own style to a ruthlessly sharp and precise standard to emphasize how his camera could do what painting could not: reproduce every leaf and fold of stone that nature presented. Take that, you lazy impressionistic brush-daubers.

But the ubiquity of photographs, especially digital images, has warped that old tradition. A painter could feed the market only by spending hours or days recreating the scenes that sold best. Adams toward the end of his career started destroying his own negatives to restrict the flood of copies that diluted his market value.

In a different way, reproduction has introduced a new curse of digital life: the addictive nature of social media sharing. Facebook and Instagram installed "like" and "follow" options in their apps knowing people respond habitually to approval. An uptick in your friends list, or notification someone shared your latest post, provides the same kind of pleasure spike as euphoric drugs like cocaine. The picture becomes more important than the experience it captures. And the social reaction matters more than the picture.

"*Pixs or it didn't happen.*" That was a popular social media slang challenge among friends chronicling everything from who showed up at the wedding to who made it unscathed down the bike trail. Because a picture is a trophy. Why shoot a selfie except to count coup on a moment when you mattered? And do you put that selfie in your own photo album, or send it to your social network? The latter, to seek their admiration through likes and shares.

Selfie rants could go lots of different directions, but I'll restrict my discussion to one ironic observation. One of the most successful ways to catch a big-game wildlife poacher is to conduct a social media search. A surprising number of convictions stem from the culprit's own selfie posing with the trophy, posted on Facebook or Instagram.

University of Montana philosopher Albert Borgman has written extensively on the hidden impacts of technology and what he sometimes calls our new artificial organ—the smartphone.

"The entire world is moving into the shadows cast by the far side of the screen," Borgman told me. "A new person you meet is only a dim outline until you Google them—and then there's a sharp picture. But we think we're illuminating the world when it's actually darkening. It's like a searchlight that picks something out and then disappears as it moves on."

That digital searchlight has no permanence. Two people on their own computers asking Google the exact same question will get different lists of responses. Google's algorithms tailor the offering of links to the individual's past searching profile, choosing sources that match political leanings, buying preferences, long- or short-read attention spans, and other quirks of our past internet activity.

◁ ◁ ◁ · ▷ ▷ ▷

If we each had a lot of direct personal experience with bears, our debates about grizzly management would have common foundations. And we all do, in an evolutionary way. Most human phobias—the hardwired fear triggers we can't escape—tend to trace back to our prehistoric threats. *Homo sapiens* became capable of hunting other species to extinction about fifty thousand years ago. For the previous five hundred million years of our existence, most other big predators considered *us* prey. They still chase us in our dreams.

This stays true even though the modern world has provided much more pervasive opponents. Biologist E. O. Wilson notes we can develop full-blown phobias to heights, running water, bears, or blood, but not usually to frayed electric wires or automobiles, even though the latter kill far more of us.

According to the Centers for Disease Control, the animal that kills most people where I live in Montana—the species that should inspire night sweats and existential dread—is the white-tailed deer. They kill hundreds of people every year, and maim thousands more, typically as a result of staring us down in the headlights of our oncoming cars.

Bears rank seventh on that list of animals that kill, and an order of magnitude below every other threat such as stinging insects or domestic dogs. Yet which animal keeps *you* up at night?

Grizzly bears suffer asymmetrically from this. Whether we mount them on a pedestal of ecological virtue and name them Blaze, or shunt them into the labyrinth of supernatural terror, our classification has little relation to the animal we're trying to describe. We wind up with a creature of our own fancy, like the misconstructed skeletons of two-headed dinosaurs put on display in nineteenth-century circus sideshows.

As creatures of imagination, grizzly bears are always *more* than what they are. Every aspect of a grizzly has an asterisk, amplifying its mythical destructive power. The grizzly of imagination has a vitality, a tingling thrill of claws on gravel, sunlight rippling across humped muscle, blood ringing in the ears. The grizzly of the Endangered Species Act occupies bear management units and depends on habitat-based criteria for continued persistence on the landscape. Which story do you want to know?

While it might seem the Internet Age has overwhelmed us with written material, studies of information consumption in the United States indicate otherwise. We use the tiny keyboards on our smartphones to compress language itself, squishing a plea to the Almighty Creator into OMG. By 2020 the fastest-growing source of news and commentary wasn't websites, but podcasts. Rather than read, most Americans prefer to download spoken presentations of everything from romance novels to economic analyses.

Millions of people with millions of easy-to-use cameras have filled Facebook and Instagram with once-in-a-lifetime experiences the rest of us can surf from the comfort of our couches. And so we've been treated to videos of Kodiak bears squeezing caviar fountains out of Alaskan salmon, grizzly bear siblings playing keep-away with a deer carcass, even a grizzly bear hopping about a porch in apparent glee as a homeowner squirts it with a garden hose.

In late 2018, one such video turned the animal-watching world on its head. Known as the "Baby Bear Video," the viral sensation showed a sow and cub trying to cross a steep snowfield. Mama makes it, but baby bear slips and skids down the snow. Three times it struggles back up, falling farther back each time until it nearly tumbles over an exposed cliff while Mama watches helplessly. Finally, the cub makes it to the top. Walt Disney couldn't have animated a more cathartic scene. In five days, more than thirty million people had watched the clip.

But by the end of that week, the headline changed from "Cute baby bear 'bearly' makes it" to "Troubling truth behind viral video." The clip was shot in Russia with a drone camera. Biologists and bear behavior experts pointed out where the camera operator flew the drone so close to the bears, it probably startled the cub and caused its fall. The mother bear's obvious distress was aimed less at her struggling cub than at the hovering gizmo that chased them onto the snow slope in the first place.

Viral Hog, the YouTube channel that popularized the baby bear video, would not reveal how much it paid for its access or how much it earned in subsequent advertising revenue. This raises several problems.

First, popularizing wildlife behavior out of context has a sordid history. Americans have cemented a belief that "lemmings" are herds of rodents that throw themselves off cliffs into the sea for no good reason. We cling to this concept in business textbooks and Far Side cartoons, despite the fact that lemmings don't do that. The idea came from a frustrated Disney producer who'd heard a rumor of such behavior in the Arctic tundra, but failing to find it, rounded up a herd of the little animals and stampeded them off a cliff while his cameras rolled. According to the debunking site Snopes, the 1958 *White Wilderness* film crew paid Inuit children to capture several dozen lemmings, which were then delivered to Alberta (where they're not native) and stampeded by the producers off a cliff into the Bow River (not the Arctic Ocean) while the narrator intones "A kind of compulsion seizes each tiny rodent, and carried along by an unreasoning hysteria, each falls into step for a march that will take them to a strange destiny. That destiny is to jump into the ocean . . ."

Lemmings do, in fact, migrate and swim. Like many small mammals, their populations swing up and down in cycles of abundance and scarcity. But the idea they commit mass suicide is a myth that refuses to leave the common culture.

And yet we legislate based on such misperceptions. A close reading of Jack Olsen's 1969 book *Night of the Grizzlies* allows even the most elementary wildlife biology fan to deduce that the two bears that killed two women in two different campgrounds on the same night were highly predisposed to doom. Each grizzly was malnourished, enfeebled, garbage-conditioned, and habituated to human presence.

But what was one of the longest lasting results of that fatal night? A woefully unsubstantiated edict against menstruating women camping in bear country. Despite the only evidence for that warning being a fourth coincidence getting stacked on top of three already improbable occurrences, it became printed policy in Glacier National Park for years. The now-debunked policy still has a residual half-life around backcountry permit offices and camping equipment displays.

The most authoritative critics of drone-caused wildlife harassment face an equal irony. They tend to be wildlife experts who diagnosed the problem while following wildlife around with drones. Montana-based filmmaker and wildlife biologist Jeremy Roberts critiqued the baby bear video for *Mountain Journal* writer Steve Primm. Roberts has used drones himself, and said the mother bear's aggressive ground-swat when the drone got too close may have caused her cub to slip in the first place.

"As the technology gets better and cheaper," Roberts told Primm, "more people are going to be out there pushing the limits of what's safe and ethical."

◄ ◄ ◄ · ► ► ►

I got my start in journalism in 1987 at the weekly *Hungry Horse News* on the edge of Glacier National Park. One of the first things publisher Brian Kennedy told me was that putting a bear on the front page bumped his weekly circulation 30 percent. Kennedy also had many bear-like aspects to his own personality, including aggressiveness, territoriality, wells of unbelievable strength and endurance, and disdain for those who couldn't keep up. My four years at the *Horse* served as a reporting boot camp. Kennedy was my drill instructor.

Yet for all that competitive incentive for more bears, I never published a photo of a grizzly in the *Hungry Horse News*. Not for lack of trying. For all the peaks bagged, rivers floated, and trails hiked as a Horseman, all my best grizzly stories came from people like Doug Peacock. Every introduction of the man includes mention that he served two tours in Vietnam as a Green Beret medic, and that he inspired Edward Abbey's lead character George Washington Hayduke in *The Monkey Wrench Gang*. Peacock began producing grizzly film documentaries and books in 1975, supporting himself as a backcountry ranger and fire lookout in Yellowstone and Glacier National Parks.

In 1989 I hadn't read any of Peacock's books. I just knew a burly, fidgety man was sitting at the prosecutor's table in a Flathead County District Court case brought against Jim Krueger, the best-known helicopter pilot in the local sky. Krueger stood accused of harassing grizzly bears with his helicopter. The Flathead County Attorney was bringing the case at the instigation of Peacock, who was the county's lead witness. Peacock had the photos of Krueger's chopper at treetop level and the eyewitness testimony of the panic that filled the bears that Peacock and a companion, a Chicago policeman, were observing at the time. But it was the second witness for the prosecution that made the courtroom memorable. It was a Glacier National Park bear biologist. "How did you know Krueger was flying too close to the bears?" the prosecutor asked the biologist.

"Because I was in the passenger seat," came the reply. "I hired Krueger to make the flight for a bear population survey." This woke the judge up. Wait: You're testifying against the pilot you asked to fly you for this project? Um, yes.

Peacock didn't look visibly amused to have jujitsu'd the National Park Service into fighting itself in a court of law. But the whole courtroom felt soaked in the surreal vibe of a con in process. In the end, the judge dismissed the charges against Krueger because Peacock's photos, while clearly showing the identification numbers of Krueger's helicopter, failed to show who was at the controls. Without convincing proof that Krueger was the actual pilot, the county attorney couldn't charge him with a crime. But like a grizzly bear's bluff-charge, Peacock's lawsuit got the National Park Service to scale back its aerial protocols.

"Between '68 and '75, it was incredible," Peacock told me when we met years later to refresh details about the helicopter case. "I was the only person in the backcountry. I would film every April, May, and June, then go work some low-level job for the Park Service, then film again through September and October. Those bears I was filming were really spooky—on the run. The few large bears I saw I presumed were survivors of those pogroms when the rangers were shooting all the bears after the dumps closed."

Peacock plunged into the grizzly debate like a Norse berserker, developing a frighteningly personal relationship with many bears along the western side of Glacier National Park. He named the area "The Grizzly Hilton." At one time, Arnold Schwarzenegger brought a TV crew to tag along behind Peacock so "The Terminator" could see grizzlies in Yellowstone.

Unlike another evangelistic grizzly documentarian, Timothy Treadwell, Peacock hasn't been eaten by a grizzly. Treadwell's advocacy career came to a fatal end in 2003 when he ignored warnings and camped inside a food-stressed Alaskan bear habitat, where a grizzly killed and consumed him and a companion. In contrast, Peacock wears the authenticity of someone who's kept his own well-being, physically and financially, secondary to his commission in the war to defend the grizzly. But he also acknowledges he's become an antisocial grizzly celebrity, able to draw crowds for lectures he'd rather not attend himself.

That's exactly how I found him the week of the federal court hearing on the Yellowstone grizzly delisting in 2018. While *Grizzly Times* cofounders Louisa Willcox and David Mattson were leading an anti-delisting rally and sold-out showing of the 1989 documentary *Peacock's War* at Missoula's Roxy Theater, the man himself was two blocks up the street in a dark bar talking to friends. While Peacock entertained audiences with self-shot documentary films like *Happy Bear*, he also tried to forge a balance between depictions of grizzlies as "fundamentally safe to be around, lovable, on occasion even cuddly" and the attack-survival stories he referred to as "ursine snuff books."

"They need tolerance from humans, which grows out of humility," Peacock told me. "Sharing the backcountry is an admission that you're not trying to kill everyone you see. It's an acknowledgement that there's something more powerful than you, that could kill and eat you any time it wanted to. It reminds the most destructive, arrogant species on Earth where it should live—in the middle of the food pyramid, not on the top."

Peacock serves as the lens many people use to watch grizzly bears. Through his experience and his writing, you view an animal that demands empathy and submission. Like watching a rattlesnake through binoculars, when it moves, you feel the thrill of terror from a safe distance. Peacock tells great stories, and has spent years telling them. In the process, he's turned himself into an icon.

That gets at a fundamental problem of living with grizzly bears. Anyone can love Peacock's Happy Bear splashing pond water on a movie screen. But as Scott McMillion wrote in *Mark of the Grizzly: More Stories of Recent Bear Attacks and the Hard Lessons Learned*, "few people have Peacock's skill or his stones, and for most of us it's hard to tell when a charging bear is bluffing, when the bear intends to cuss you out, and when it means business."

And what about those who don't live with grizzly bears, whose only experience with them comes through a screen or a book? There's a joke in newsrooms about the difference in attitude between people who go to city council meetings and those who attend school board meetings. Few have any extensive encounters with building codes or municipal water sanitation, but everyone has been to third grade. That sense of personal experience—"I know what a good/bad education policy is because it happened to me"—endows people with a sense of authority regardless whether they've glanced at a page of pedagogy.

Technology let us peer into the grizzly bear's den and learn what helps and hinders its survival. In a way, it has also removed the real bear from our lives. The grizzly-dedicated land trust Vital Ground was cofounded by Doug Seus, who in the 1980s and '90s trained a massive grizzly named Bart to star in dozens of movies, TV shows, and commercials. Talented as Bart was, he never stood a chance in the 2017 production of *The Revenant*, where Leonardo DiCaprio won an Oscar for getting mauled by a super-realistic motion-capture simulation of a grizzly. The moviemakers passed over the real animal in favor of a virtual one, at once more terrifying and more controllable.

In this way, *Facebookii* grizzly bears suffer from this in their status as virtual charismatic megafauna. On my cell phone, I've seen a coyote bite a grizzly bear in the butt. I've watched a grizzly excavate a black bear family out of a den and kill one of the cubs. I've watched grizzly bears have sex. That makes for great cocktail party conversation, but it doesn't make me an expert on grizzly bears.

At the same time, I've become a member of a massive community of fellow watchers, who have become invested in grizzly bears as a part of their lives. Does that qualify us to debate someone like Kerry Gunther at the scene of a Yellowstone National Park fatality? Conversely, by law grizzly bears in Montana, Idaho, and Wyoming belong to the public trust of the whole United States. Does Gunther owe any sort of political or social allegiance to Peacock and the millions of grizzly fans that might contradict his biological experience or policy directive? The Yellowstone administrators investigating Lance Crosby's death all got their scientific training at the dawn of the digital age. The first digital photo got uploaded to the World Wide Web in 1992. Digital cameras outsold film cameras in 2003. By 2010, digital camera production peaked as cell phone cameras replaced the market. By 2020, digital photographers snapped more pictures every two minutes than existed in the first 108 years of photography.

Facebook in 2020 claimed 2.45 billion users. If it were a nation, it would be the largest on earth—twice the size of China or India. In less than two decades, Facebook got more people to participate in its community than worldwide Christianity congregated in two thousand years. Facebook's sustenance depends on finding and sharing stuff that those followers create, and then selling access to the marketplace that this social community creates. In the ethics of social media, getting thirty million views of a baby bear's near-death experience in five days goes in the "good" column, along with celebrity misbehavior, freakish sports incidents, and practical jokes.

To borrow another Disney reference, this inundation of imagery has left me feeling like the sorcerer's apprentice in *Fantasia*, who used his master's magic to enchant a broom to fill the water basin, only to find himself washed out of the castle when the magic wouldn't stop gushing. Like the *Facebookii*, I enjoy a virtual world that beguiles my understanding of the dangers beyond.

3

The Only Good Bear

THE ONLY PREDATORY ANIMAL TO RECEIVE MORE MENTIONS IN
Lewis and Clark's journals than the grizzly bear was the mosquito. But
while many consider the Voyage of Discovery to have begun the written
history of the grizzly bear, the species' first log entry actually appears two
centuries earlier. Spanish explorers reported grizzly bears eating beached
whales near what is now Monterrey, California, in 1602. The record stays
thin until 1691, when Hudson's Bay Company apprentice trader Henry
Kelsey noted "This lain affords nothing but short, round sticky grass and
buffalo and a great sort of bear which is bigger than any white bear and
is neither white nor black but silver haired like our English rabbit." Kelsey
was also the first white settler to record killing a grizzly bear, noting it "is
good meat. His skin I have used all the ways I can." But he added local tribes
"said it was a God and they should starve" before hunting one for food.

Meriwether Lewis entered his first notes about grizzlies on April 13,
1805, with the observation of enormous tracks near the winter-killed
carcasses of bison along the Missouri River in what is now North Dakota.
His Minatare Indian hosts warned him of the bear's ferocity, adding they
only hunted it in parties of six to ten warriors.

Six members of the Corps of Discovery put a stalk on a grizzly with nearly disastrous results. After getting within forty paces, four of the men fired their rifles while two held their powder in reserve. All four hit their target, two putting balls through both lungs. The bear charged, and the reserve duo fired.

"[B]oth of them struck him, one only slightly and the other fortunately broke his shoulder," Lewis journaled. "This however retarted [sic] his motion for a moment only, the men unable to reload their guns took flight, the bear pursued and had very nearly over taken them before they reached the river."

Two men made it to the canoes and paddled away. The rest scattered in the riverside bushes to reload their single-shot rifles. Although they hit it several more times, the bear kept up pursuit and "they were obliged to throw aside their guns and pouches and throw themselves into the river although the bank was nearly 20 feet perpendicular; so enraged was this animal that he plunged into the river only a few feet behind the second man."

A bullet through the grizzly's head finally ended the battle. An autopsy revealed they had put eight shots into the bear from different directions. The Voyage of Discovery killed twenty-three white bears on its trek west, the last one shot near present-day Three Forks, Montana. From there to the Pacific Coast, the journals report no more grizzly sightings. But on the eastward return, the tally resumed with six shot along Idaho's Clearwater River and another fourteen killed as they recrossed the prairie beyond the Rocky Mountain Front.

Exactly why the voyagers killed so many grizzlies has fostered a lively historical debate. The bears provided some practical resources, especially fat that had useful lubricating qualities for their gear. But being an essentially unknown species at the time, the explorers couldn't claim a custom or tradition of seeking grizzlies out for grease. They did eat some of the meat, but didn't find it notably preferable, and it was certainly a risky investment in their daily search for food. President Thomas Jefferson's mission orders included collecting samples of all interesting fauna discovered along the way, but that didn't seem to justify killing forty-three grizzlies (and wounding an uncounted additional number of bears) in pursuit of the perfect museum specimen.

Historian Dan Flores considers this an example of Western humanity's faith in technology over nature. Lewis and Clark tested a variety of innovative concepts on the trek, from newfangled air rifles to astrological observation protocols used for map-making. Along the way, their charge was to display the engineering superiority of the "Great Father in Washington" to anyone who might challenge His title to the Louisiana Purchase.

"What is striking upon reading [Lewis and Clark's] accounts is their repeated disbelief that America held an animal so powerful and with so tenacious a will to live that Western scientific technology was incapable of easily conquering it," Flores writes. Lewis assumed the Indians he met lacked sufficiently advanced technology capable of killing grizzlies, but Flores adds "you have to note in this regard that Columbian mammoths were pretty formidable too, yet the Clovis people apparently still managed to push them into extinction."

Spanish colonists on the Pacific Coast had also encountered grizzly bears. They reported killing hundreds of them in the early 1800s, as well as capturing some for bullfights. The vaqueros usually used a variation of the culvert trap—a stout log cage baited with cow guts. Once captured, the bear would be prodded into an iron cage on a wagon and hauled to the bullring. Period accounts told of grizzlies taking a bull's charge straight to the chest, gripping the head in its paws, and breaking the bull's neck. An 1840 report stated "When the bull approached, the bear thrust a paw in its face, or caught a leg in its jaws. In this way the bear forced the bull to lower its head, and when it bellowed, caught it by the tongue. It was then necessary to separate the contestants quickly to keep the bear from killing the bull immediately."

Nevertheless, grizzly bears from then on were considered the biggest pest in the West. As incredible as a thousand-pound predator with five-inch claws and a cruising speed of thirty miles per hour seems in real life, the grizzly grew even more fearsome in the tall tales that traveled back East, a Wild West Grendel defying Beowulf's duty to impose peace and order in his lord's domain.

And like Beowulf, the pioneers and settlers won. But their stories had little room for the role Grendel, or the grizzly bear, played in the domain. As Flores puts it, the specter of wildness in the American frontier "produced enough unease about the thinness of civilization's veneer that we reacted with a numb orgy of destruction aimed at the animals that we subconsciously saw as exposing in raw form our own base instincts as animals."

It was a numb but systematic orgy. In 1756, future president John Adams described North America before his kind arrived as "one continuing dismal wilderness, the haunt of wolves and bears and more savage men. Now the forests are removed, the land covered with fields of corn, orchards bending with fruit and the magnificent habitations of rational and civilized people."

The United States' westward expansion helped construct the perversely split political personality of its future residents, according to historian Megan Black. The Louisiana Purchase of 1803 added 820,000 square miles to the young nation, doubling its geographic reach. Then the decade of the 1840s brought the annexation of Texas, territory captured in the Mexican War, and the addition of Oregon Treaty lands to append another 1.2 million square miles.

The impact on American society was schizophrenic. All that new land pushed a pile of work at the federal government, which had to rapidly expand to survey, inventory, and administer its coast-to-coast possessions. This aggravated the public factions hoping to keep the federal system small and weak; at the same time the population demanded access to those lands which only the federal system could provide. Fur trappers, gold miners, ranchers, and farmers swarmed into the West, seeking independence and personal fortune supported by subsidized railroads, militarily enforced Indian eviction, and free homesteads and mineral rights provided by the federal estate.

Most native wildlife was considered little more than undomesticated groceries by the wagon trains of pioneers departing the East. But the predators fell into a different category: less a resource than an obstacle to be removed. Where grizzlies were concerned, options included baiting, poisoning, dog-chasing, and occasionally using explosives.

◄ ◄ ◄ · ► ► ►

Fair warning: This will be a bloody and bloody-minded chapter. Its title comes from a 1986 book edited by Jeanette Prodgers titled *The Only Good*

Bear Is a Dead Bear: A Collection of the West's Best Bear Stories. In the introduction, wildlife biologist Les Pengelly states the stories give insight "into our preoccupation with our continual attempts at their destruction, exposes the exaggerations and excesses, and casts doubt on the sportsmanship involved."

Prodgers's archive also reflects a time when "the monstrous predatory beasts" mounted "a reign of terror," "haunting the caves and ledges" of the pioneers' Promised Land. The storytellers' language condemns the grizzly without a trial. Even the cover prejudges. The title of her book echoes a quote variously attributed to Presidents Andrew Jackson and Theodore Roosevelt: "The only good Indian is a dead Indian." Or to borrow an Ozark hillbilly phrase from Pengelly: "We'uns is generally down on what we ain't up on."

To get that advantage, ranchers in the Southwest sought government help. The Department of Agriculture responded with the Predatory Animal and Rodent Control Division. PARC agents spread chunks of beef suet laced with strychnine by the gunny-sack load across thirty million acres. The nerve toxin causes painful muscle spasms and can take half an hour or more to kill. It also remains lethal for years. Flores cited Indian reports of horses dying after grazing at sites where poisoned wolves had vomited on the grass. Grizzly bears, naturally attracted to carrion, were particularly vulnerable.

Some preferred more elaborate methods against the bear. A 1927 *Rocky Mountain Husbandman* magazine story credited Butte shoe salesman J. H. Baker with perfecting the "honey roll" which involved a pile of blasting caps wrapped in burlap and coated with honey. The first grizzly to bite one "had its entire head blown off." A cowboy on a grizzly-afflicted ranch found a grizzly cub that had swallowed a honey roll whole and chased it over a cliff, whereupon it exploded and his companions "were deluged by a shower of fur and warm flesh." The cowboys considered the Baker's Bear Exterminators a hazard to themselves: "No one would shoot a bear unless the animal happened to be at least half a mile away."

The stories debate the means but rarely the ends. A few bears get credit for killing trappers or gold miners who'd cheated their fellow humans, serving as the claw of fate bringing retribution on the unworthy. But as a rule, the grizzly in the Wild West is both inhuman and inhumane. When a bear uses its strength, teeth, and claws to dispatch a human threat to its territory, it gets portrayed as a terrorist or demon. If J. H. Baker fed one of his bear exterminators to a banker who foreclosed on his shoe store, who would be the villain of the story?

More important, *why* is there a villain in the story? These tales set the foundation for how humans relate to the world they inhabit. Rivers and trees killed far more settlers than grizzlies ever did. Yet rivers and trees aren't demonized as agents of evil to be destroyed (although we are willing to exploit them through dams and logging). They are agents deserving respect.

Grizzly bears make ferocious opponents. Does that justify the pre-emptive offense settlers tended to take when a bear enters *their* territory? Before the grizzly bear was listed as a federally protected species in 1975, big-game regulations of Montana, Idaho, and Wyoming all classified it as a predator available to be shot at any time of year without a license. Unlike hail or heatwaves, the agriculture industry considered grizzlies a hazard it was almost obligated to confront.

In an interview I had with a county extension agent in northern Montana, the topic of grizzly bears came up. A national organization called the American Prairie Reserve was introducing bison to the remote Missouri Breaks country, and ranchers there were angry about their traditional dominance getting displaced. Part of APR's rewilding vision included returning grizzlies to the landscape where Lewis and Clark first encountered them.

"You know that when grizzlies started showing up in the next county west of us, they killed twenty cows last year," the extension agent told me.

"OK," I replied. "The state Board of Livestock also just published a report saying eleven thousand cows died of exposure last winter in Montana."

"True," he said. "Seven thousand of them here in Phillips County."

"Help me put that in a ranching business context. If you're losing seven thousand cattle to the weather, why are you so concerned about twenty more?"

"Well, a grizzly killed that woman and her baby in the Yukon last week," he answered.

"Still, drunk drivers kill that many people every month in Montana. How do you balance seven thousand against twenty?"

"We'll just have to agree to disagree," was his riposte.

A grizzly bear did kill Valérie Théorêt and her ten-month-old daughter Adele that November at a remote cabin on Einarson Lake, in Canada's Northwest Territory. Théorêt's partner and Adele's father, Gjermund Roesholt, killed the bear when it charged him while he was checking his trap line, *before* he discovered the dead bodies of his family. Canadian television hunting show host Jim Shockey claimed British Columbia and the Yukon were "facing a grizzly bear plague" and called for more bears to be killed in wilderness areas around Einarson Lake. However, the Canadian Yukon Environmental Department refuted his charge, showing the grizzly population there was stable or declining.

◄ ◄ ◄ · ► ► ►

This divide separating emotion and economics confounds grizzly bear management. In a burger joint, if the stove catches fire and the waiter shows up late for a shift, which problem does the owner focus on? Losing thousands of cattle to weather versus dozens to grizzlies seems like a no-brainer on the list of things to worry about today.

On the other hand, humans can kill the grizzlies that threaten them, and the persuasive power of action often overrides the practical result of the act. US Fish and Wildlife Service grizzly bear recovery coordinator Chris Servheen once told author David Knibb that his efforts coincided with local economies throughout the Rocky Mountain states losing their logging jobs, timber mills, mines, and farms in the 1990s. "Species recovery is not responsible for these problems," Servheen said, "but it's happening at the same time, so it tends to get blamed."

That blame metastasized into fury. Knibb recounted a 1993 meeting in Okanagan, Washington, where federal bear managers were presenting plans to revive the struggling grizzly population in the North Cascades Recovery Area. Biologist Doug Zimmer got spit at by a grandmother, cursed by a man in a cowboy hat announcing "You son of a bitch! I'm going to go out to my truck and get a rifle and come back in here and shoot you!" and finally threatened by another man who told Zimmer he was "of a good mind to get his lariat and take three turns around me and three turns around his trailer hitch, and three turns around town." Zimmer gave that "the award for the evening's most imaginative death threat."

But grizzly bears didn't create the punishing economics of the cattle business in the northern Rockies. Texas alone provides almost 15 percent of the nation's beef cattle, and the top five beef states (none of which are in today's grizzly country) produce more than 40 percent of the thirty-two million cows we turn into meat each year. Montana ranks seventh on that list, with about one and a half million beef cattle (slightly more than one and a half cows per Montanan). Federal labor statistics for 2018 report that of Montana's almost seven hundred thousand workers, just thirty-one thousand work on a ranch or farm. The grizzly habitat states of Wyoming and Idaho fall even farther off the balance sheet, ranking fifteenth and twentieth respectively, on the list of cattle producers by state. Combined, Wyoming and Idaho ranchers together raise barely as many cows as Montanans do.

"The public wants me gone, not the bears," Montana rancher Wayne Slaght told me. "So the only reason I can be here is because I tolerate them. I'm willing to try anything. Bottom line—I want to stay here and the only way is to learn to live with them. The public would be fine with me gone. I moved onto this ranch when I was four. My three kids have grown up here. It's a way of life. It's not about the money."

Slaght runs the Two Creek Ranch near Ovando, an hour's drive from my home in Missoula. Its two namesake creeks pour out of the Bob Marshall Wilderness Complex—the nearly two-million-acre heart of the Northern Continental Divide Ecosystem and grizzly recovery area. Sitting in the knotty-pine paneled office of his home on a spring morning, Slaght confidently estimates he has ten grizzly bears roaming his twenty-one-thousand acre spread as we speak.

Slaght has been active in one of the most successful predator conflict management efforts in all of grizzly country. After growing up virtually bear-free in the late twentieth century, Slaght lost three cows to grizzlies in three years at the turn of the twenty-first. The first one died just five hundred yards from his house. All he found was the crushed skull and part of the backbone. Grizzlies have distinctive ways of killing cattle, as documented by biologist Adolph Murie in 1945. They usually bite through the cow's skull or neck to kill it, and then tear open the stomach. Murie had investigated ten cattle depredations on a Wyoming ranch during one summer, noting that each had its stomach and intestines cleanly removed before any other part was consumed.

"Emotions run very high," Slaght said. "When you have a grizzly depredation close to the house, you want to kill all the bears. That's your bottom line for a while. I don't know how long it took to get over it. I just wanted to shoot them all."

Instead, he partnered with the Montana Fish, Wildlife and Parks Department and the US Fish and Wildlife Service and private organizations to build an electric fence around his most vulnerable cattle pastures. That kept the bears out of the cows, but they still tore the doors off his barns seeking cattle feed. So he brought in steel shipping containers.

While showing me around the ranch, Slaght noted grizzlies key on anything salty, including creosote-soaked fenceposts. He's even had a grizzly snatch the sweat-soaked seat off his all-terrain vehicle.

The most effective change, Slaght said, was the carcass pick-up program. Ranchers traditionally kept a death pit on their property where they'd dump livestock that died of disease or injury, as well as other decomposable debris for scavengers to clean up. This worked fine until the crows and coyotes got crowded out by wolves and grizzly bears. So Slaght now dumps his carcasses on a huge hay roll in his driveway and calls a pick-up service to haul it to a composting pit at the nearby state highway gravel yard, where it's grizzly-proofed by concrete-reinforced chain-link fence. The Two Creek Ranch hasn't lost a cow to grizzlies in nineteen years.

Despite that track record, Wayne Slaght and his son Ben said it's been a hard sell getting others to participate.

"It's a pride thing," Ben Slaght said. "A lot of ranchers don't want anyone to know they lost a calf. The pick-up guy isn't supposed to tell anyone who is getting a pick up. But they're afraid word will get around."

Working with government bear managers and nongovernment organizations like Defenders of Wildlife (which help pay for those electric fences, shipping containers, and pick-up services) risks getting you labeled

A tuft of grizzly bear fur clings to a barbed-wire fencepost on a Montana ranch whose owners have participated in numerous programs to keep grizzlies from killing their livestock. Despite the success of such programs, many ranchers and farmers prefer expanded opportunities to kill the bears. Photograph by the author.

as a bear lover by fellow ranchers, Wayne Slaght added. It makes for awkward conversations, especially with someone who lost a yearling just last week instead of two decades ago. Even the idea of getting cash compensation for livestock lost to predators—something several pro-grizzly organizations started doing with donated money in the 1990s—isn't a simple economic decision.

"We're not in the business of getting paid for dead animals," Slaght said. It's called animal husbandry for a reason; losing a cow to a predator, to something you could have or should have fought off, feels like losing a member of the family. Slaght's parents and grandparents couldn't get rid of blizzards, but they could and nearly did get rid of grizzly bears and wolves. Slaght said the national effort to restore those animals (using his tax dollars) "sticks in your craw."

Furthermore, the process of getting compensated for a predator kill is nothing like filing an insurance claim for a weather incident. A US Wildlife Services agent must come out to inspect the scene. The investigator looks for things like hemorrhaging around the bite marks on the skin, showing that the animal was still alive when bitten. Wildlife Services won't pay for carrion, only depredations. And it won't accept camera evidence from a cowboy—only the federal agent. By then, the carcass may have been too decomposed, damaged, or consumed to determine any cause of death. Plus, at the time of the attack there was probably a single grizzly involved. When the investigator arrives, five or six grizzlies might be prowling around waiting for a chance at the remains.

"If you've got a dead calf ten miles away from the house, and there's not enough left to prove anything, you get nothing out of it except you lost a calf and you got madder," Slaght said. "I think a lot of ranchers have quit turning in death loss reports. They're a pain. They're time-consuming. And that makes the (livestock loss) numbers different. The true numbers aren't there. What looks like a decline in livestock reported killed is just a decline in reporting."

A tool Slaght and other ranchers would like to see return is a hunting season. Even after grizzlies made the Endangered Species Act in 1975, until 1991 Montanans could legally hunt them in the Bob Marshall Wilderness Complex. Slaght said he thought that contributed to the paucity of bear incidents when he was a younger rancher; bears had a fear of human hunters and stayed away. While that idea doesn't have either science or history to support it, it remains top-of-mind among grizzly delisting advocates.

"The bears aren't going anywhere and we don't want to go anywhere either," Slaght said. "So we're living with them."

Canadian outfitter and naturalist Andy Russell recounted an incident when ranchers' control efforts backfired spectacularly. A stock association's effort to capture a cow-killing sow grizzly with an undersized trap only injured its paw. "Perhaps she blamed this discomfort on the dead cow, for she promptly went on a cattle-killing spree as though she had invented the pastime," Russell wrote. In favoring her bad leg, the sow developed a distinctive method where she'd run alongside the cow, bite it by the ear, set her feet and flip the victim end over end. She also became so wary of people that any trap or human scent would make her abandon the carcass and seek another. "Thus a killer of truly psychopathic proportion was developed by a misdirection of thrift and further cultivated toward new heights of bovine murder by the very men wishing to destroy her."

⊰ ⊰ ⊰ · ⊱ ⊱ ⊱

Even when the grizzly was the focus of a Western sporting hunt, the hunters tend to smudge the image of fair-chase principles. The exertions necessary to kill a grizzly bear often don't justify the results either. Ernest Hemingway sets a prime example when he shoots his own favorite horse in the head to bait a grizzly in the Beartooth Mountains north of Yellowstone National Park. Hemingway natters on about how "Old Kite" had a split hoof and was too weak for the author to ride yet still wanted to be part of the adventure. Papa receives a rubber-lipped kiss from the horse just before putting a bullet between its eye and ear: "and his feet went straight down under him and all of him dropped together and he was a bear bait." The actual shooting of the grizzly doesn't appear in the story.

Hemingway's son Patrick described a somewhat different hunt in 1936 at the upper end of Crandall Creek above the Clarks Fork Valley in the Beartooths. He was eight years old and got to tag along on a two-family, two-week hunting trip. He recalled "the very first day's encounter with a mature grizzly sow and two almost fully grown cubs and the resulting firefight that lead to sow and one cub, in the words of the hymn, blood-stained, distended, cold and dead." The hymn was *The Most Holy Winding Sheet*, and refers to the crucified body of Jesus Christ.

Other Montana grizzly killers had much less compunction about heroic combat. A Darby rancher named George Solleder claimed to kill his first grizzly in the Big Hole Valley, three or four years after Chief Joseph and his band of Nez Perce Indians fought the Battle of the Big Hole there ("hole" was a common term for "valley" among nineteenth-century trappers). After homesteading at the foot of the Bitterroot Mountains, Solleder lost a cow to a grizzly and began a vendetta against the bears. He reportedly killed five to ten grizzly bears a year for twenty-seven years. On one occasion, he tried to chloroform a hibernating grizzly and drag it from its den for a photograph. The project nearly ended in disaster when the bear woke up as Solleder was trying to focus his box camera under its cape cover. His companions shot it to death.

The story was printed in the *Anaconda Standard* on July 18, 1909. It was one of a plethora of grisly grizzly encounters the paper published, leading to suspicions of pandering to an action-starved audience, in the days before televised car chases.

Two of the men most associated with the concept of fair-chase hunting backed up their ethics with an epic safari within Yellowstone National Park itself. They were Sexton Pope and Earnest Young, whose legacy Pope and Young Club remains court of honor for big-game archery hunters around the globe.

The California Academy of Sciences had wanted a display of grizzlies for its museum in Golden Gate Park, but had failed to acquire a California grizzly before it was extirpated from the state. The last golden bear in California was reported killed in 1922, shot by a cattle rancher eleven years after the state legislature adopted its image for the state flag. In 1917, *Forest and Stream Magazine* editor George Bird Grinnell had written for an American Natural History Museum exhibit that grizzlies "have become the shyest of game animals and are well-nigh extinct." The academy commissioned Pope and Young to fill its desire for a mounted grizzly bear in 1920.

True to their idiom, the hunters decided to fill their tags with archery equipment. In his *Forest and Stream* write-up, Pope noted that "a great many people will say shooting bears in Yellowstone Park is rather a tame proposition. These people think that bears are all over the park, playing around the hotel garbage pile and pillaging camps."

They consulted William Wright's 1909 *The Grizzly Bear* ("the best authority we have"), and hired local guide Ned Frost, who had reportedly killed more than three hundred bears, and himself been mauled by a grizzly. Pope and Young armed themselves with seventy-five-pound-pull

Oregon yew bows—five-foot-eight inches long—shooting birch dowels twenty-eight inches long done up with turkey feathers and tempered steel broadheads. They entered the park in early May.

About four days into the expedition, they spy-glassed a group of five grizzlies: a sow and three cubs followed by a large male. They stalked the grizzlies for three miles, eventually closing within fifty yards. Frost backed them up with "his modern destroyer, a .35 automatic rifle," but was under orders to fire only in desperation: "such an exigency must be considered a failure in our eyes."

The final creep brought them downwind within twenty-five yards of the sow and cubs (or as Pope called it, "four intermingled hearth rugs"). Each man took three arrows.

Pope hit one of the cubs with his first arrow. Young hit the sow with his first. Pope shot her with a second arrow, and she charged both men. Then Frost fired his rifle, breaking her right shoulder. The archers shot at her four more times, hitting twice.

They weighed the female at three hundred and five pounds. The cub weighed one-thirty-five. The men weren't satisfied. They still had ambitions to bring back a large male.

For several more weeks, they scouted unsuccessfully. Pope offered "the sneaking idea that the bear had all been killed off. We knew they had been a pest to campers, wrecking automobiles and chasing visitors up trees. We suspected the Park authorities of quiet extermination."

Finally in early June, elk herds began to fill the valley bottoms as they gave birth to new calves. And grizzlies started to appear, hunting the calves and occasionally the cows. Near Dunraven Pass they spotted boar grizzly bear tracks eleven inches long.

They set up a blind and shot another one hundred-twenty-pound grizzly cub. A few nights later, another family group appeared and the men decided to take them all.

They shot the sow and two cubs, and just as the mother started to charge them, a huge male appeared. Pope shot the sow again and told Pope to shoot the male. The two men fired five arrows and saw him run away clean. They'd missed.

After waiting an hour to make sure the boar wasn't coming back, they set about processing their kills. The sow they logged at five hundred pounds. One cub they found, the other they lost.

Then they went to recover the arrows they'd shot at the boar. One was missing, leading them to believe they might have hit it after all. They spent the rest of the day tracing a blood trail.

"We clambered down, and there he lay, great hulk that he was, on a rock straddled across a tree!" Pope wrote. "He was dead as Caesar, cold and stiff! His rugged coat was matted with blood. Well back in his chest the arrow wound showed clear. I measured him; twenty-six inches of bear had been pierced through and through. One arrow killed him. He was tremendous. His great wide head, his worn and glistening teeth, his massive arms, his vast, ponderous feet and long curved claws—all were there. He was a wonderful beast. It seemed incredible. I thumped Young on the scapula. 'My boy! I congratulate you!'"

They claimed the carcass weighed a thousand pounds. It took nine hours to skin and debone the bear for museum transport. They sustained themselves with broiled grizzly cub steaks and canned beans: "We have the extremely gratifying feeling that we have killed five of the finest grizzly bear in Wyoming—killed them fair and clean with the bow and arrow."

◄ ◄ ◄ · ► ► ►

The Dakota states lost their grizzlies near the turn of the twentieth century. Kansas, Nebraska, Oklahoma, and Texas had all claimed bear populations up until then as well. Utah reported its last grizzly killed in 1923. Oregon's grizzly bears winked out in 1931, along with those in New Mexico and Arizona. Idaho actually moved to protect its remaining population in 1947—the first state to do so.

In Colorado, a lone grizzly was reportedly killed by a black bear hunter in 1979, lending credence to a rumored holdout colony in the San Juan Mountains there. Dedicated searching failed to return confirming evidence, although the Interagency Grizzly Bear Committee briefly considered making the San Juan range a future recovery habitat.

Farm and ranch communities in the grizzly recovery areas of Montana, Idaho, and Wyoming have sent delegations to IGBC meetings with fearful stories of grizzlies menacing their livestock, their senior citizens, and their peace of mind. They demand assurance that any grizzly prowling around a child's school bus stop will be found and removed. And as this book went to press, about half the grizzly bears in the contiguous United States that die by human hands do so in the custody of those who know them best: the state and federal wildlife biologists who respond to bear conflicts. Captured grizzlies suspected of habituation to human food or livestock depredation are usually euthanized with an overdose of the immobilizing drugs used for research activity.

Americans tend to fight with grizzlies to the death, and given our technological superiority, we tend to win. We usually do so either to replace the grizzly with something we prefer, like cattle, or peace of mind at the fishing hole; or to confirm our dominance, both among species and among ourselves. To kill a charismatic megafauna is to become a charismatic megafauna.

Natural history author David Quammen posits another reason: conquerors kill these creatures to show their culture outranks the conquered culture. Colonists around the globe follow a particular pattern when subjugating the locals—they also trammel the landscape. As he put it in *Monster of God*, "it means rooting out those big flesh-eating beasts that rule the woods and the rivers and the swamps, that offer mortal peril to the unwary, and that hold pivotal significance within the belief systems of the natives. Kill off the sacred bear. Kill off the ancestral crocodile. Kill off the myth-wrapped tiger. Kill off the lion. You haven't conquered a people, and their place, until you've exterminated their resident monsters."

Yet if you come to kill the king, you best not miss. Another of Chuck Jonkel's students, Carrie Hunt, built her career refining a skunk-like spray that would deter a charging grizzly. The winning formula uses capsicum, the substance that gives heat to hot peppers. Research has shown bear spray to be highly effective, with a crucial report finding 98 percent of users walking away from their encounter unharmed, and zero fatalities to people *or* bears.

In contrast, a much larger study of grizzly encounters involving firearms found 56 percent of the users were subsequently injured, and 61 percent of the bears died. As Montana bear manager Mike Madel put it at the fourth International Human-Bear Conflict Workshop in 2012, "If you do all the wrong things and end up in an aggressive encounter with a bear, the next wrong thing on the list is hoping to shoot your way out with a gun. Still, I know a lot of bear managers who would like to rely on their firearm."

Bear spray doesn't work the way many people assume. It doesn't incapacitate a grizzly the way mace or tear gas turns a human attacker into a writhing ball of pain. Instead, the cloud of irritation degrades a charging bear's senses of smell and vision as it is attacking. The result is like a jet fighter pilot losing radar in a dogfight: Better to break off and retreat than risk losing the plane while flying blind.

Combat matters. Canadian bear-attack expert Stephen Herrero told me he frequently encounters people who prophylactically douse their tents or backpacks with bear spray like it was mosquito repellent. One man he interviewed drew a circle of spray around his campsite, only to spend the night in a tree while several bears came to investigate. On a hike into Harrison Lake in Glacier National Park, I found a bear spray canister on the trail with a hole the size of a grizzly canine tooth punched in it.

That's because the solution transporting the capsicum is usually something like vegetable oil. In other words, bear spray is an aerosol canister of high-calorie hot sauce. In the rush of combat, it affects a bear's choice to fight or flee. Otherwise, it's food.

The rush of combat also affects a person's ability to handle a firearm. The national debate over gun safety and firearm deaths in school or workplace shootings glosses over how really difficult it is to put a piece of lead the size of your pinkie fingertip exactly where you want it. And that assumes you've done everything properly before pulling the trigger. In a fatal grizzly attack in Wyoming in 2018, a hunting client tried to throw a pistol to his guide as the guide was getting mauled. But the client accidentally ejected the bullet magazine from the gun before he threw it.

Furthermore, as the previous accounts of Chuck Jonkel and the Voyage of Discovery shooters attest, a bullet to the head is about the only way to stop a charging grizzly with a firearm. In contrast, bear spray deploys a defensive wall between opponents, giving both sides opportunity to survive.

◅ ◅ ◅ · ▻ ▻ ▻

The year before Montana ended its legal hunt, I met one of the state's most remarkable grizzly fighters. Nothing about the encounter fit the stereotypical "dead bear" story. Leo Turner killed a five-hundred-pound grizzly bear, in the dark, with a knife.

That made the prospect of finding him for an interview almost as scary as finding the bear. Details of the incident were sparse. The game wardens weren't releasing his name, and only gave vague hints about where the killing took place. The whole thing was "under investigation."

Still, rumor was that a hermit had single-handedly killed a griz with a knife in the night. Brian Kennedy, my boss at the *Hungry Horse News*, knew a great story had to lurk behind that buzz. He challenged me to go find it.

I drove out to the Echo Lake area east of Bigfork, Montana, and started asking people if they'd heard about the grizzly killing. One tip after another narrowed the search down to LaBrant Road. Find the old war vet who raises Rottweilers. He's as mean as his dogs. Crazy, too.

The Rottweilers let Turner know I was coming long before I got to his door. First appearances deceived. A short, thin, quiet man with a trimmed beard politely opened the door, and told me not to worry about the four-legged block of muscle and teeth at his side. Come on in.

Turner was wearing a Montana Centennial sweatshirt with a mountain man printed on the front, and he could have played the part if he scuffed himself up a bit. Outside his house, a thirty-three-by-twenty-foot dog kennel with a six-foot fence stood in disarray. The two-by-eight beam supporting the center of the fence was shoved down nearly to the ground, supported only by a cobweb of wire mesh.

About 11 p.m. April 30, 1990, Turner had gone out to feed his dog pack. They'd been making odd barks, but Turner wasn't concerned. A neighbor had mentioned coyotes were in the area. The first dog he found changed that assumption.

A five-hundred-pound grizzly bear smashed the top of the kennel where Leo Turner penned his rottweiler dogs. A disabled Vietnam veteran, Turner fought and killed the bear with a shotgun and K-bar knife in the dark without realizing exactly what was attacking his dogs. Game wardens ruled the 1990 incident a justifiable killing. Photograph by the author. Courtesy *Hungry Horse News*.

"His chain was tangled around the tree and he wasn't barking or anything," Turner told me. "But he seemed scared. I got him a bowl of food and set it down, and all of a sudden, I heard something ram the back of the kennel."

Grizzly bear No. 149 was a known entity along the Swan Range, having been trapped and collared five years before. He'd rarely been in trouble since, but the spring of 1990 was different. No. 149 had turned up in several reports, including a bizarre incident where two grizzlies had a tremendous battle that coincidentally killed a small poodle. That Monday night, No. 149 had squeezed his bulk through a tiny dog door in the kennel, intent on stealing kibble.

"I saw something black in there and I just thought—it's got to be a black bear," Turner said. A black bear had recently killed one of his puppies and injured two mature Rottweilers.

"I ran to the house and grabbed the only gun that was around loaded, a shotgun," he said. "And a flashlight. But the flashlight was dead and I couldn't see what it was."

The house light didn't help much either. Turner was about four feet from the kennel's corner when he heard the two-by-eight top boards of the fence crack.

"All of a sudden, the whole top of the kennel collapsed," he said. "Something had come right over the top. The game warden said I jumped backwards two yards. He could tell from where he found the hull (of the shotgun shell) I was only about twelve feet away from it when I shot. I'm a disabled veteran. I've got bronchitis and don't do very well on the treadmill any more. I never knew I could jump backward that well."

The evidence on the ground showed Turner had shot once, jumped backward, and fired a second time. His shotgun was loaded with oo-buckshot, and both rounds hit the target he could not see but only sense. A third round jammed in the gun, but he was able to free it with a jerk of the action for a last shot.

Neighbor Chris Lambaise came out with a working flashlight and the two men went back to Turner's house to rearm. Together they went back into the dark woods behind the dog kennel. Lambaise brought a double-barreled shotgun. Turner advanced with a .357 Magnum pistol in his belt and K-bar combat knife in his hand. They could just see a large, dark shape on the ground, facing away on a slight slope.

"I got about halfway up along the body and I saw its right ear," Turner told me. "When I saw it twitch, I jumped up and stabbed it where I thought its heart would be."

Turner stabbed a grizzly bear in the dark. I photographed the knife, still spotted with dried blood. He drove the eight-inch blade behind the bear's shoulder all the way to the hilt and jumped back. The grizzly didn't move again.

In the glow of Lambaise's flashlight, Turner then made out the long claws, white ear-tag, and black radio collar around his victim's neck. He said it wasn't until that moment he realized he'd killed a grizzly bear.

Scribbling notes on my pad, it was that moment I realized I was talking with a man who'd fought a grizzly and won. The details thumped like drum beats. Dark forest. Fenceposts snapping. Something huge. Pistol in belt. Knife in hand.

You went after a monster in the dark with a knife?

Little Leo Turner with bronchitis told me that's what his training told him. Did I remember the TV show *The A-Team*? Mr. T? "I pity da fool!" "I love it when a plan comes together." In the dark, when you're unsure of your opponent, a knife is best.

Leo Turner was an A-Team fighter? There really was an A-Team?

Leo Turner took a framed certificate off his bookshelf. It testified he had passed the requirements to serve in the US Army's A-Team special combat unit in Vietnam. It testified that the silly shoot-em-up action show had origins far darker than actor Dirk Benedict's "Face" Peck implied.

The mountain man on Turner's sweatshirt had more Hollywood chutzpah than its owner did. He told his story without a trace of bravado. Just the opposite.

"He had a magnificent head," said the man who'd given up hunting several years before. "There was no way I could have killed that thing in the daylight, unless he was attacking me and my dogs. He was too pretty."

Seeing Turner with his Rottweilers, that made sense. A Rottweiler's head looks like a fur-covered bowling ball with teeth. It radiates violence. Yet Turner waded into swarms of black-and-brown mayhem like a kindergarten teacher at story time. If you wanted to understand the canine perspective—Dog's Best Friend—you looked at Leo Turner. The only thing military about him was the aura of command and loyalty he displayed among his pack. If something terrified his Rottweilers, Leo Turner would fight that enemy to the death for them. And he did.

It took four men and a winch to get No. 149 into the game warden's truck. It filled the eight-foot bed. Turner was never charged with killing a federally endangered species.

"The warden said it was obvious I didn't know what it was, because nobody would go after a grizzly with a knife," Turner said. "Man, I'm the only guy in the world who can stay at home and still get in trouble."

4

Spirit Animal

IN HIS GREETING TO THE INTERAGENCY GRIZZLY BEAR COMMIT-
tee, a man named Standing Grizzly Bear demonstrated the multifaceted
perspective some cultures have toward animals.

Standing Grizzly Bear is also known as Joe Durglo, and he is the
Confederated Salish and Kootenai tribal historical preservation director.
At the meeting, he greeted the committee with a story from his early
career as a game warden. Durglo worked under Chuck Jonkel from 1977
to '79 on the Border Grizzly Study. He had captured grizzlies and brought
them to Missoula where Jonkel and Carrie Hunt were developing the first
successful bear spray deterrent. For thirteen years, he was the Flathead
Indian Reservation's tribal grizzly bear manager—"only bitten once."

In his younger days, Durglo patrolled the reservation's tribal wilderness area for three days at a stretch, usually solo. Once, heading to Summit
Lake behind McDonald Peak, he was working his way up a set of rocky
switchbacks on the side of a cliff. He heard a *grrrrr*. A grizzly bear was
coming down the same switchback.

"My grandfather had told me what to do, if you ever meet a bear and
have nowhere to run or go," Durglo said. "He said wait for the bear to

charge you. So I did. And just as he was ready to bite me, I reached into his mouth and grabbed his tail and pulled so hard I pulled him inside out. And he turned around and kept running the other way.

"I kind of feel bad about it," he added. "One of these days, I'm going to have to sneak up behind him and make him right."

At the 2018 IGBC meeting where Durglo told his joke, most of the mostly white audience wasn't accustomed to pulling pranks on God. A spirituality where other creatures, and even creation itself, can have a holy relationship with humans in the here and now doesn't fit comfortably with mainstream American Christianity, where people are on earth and God is in heaven.

The Pew Research Center on Religious and Public Life reports 70 percent of the United States identifies as Christian, with only 6 percent avowing "non-Christian" faiths such as Judaism, Islam, Buddhism, and Hinduism. One-fifth of those surveyed claimed they were unaffiliated: either agnostic, atheist, or "nothing in particular."

The numbers of followers of Native American spiritual traditions don't even rank on the survey. But they may play an outsized role in grizzly country.

Durglo spoke shortly after a US Fish and Wildlife Service representative announced that the final rule for removing federal protections from about a thousand grizzlies in the Northern Continental Divide Ecosystem would be published by the end of that year. A few days later, official representatives of the Blackfeet and Confederated Salish and Kootenai tribal governments said they had no intention of meeting that deadline. Furthermore, the tribes said that allowing states to set trophy hunts for grizzlies was a "showstopper," in the words of CSKT Wildlife Program Manager Dale Becker.

"There's more than just biology related to species recovery here," Becker told me. "The larger audience is strictly thinking about wildlife. But grizzly bears are a cut above pretty much every species on the reservation. They have a role in the tribes of tremendous cultural, spiritual, and ecological significance. Travel all over our land looking at petroglyphs, and sooner or later the bear turns up. He's in our elder stories, our grandparents' stories. He's the guardian of our ancestral lands."

The Confederated Salish and Kootenai Tribes (CSKT) were among the first stakeholders to acknowledge and react to the grizzly's listing as a threatened species under the Endangered Species Act in 1975. The tribes designated ninety thousand acres of their Flathead Indian Reservation as tribal wilderness, banned grizzly hunting and imposed seasonal closures on the most popular climbing peaks when grizzlies congregated there to feed on high-altitude ladybugs and moths. Yet 2018 marked the first time the Interagency Grizzly Bear Committee had held a meeting on reservation land since the bear received federal protection.

That matters, because the CSKT and Blackfeet tribal governments have active membership in the Interagency Grizzly Bear Committee, as well as oversight of 2.8 million acres of prime grizzly recovery habitat—more than the entire Bob Marshall Wilderness Complex that forms the core of the Northern Continental Divide Ecosystem for grizzly recovery.

However, American Indians were systematically erased from the grizzly bear story of American settlement. In his influential 1901 essay "Our National Parks," John Muir observed "as to Indians, most of them are dead or civilized into useless ignorance." In that same paragraph, Muir sympathized more with the parks' remaining bears: "Poor fellows, they have been poisoned, trapped and shot at until they have lost confidence in brother man."

‹ ‹ ‹ · › › ›

American Indians hold a complicated position in the recovery of the grizzly bear. Where dominant American society had almost no recorded encounters with grizzlies before 1805, Joe Standing Grizzly Bear Durglo claims a family relationship pushing back ten thousand years, give or take a millennium. He can recite cultural traditions and beliefs regarding grizzly bears that have just as much relevance and durability as the Virgin Mary has to a Christian or Ganesh has to a Hindu. The grizzly shows up in his world creation stories like Adam and Eve and teaches lessons like Siddhartha Buddha. With one whopping difference. Standing Grizzly Bear, and anyone else, can occasionally meet a grizzly bear standing in the trail, word made flesh.

Representatives from hundreds of American Indian communities have declared their stake in the grizzly's future, and many have treaties with the United States government backing their claims. This sets up an engagement between what Harvard biologist and author E. O. Wilson called "the separate magisteriums of science and religion." The declared measuring stick for grizzly bear recovery under the Endangered Species Act is "the best available science." But the decision-makers, by law, include Native American tribes who argue their spiritual and cultural traditions also deserve inclusion in the measurement. And to complicate matters further, many tribal governments have their own wildlife biology programs interacting with cultural committees, distinct from the state and federal wildlife agencies and non-Native society's spiritual and political channels. So while Native American tribes have legal standing in the grizzly bear debate, they often can't speak with one voice. Yet considering their complex relationship with wildlife has ramifications for how all of American society manages its natural resources.

The Interagency Grizzly Bear Committee (IGBC) formed in 1983 to keep all the national, state, local, and tribal stakeholders on the same page regarding grizzly recovery. Although the Endangered Species Act lives in the bureaucracy of the US Fish and Wildlife Service, the creatures touched by the law touch the jurisdictions of many other entities. In the grizzly bear's case, the IGBC has ratified and endorsed recovery strategies and delisting rules. It has directed research in response to court decisions overturning some of those plans and rules. It wears the public face of grizzly bear management in the United States.

But the IGBC has no authority to tell the Fish and Wildlife Service what to do. That left everyone unsure what could happen if the Blackfeet and CSKT didn't endorse a 2018 conservation strategy before the federal agency published a delisting rule for grizzlies in the Northern Continental Divide Ecosystem, which includes the tribes' reservations.

And that's just the procedural part of the story, the administrative conundrum. While officials from those two reservation governments debated their position, at least 277 other Indian representatives published a treaty demanding continued federal protection of grizzly bears. That move struck at the heart of what it means to be Indian in the United States. When someone like Joe Standing Grizzly Bear Durglo can speak with authority as a biologist, cultural elder, sovereign government representative, and United States citizen in the same instant, his testimony fits in no single box. Unlike the cloudy social world of *Facebookii* grizzly fans, Durglo's words live in IGBC testimony, lawsuits, and scientific reports at the crux of grizzly politics in North America.

◄ ◄ ◄ · ► ► ►

Anthropologists and archaeologists have several competing theories describing how and when *Homo sapiens* colonized the continent of North America. Most revolve around the retreat of massive glacial ice fields that blocked passage between what's now called Siberia and Alaska, through an area described in the Pleistocene epoch as Beringia. Now just a necklace of islands in the Bering Sea, Beringia thirteen thousand years ago was a land-bridge allowing migration from humans' Old World to the New. Those ancestors just had to wait until the ice fields shrunk enough that explorers could cross them and find food on the other side before they starved to death.

Paleobiologists propose another impediment: the prehistoric short-faced bear. Don't let the diminutive name mislead. *Arcodus simus* was to *Ursus arctos horribilis* as *Tyrannosaurus rex* was to allosaurus; a two-thousand-pound predator standing seven feet at the shoulder, like a cross between a draft horse and the Terminator. Competing with saber-toothed cats and packs of dire wolves, the short-faced bear of the Pleistocene was the maître d' of the North American carnivorous welcoming committee.

So how did those early humans get past those obstacles of ice and teeth to eventually reach the beaches of Tierra del Fuego at the tip of South America? In English-language folklore, stories start with the ritual "Once upon a time." A Crow Indian storyteller I met has a different tradition: Her tales begin "Long ago, when the animals were bigger."

Archaeological evidence indicates humans may have made several unsuccessful attempts to colonize North America before a technological breakthrough changed everything. This was the perfection of a stone blade now known as the Clovis point. Combined with our strategizing pack societies, the lethal six- to eight-inch-long spear tips helped *Homo sapiens* outcompete the Pleistocene megafauna around the beginning of the current era geologists call the Holocene.

Whether we as a predatory species can take responsibility for exterminating the short-faced bear, wooly mammoth, giant sloth, and other enormous inhabitants of North America remains debatable. What is clear is that about two thousand years after Clovis-equipped hunting parties appeared in Beringia, the bigger animals were gone and *Homo sapiens* was established. And across most of the western half of the continent, the one remaining competitor to human dominance—the one mammal still willing to push us around—was the grizzly bear.

In the Holocene era, *Ursus arctos horribilis* dominated the North American food chain from Alaska to Mexico and east across the Great Plains to the beaches of the Pacific Ocean. Almost every Indian tribal culture in that half of the continent built grizzly bears into their cosmology. But while the grizzly consistently appears among the most powerful of spiritual beings, it rarely plays a leadership role.

Around the world, many Indigenous traditions about the grizzly bear suppose the bear's winter hibernation gives it access to both the common and the spiritual worlds, light and dark. That makes it the intercessor, the same role saints serve for Roman Catholics seeking the guidance of God. Eighteenth-century European philosophers like Immanuel Kant and Edmund Burke imbued certain wild landscapes with this quality of the sublime—places so emotionally resonant that holy presence must be woven into towering mountains and cascading waterfalls. Seeing a grizzly bear in such a place concentrates that abstract wonder in a way reminiscent of the Israelites in Exodus 16:10, who "looked toward the wilderness, and behold, the glory of the Lord appeared in the cloud."

Yet those who have tight connections to grizzlies often get pushed to the fringe in many Native American cultures, including the Salish, Kootenai, and Piegan Blackfeet whose present-day nations surround grizzly bear recovery areas. The grizzly carries too much power, too much chaos, to traffic in common society. That's not a sign of disrespect for the grizzly—just the opposite. It contains a force beyond human control or comprehension. And while a spiritual seeker doesn't need to go there; they might want to. The grizzly is Nature's performance-enhancing drug.

Yet taking that drug, while it may make you better, it will also extract a price. Because what do you do when you enter the wilderness? You meet the wild. You meet thunderstorms that rattle your teeth, rivers that rip your boots off, and, just maybe, a grizzly bear that might maul you. You measure yourself against the Universe, see how infinitesimally tiny you are compared to the indifferent cosmos, and yet you come out somehow enlarged.

Take the bear out of the temple, and the magic becomes indifferent. The thunderstorms and rivers and mountain peaks don't look you in the eye. They don't pass judgment on your worthiness, or edibility, or threat potential. It's not anthropomorphizing to say the grizzly makes a decision about any encounter between the two of you, one in which you have virtually no standing to justify or sway. As the Glacier Park T-shirt says, "Some days the bear gets you; Some days it just walks away." Get sanctified by a grizzly bear, and you wear a pan-denominational robe of glory.

Anyone with any affinity for wilderness longs for that kind of transfiguration. That promise that if I go in deep, I will return empowered, enlightened—or at least verified as beyond merely human.

◄ ◄ ◄ · ► ► ►

In twenty-first-century American culture, that experience gets tangled up in woolly-headed self-realization efforts along with drum circles and corporate team-building exercises. Americans have long been suspicious of such semi-secular enrichment attempts. Even wilderness philosopher Henry David Thoreau mused about the "savage and dreary" summit of Mount Katahdin; "a place of heathenism and superstitious rites—to be inhabited by men nearer of kin to the rocks and wild animals than we." A century later, Emma Marris wrote in *Rambunctious Garden*, "To my mind, the wilderness cult can also be seen as the Americanization of an essentially European romanticism, with less swooning and more shooting, less poetry and more adventure stories."

Environmental historian William Cronon points out this fundamental obstacle to debating about wilderness: No one has agreed to the basic terms. For example, does "natural and unnatural" mean the same as "good and bad"? Is something that is natural automatically good? If nature is natural, is civilization unnatural (and therefore bad)?

Before we should have ever gotten to this point in the debate, Cronon reminds us to reflect on our respective definitions. What we find to be "natural" tends to be highly specific to the individual, and often grows from the kind of place each of us grew up in. A city-dweller might consider a sycamore tree growing on one side of a sidewalk natural compared to the office tower on the other. Someone living near Redwood National Park might consider that same sycamore unnatural and out of place compared to a giant sequoia. Cronon himself questions whether the designation of national parks imposes an unfounded "natural" quality on the landscape contained inside, given the level of "unnatural" human management that goes on there.

And even Cronon can get tangled up in terminology when he writes "wilderness fulfills the old romantic project of secularizing Judeo-Christian values so as to make a new cathedral not in some petty human building but in God's own creation, Nature itself." Ironically, the term "Judeo-Christian" has little historical reference to some scriptural foundation in the Bible of the Jews and the New Testament of the Christians. Religion historian Healan Gaston and others have shown that the term expanded into American conversation in the 1930s, when an interfaith coalition of Jewish and Roman Catholic activists popularized it as a counter to the rise of the Ku Klux Klan, Nazis, and "godless" Communists in Europe (while simultaneously claiming allegiance with the American White Anglo-Saxton Protestant power structure that discriminated against Jews and Catholics).

Another perspective exists, one that pervades the ethos of thousands of non-Western cultures. The Creator did not give Man dominion over the earth and all its creatures (as the Book of Genesis puts it) in every community of humans. Many perceive people as coequal inhabitants to the surrounding plants and animals, and quite a few consider us subordinate to them. For example, creation stories told on both the Blackfeet and Flathead Indian reservations begin with the arrival of animal *persons*, such as the Grizzly Bear Person, who prepare a place for and assist the survival of the pathetically naïve human *people* that appear later. The distinction between animals as individual characters and humans as a group stays consistent across many tribal cultures.

Inuit communities north of the Arctic Circle named their bear god Nanuq, one of the oldest members of their spiritual world. The Haida tribe along the Alaskan coast told of Rhpisunt, a bear-mother-goddess with awesome supernatural powers. Tribes in the American Southwest often describe the House of the Sun typically guarded by a bear and a serpent. The Navajo deity Estanatlehi sent a bear to protect new clans of humans and teach them how to hunt.

A remarkable note about these grizzly traditions is the variety of attitudes a bear might display. They can be ferocious, benevolent, greedy, rude, nurturing, fumbling, wise, ignorant, and comic. The Medicine Grizzly of the Blackfeet taught people how to use plants for healing. Giant bears terrorized a group of Kiowa girls so terribly that the Rock Spirit took pity and lifted them to safety onto a massive tower of stone; the bears carved deep grooves in the tower with their claws, trying to catch the girls. The Kiowa call the formation Tso'Ai, or Bear's Lodge; modern tourists visiting Wyoming call it Devils Tower National Monument. A Romanian folktale recounts the Devil's attempt to win a man's soul in a wrestling match. The man persuades the Devil to wrestle his "Old Uncle" first and sends him into a bear's cave, where the bear thrashes him.

"The grizzly was the leader of all the animals with the eagle before people arrived," Salish traditional elder Johnny Arlee explained to me. "He was always the grouch."

◁ ◁ ◁ · ▷ ▷ ▷

Two caveats here. First, I don't intend to argue that Indigenous American spirituality somehow outranks the religions or philosophies imported from across the oceans. That's especially true when discussing how these animals might play roles in human affairs. As historian Dan Flores observed, animistic and shamanistic religions "accord admirable respect to entities outside the human sphere . . . but the ceremonial lives and cosmologies of most primary cultures are actually extremely human-centered." That said, I don't believe that a people's traditions can be dismissed as inferior just because its culture doesn't have a legacy of universities, courts, and libraries recording its opinions. I would not want to be the person claiming the Creator gives preference to supplicants with scribes over those without.

And second, I'll stake my credentials as a journalist that I have tried to transparently observe and report on the forces at play in the fate of the grizzly bear. But I don't claim any authority or qualification to handle the spiritual tools of various cultures, any more than I could sanctify a Jewish wedding or turn bread and wine into flesh and blood before a Christian altar. For example, when I asked Arlee to share some stories about grouchy grizzlies on an August afternoon, he explained he could not because there was no snow on the ground: in Salish (and many other tribal) practice, such stories are only told during winter months.

With that in mind, I do intend to boldly go where others have publicly gone before. In the clash of cultures, competing religions often claim their occult qualities can overcome the resources of others. What they do in their sacred sanctuaries is up to them. I intend to show how their stories about bears compete in the marketplace of ideas.

In his ethnological study *Giving Voice to Bear*, David Rockwell notes that bear-hunting traditions present remarkably similar details around the globe. The hunt almost always has an explicit spiritual or ritual purpose, never just a subsistence exercise for another source of meat. The hunter usually asks permission to kill the bear, and the bear either grants it or finds the hunter unworthy. If successful, hunters in both North America and Eurasia make elaborate apologies or thank-yous to the bear's spirit. Lengthy lists of procedures and taboos surround the field-dressing, delivery, and eating of the meat. Killing a bear often means hosting a feast, and the circumstances and observance of rules throughout the occasion may foretell the fate of the whole clan in the coming year.

Women have particularly complicated roles. An Ojibwa girl experiencing her first menstrual period was considered "going to be a bear," a time Rockwell described as so powerful "that her glance or touch could bring paralysis to another, death to a child or the destruction of the year's berry crop." This wasn't a liability so much as an acknowledgment of the girl realizing her true power as a woman.

Nevertheless, contact with bear items, even stepping over blood on the ground or breathing steam from a pot of bear stew, "would make a woman mean, insane or physically ill," according to Alaskan anthropologist Richard Nelson. Bear items retained power for a long time as well. Nelson's Yukon elders told him:

> When a brown bear has been killed, none of its meat should be brought into the village for some days or weeks; it is too fresh and potent with easily affronted spiritual energy. During earlier years, in fact, it was left in a cache at the kill site until the midwinter potlatch memorializing people who had died in the previous year. The meat was finally brought in just before it was cooked. Nowadays it is left "out there someplace" at least until it is frozen. Doing this ensures that the meat is fully dead before it comes near the dangerous presence of women. And it eliminates all chances of getting the animal's blood on the sled, canvas cover or anything a woman might later touch or step over.

The bulk of these writings come from male authors—something anthropologist Barbara Tetlock calls out for possibly missing important nuances. For example, she cites an account of an Iglulik seance recorded by Danish ethnographer Knud Rasmussen in the early twentieth century, where the male shaman assumed the role of a spirit bear while his wife served as "his assistant":

> Then came a fierce growl [from the husband], followed by a wild shriek, and at the same moment, Tuglik [the wife] dashed forward and began talking to the spirits. She spoke in her own particular spirit language. . . . Tuglik informed us that her husband, in the shape of a fabulous bear, had been out exploring the route we were to follow on our long journey. All obstacles had been swept aside, accident, sickness and death were rendered powerless, and we should all return to the safety of our house the following summer. All this had been communicated in the special language of the spirits, which Tuglik translated for us.

Tedlock also chronicled numerous encounters with husband-and-wife shamanic teams. In most, she notes the man would be possessed by the bear spirit while the woman remained "intellectually alert and interactive with both the spirits and the audience." Folklorist Ella Clark's *Indian Legends from the Northern Rockies* adds how grizzly bears choose women over men to receive wisdom and advice. Clark recounts numerous stories from Salish Indian women about dream visits by female grizzly bears who taught lessons in herb lore and midwifery. The dismissal or omission of women's shamanic presence in many anthropological records may stem from the common association of wildlife with hunting, which many historians presumed was a mostly male activity. Tedlock and others, however, have expanded the historical record with accounts that not only present female participation in hunting, but indicate a long-standing tendency of scholars to willfully ignore those stories in favor of more traditional male-dominated versions.

◄ ◄ ◄ · ► ► ►

In the United States, environmentalists often face criticism for bringing up Native American traditions at all. Doing so troubles the popular reliance on Christian principles, including its rejection of pagan earth-worshiping. Indigenous knowledge also competes with mainstream scientific and historic interpretation, without the advantages of universities and institutions that have spent generations setting out the rules of public debate. Furthermore, relying too much on tribal spirituality's novelty and mythic purity ignores the fact that various tribes have found one another's practices as suspect as they found the Christianity of white society.

That said, losing the grizzly along with everything else related to their former precedence in the American West has left deep wounds in many tribal communities. And their members have mounted campaigns for retribution.

Blackfeet musician and activist Jack Gladstone went from Stone Age to Space Age when he chastised an IGBC meeting in 2017. He reminded them that just a half-century before, Apollo 8 astronaut Bill Anders took the iconic "Earthrise" photo of his home planet adrift in empty space.

"We saw our home for the first time from a different perspective," Gladstone said of Anders's image. "From time immemorial, there were bears that were here before us. And for at least the fifteen thousand years that people have been here, bears have always been a part of our ecosystem, part of the original palette of creation."

Gladstone didn't deploy that palette for a painting of interspecies harmony. In fact, he considered problem bears a crucial part of the picture.

"We have to expand our own comfort zone a little bit more. I have bears all around me. When they get too close to the house, the dogs go out and give them a bad time. All Crazy Dogs [the Blackfeet protective society] is modeled after that sense. Let us find ways where we can be neighbors, allies on this shrinking earth in however much time we have left."

About 5.4 million people describe themselves to the US Census as "American Indians," "Alaska Natives," or some combination thereof. That roughly accounts for 2 percent of the United States population, and represents hundreds of different Native nations and communities, with distinct cultures, traditions, languages, treaty rights, and political positions. Blackfeet Jack Gladstone and Salish Joe Durglo stand affiliated only in their respective sovereign relations with the United States government. To say either Gladstone or Durglo presents the "Indian" perspective in this debate would be both incomplete and inaccurate.

Canadians, Indigenous and otherwise, have produced a different solution with the term "First Nations." That incorporates both primacy of residence and sovereignty. Because where the grizzly bear is concerned, both history and agency matter. One gives you something to contribute. The other gets you a seat at the table. The Endangered Species Act confers rights of consultation to Indian tribes that have a verified stake in a recovery process.

So where is this table around which we debate the fate of the grizzly bear? Before anybody sits down, we'd better lay out some ground rules. Because by participating in the formal grizzly bear recovery process, tribal members add some value perspectives very different from the assumptions mainstream American agencies proceed from.

Yale School of Forestry and Environmental Studies scholar Stephen Kellert described nine separate ways people make value decisions about wildlife. Knowing which system someone believes in can head off apples-and-oranges arguments that otherwise bog down management debates. Kellert's categories boil down into three general approaches.

The first approach or group of methods starts with utilitarianism, the most common framework used in American wildlife agency management: the greatest good for the greatest number for the longest time. The idea was codified by Gifford Pinchot in his wise-use philosophy of public lands at the turn of the twentieth century. It commonly crops up in position papers where someone argues that grizzly-related tourism contributes $X million dollars to the local economy, or grizzly livestock depredation costs ranchers $Y million a year. Resolve the cost-benefit analysis and get your policy.

When biological processes can't be reduced to dollars—and they often can't— policy makers shift to eco-scientific values. Does recovering the grizzly bear enhance or improve an ecosystem? Does it fulfill Aldo Leopold's dictum of intelligent tinkering—to first save all the parts? Does the bear's presence keep a check on wolf populations? Does its scat fertilize and reseed landscapes?

Combining these two methods often results in a third hybrid: symbolic value. This gets brought up a lot in Endangered Species Act arguments—the need for a victory. Getting the grizzly bear across the finish line from protection to "delisting" counts as a political touchdown, proof that there's an end to the long trial and tribulation and the expense of resuscitating the species, marking a time to celebrate and pass out plaques of appreciation. Declaring a symbolic victory in eco-scientific matters often allows utilitarian interests to progress. Once we've commodified the ecology, we know where it's safe or allowable to make money.

Kellert's second approach starts with naturalistic values, measured by emotional satisfaction. Did seeing a grizzly bear on a tour of Yellowstone Park become the high-point of the vacation? Did it make the journey worth the gas and hotel rooms and the kids whining "are we there yet?" Recreation managers swim in these waters, trying to equate the satisfaction of experiencing nature with the need to expand roadside parking pullouts in national parks.

One way they do that is through aesthetic values, which combine naturalistic and eco-scientific principles. Does the grizzly complete some sense of correct or functional order in the landscape? Does it add beauty? Aesthetics assume the ecosystem has its own standards of perfection, regardless whether it makes us humans feel good about its improvement. Restoring a threatened predator may trigger a trophic cascade, where grizzly bears and wolves keep herds of elk moving around, which reduces the grazing impact on creek sides, which increases the survival of trees favored by songbirds. The trouble with the trophic cascade hypothesis is that, given the massive number of moving parts, it is really difficult to test scientifically. But it works out intuitively in an aesthetic sense: This is how the ecosystem was set up before we started tinkering with it, so returning it to that original state must be good. Scientists themselves get sucked into aesthetics, often depending on the "elegance" of an equation to support its veracity.

Kellert's third values approach looks more inward than outward. They offer ways for an individual to rank his or her place in the system—an internal scorecard.

The most obvious are moralistic values: I have followed a code I believe in, that orders my life, and that I benefit from by accomplishing beneficial tasks. Many Native American spiritual cultures feature moralistic motivations, because the grizzly plays an intrinsic part in their perception of the sacred. The extirpation of the grizzly from the American West erased a significant character from their creation stories, cultural guidance, and traditional understanding of the world. Restoring the grizzly to the landscape attempts to mend a broken seam in the spiritual fabric.

The culture of the settlers and pioneers who displaced the Indians tended to be more dominionistic: Did I show I'm in charge? The driving principle of Manifest Destiny was to dominate the New World from coast to coast, with specific details to be worked out on the trail. It also brings in a Darwinian survival-of-the-fittest resolution: If it wins, it is good.

Dominionism's kid brother is negativism: I kill what I hate or fear. That may not seem like a guiding value, until you think about attitudes of racism, bigotry, and political polarization. Responding negatively tends to be the baseline reaction to "the other" when something outside our group challenges us for space or possessions (which often happens when we meet grizzly bears).

Which gets us to the most complicated of Kellert's inward-looking values: humanistic. The bear is my brother. I owe it respect and honor. By showing the bear mercy, I am becoming a better person. By acknowledging the grizzly's intrinsic worth, I understand my place in the council of life.

In college, I earned a degree in political science. In practice, political science examines the use of power, whether by cash, campaigns, or culture. One of my more cynical professors referred to it as "professional cocktail party conversation."

Here's where we professional cocktail party conversationalists start spilling drinks. Humanistic values, by etymology, originate from humans. To apply them to creatures outside our species crashes into all kinds of assumptions unconsciously built into the original premise. In an essay titled *The Uncanny Goodness of Being Edible to Bears,* philosopher James Hatley pokes at our perceived place on top of the food chain. How, he asks, can humans eat anything they want on the planet, and yet declare themselves so inedible as to make it a crime for something else to eat us? When a grizzly bear kills a human and eats it, we call the act "inhumane."

"One can think while entering a wilderness area of how inhumanely one would be treated if attacked by an animal," Hatley writes. "Whether the animal is a vicious human or a morally oblivious grizzly bear is irrelevant to this sense of the inhumane. . . . The bear is seamlessly woven into the natural world in which one flesh eating another is the very condition by which any flesh finds itself living."

Applying humanistic values also stomps muddy feet into a debate roiling scientific cocktail parties: the emotional lives of animals. Attributing motivations to animal behavior beyond instinct or environmental conditioning remains a controversial practice in zoological circles. Yet their records bulge with examples of animals acting in ways that can't be explained by such deterministic mechanisms. Look through the annals of wildlife conflict management and try to excise the descriptions of grizzlies with individual personalities that game wardens cite when deciding whether to relocate or kill a captured bear.

This matters because decisions about grizzly bear recovery typically get made at the Interagency Grizzly Bear Committee in a three-ring circus of competing values. A policy might get approved on the basis of utilitarian or eco-scientific values, but get challenged from negativistic, moralist, or symbolic vectors. How do you judge between my claim that the beauty of a mountain lake is improved by the presence of a grizzly against your charge that the bear has scared you away from your favorite fishing spot? Does the grizzly's restraint of ungulate overpopulation by gobbling elk calves in the spring offset the loss of guided hunting trips for elk in the fall?

◄ ◄ ◄ · ► ► ►

Kellert's categories get reprinted in dozens of environmental policy papers. But they have two shortcomings. I'll call them the majority and minority reports.

Mainstream American society, being predominantly Christian, imparts a subconscious theological spin on environmental issues. For many Christians, God has the ultimate, highest possible value against which everything else gets measured. That includes creation, which comes from the Creator.

That sounds esoteric until you open the first chapter of the first book in the Hebrew Bible, Genesis 1:26: "And God said, Let us make man in our image, after our likeness, and let them have dominion over the fish of the sea and over the fowl of the air, and over the cattle, and over all the earth, and over every creeping thing that creepeth upon the earth." Dominion quickly becomes political.

If you hold that only God has intrinsic value, and we humans have inherent value because God loves us above all the rest of creation, then creation has only instrumental value as an asset given by God for us to use. As Kant put it, nature "receives the dominion of Man as meekly as the ass on which the Savior rode." Ergo, the US Fish and Wildlife Service has God-given authority to decide the fate of the grizzly bear.

Environmental ethicists struggle with this mindset for a couple of reasons. In 1967, as Congress debated early drafts of the Endangered Species Act and the Clean Water Act, Lynn White wrote an essay, "The Historical Roots of Our Ecological Crisis." It declared Western Christianity "the most anthropocentric religion the world has seen . . . [which] not only established a dualism of man and nature but also insisted that it is God's will that man exploit nature for his proper ends." This anthropocentric, religious assumption has woven through land-use politics for decades, despite the fact that many religious leaders have since disavowed it. In his 2015 encyclical *Laudato Si'*, Roman Catholic Pope Francis stated "Clearly the Bible has no place for a tyrannical anthropocentrism unconcerned for other creatures." Or as Wendell Berry put it, "In the hereafter, the Lord may forgive our wrongs against nature, but on earth, so far as we know, He does not overturn her decisions."

Politicians usually accomplish and justify that exploitation without religious reference, using other methods in Kellert's system of values. Do we prefer a utilitarian balance weighing the dollars earned from tourism compared to logging in grizzly habitat, or an eco-scientific analysis of a landscape functioning with or without its keystone predator species?

The key word in all of that is *we*. Here's where the minority report weighs in.

Christian environmental ethicists such as Andrew Spenser insist on keeping God as the *summum bonum*—the ultimate good—and consider it a theological error when "the God of the Bible is replaced with Gaia, and the created order becomes something that should be treasured as an end in itself—perhaps even worshiped."

However, Americans must render unto Caesar what is Caesar's and unto God what is God's. Christians may exert majority rule over the United States, but according to the US Constitution the Bible is not a founding legal document. Other interest groups exist, some with different theological foundations and some with sovereign legal rights. Some of them get to sit at the grizzly fate table.

That's why considering how differing cultures view the grizzly might help guide what *we* (that word again) decide to do about it. Because—religious, legal, and ethical presumptions aside—*we* have appointed ourselves the deciders of the grizzly's future survival.

Some people derive life-changing benefit from seeing a grizzly. What is that worth? How does a Hindu explain to a Muslim that in India a cow is sacred and must be allowed to wander in the streets unmolested, until it wanders across the border into Pakistan, where it's a commodity to be eaten and tanned into leather? How do I tell a Hutterite farmer on the Rocky Mountain Front that my grizzly sighting is worth his family having to live behind electric fences? All those precepts get thrown in a blender when North America's sovereign Indian nations get involved. And they have, in a big way.

⊰ ⊰ ⊰ · ⊱ ⊱ ⊱

In 2016, a small group of grizzly bear protection advocates started a campaign to drive a wedge into the delisting debate. It resulted in the Piikani Grizzly Treaty, bearing signatures of more than 150 tribal groups and nations as of mid-2020, demanding the grizzly bear retain protection under the Endangered Species Act. It also condemned any attempt to return to a hunting season for grizzly bears. The Guardians of Our Ancestors' Legacy (GOAL) Tribal Coalition spoke for many of the participants.

"What they (state wildlife agencies) are wanting to do with the grizzly bear is an extension of Manifest Destiny," GOAL council leader Jay Old Coyote wrote in a statement to then-president Barack Obama. "Their ancestors' solution was killing, and so is theirs. They harbor the arrogance of colonialism. These state game agencies are run by great white hunters for the sole benefit of other great white hunters at the exclusion of everybody else. But they forget that this will always be our land. We will always be the first people to call this land home."

The treaty signers insisted they had a right to participate in the grizzly recovery process. Here's where things get complicated. The signatories fall into a variety of categories. Many tribal nations, elected by specific tribal communities, have backed the treaty. The Standing Rock Sioux Tribe, Crow Tribe, and Northern Cheyenne Tribe all signed through their respective tribal business councils or executive offices.

Then come tribal cultural groups such as the Blackfeet All Crazy Dogs Society. That private group may represent the social power structure of a reservation, but it doesn't have government-to-government sovereign standing to address the US Fish and Wildlife Service.

That results in scenes like an IGBC meeting in 2017 when a self-announced Blackfeet tribal medicine chief named Jimmy St. Goddard claimed standing to argue the bears deserve far more protection than his tribal government seemed interested in providing.

Blackfeet Indian activist and medicine chief Jimmy St. Goddard argued for the grizzly bear's religious significance in a federal lawsuit challenging the US Fish and Wildlife Service's effort to delist the bear in 2018. Photograph by the author.

"They've got a gun to my grizzly's head," St. Goddard said during the meeting in Choteau, Montana, with a delegation of those Hutterite farmers in the room. "All of this is because of money. This is wrong what you're doing to the grizzly. I could pay you when the government pays me all the trillions of dollars they owe me. I think you guys should come to your senses."

At the same meeting, Blackfeet Tribal Fish and Wildlife chief Donna Rutherford represented the tribal leadership and said the Blackfeet Tribal Business Council was not opposed to delisting grizzly bears, although it also did not support allowing anyone to hunt them on the Blackfeet Reservation. Just two months before, two opposing factions of Blackfeet elected leaders each claimed to be the tribal business council, with one locking the other out of the government offices in Browning for almost a year. Then in 2019, a new iteration of the Blackfeet Tribal Business Council endorsed the Piikani Treaty. That year, another Blackfeet tribal member named Kristin Kipp became a member of the Montana governor's Grizzly Bear Advisory Committee and testified that her kids couldn't play in the yard for fear of grizzly bears and called for delisting, state management, and lethal control.

The Northern Arapaho and Eastern Shoshone tribes of the Wind River Reservation bordering the southeast corner of Yellowstone National Park have grizzly bears on their land, but lack voting seats at the IGBC. In 2009, their combined tribal wildlife agency declared the grizzly bear was a game animal. Northern Arapaho elder Lynnette Grey Bull repudiated that rule in testimony to Congress. The Shoshone-Bannock Tribe claims heritage on the Wind River Reservation, although it is located on the Fort Hall Reservation in Idaho, two hundred air-miles to the west. All three tribal governments have signed on to the Piikani Treaty.

The Crow Tribe has no known grizzly bears on its reservation, which lies outside the demographic monitoring area of the Greater Yellowstone Ecosystem (GYE), but it is the lead plaintiff in the most salient legal challenge to the GYE's delisting decision, *Crow Tribe v. Zinke*. It's one of twenty-six tribal nations that have raised claims of sovereign consultation in the GYE delisting based on historic and prehistoric association with grizzlies in that conjunction of modern-day Montana, Idaho, and Wyoming. All told, at least fifty-three tribes have declared a cultural and historical connection specifically to the Greater Yellowstone Ecosystem. Keep in mind that the Crow are historic enemies of the Northern Cheyenne Tribe, even though their tribal nations border one another and they stand together in the lawsuit.

Then what about the Hopi, Navajo, Pawnee, and dozens of other tribes who claim traditional and ancestral kinship to the grizzly? They've signed the treaty, declaring their own sovereign authority to participate in the bear's fate as it grinds through the delisting process.

The Piikani Treaty exists as a manifesto more than a legal commitment. Lots of other treaties, however, give Indian tribes the standing and authority to participate in the grizzly's future with the US government. As sovereign nations, the tribes have some intriguing cards to play.

"[T]here has been no discussion in this process related to the impact delisting the grizzly bear, and the subsequent trophy hunting of the grizzly, will have on Native American spirituality, namely the religious practices of traditional tribal people," Standing Rock Sioux tribal chairman

Dave Archambault said in 2015 as the Piikani Treaty gathered attention. The American Indian Religious Freedom Act and the Endangered Species Act each grant Indian tribes consultation rights greater than that afforded the general public. Those commitments, Archambault insisted, had not been met. While the Fish and Wildlife Service did provide consultation meetings in 2014, GOAL members ridiculed the effort for reaching just four of thirty-three tribes seeking participation.

That consultation request arms an explosive new concept in Indian legal deliberations. As of 2019, tribal arguments under the American Indian Religious Freedom Act and Religious Freedom Restoration Act haven't found much courtroom traction in efforts to reclaim land territory, even when tribes presented evidence of sacred or cultural landmarks that had been excluded from their reservations. Claiming spiritual ownership of the grizzly bear opens an entirely different door.

Montana's Blackfeet, Fort Belknap, and Fort Peck reservations have already started efforts to restore wild bison to their lands. A growing body of science shows that bison and bears shared a tight ecological and evolutionary relationship in the western prairies where they roamed when Lewis and Clark first depicted them to the larger American public. The Blackfeet already have both bison and bears on the east side of Glacier National Park. So do the Confederated Salish and Kootenai Tribes southwest of Glacier, although those buffalo live behind high fences on the National Bison Range (another Fish and Wildlife Service institution with its own complicated story).

The Northern Cheyenne, Crow, Rocky Boys', Fort Belknap, and Fort Peck reservations together encompass more than five million acres of historical grizzly bear habitat. What if they decide they want bears back? That's not idle speculation. The *Crow Tribe v. Zinke* initial complaint specifically said tribes wanted to restore the grizzly bear—not just to recovery status, but as a resident species on several reservations. They argued that sport hunting "profoundly disrupts, if not entirely prevents, the GYE grizzly bears' sustainable recovery to its full habitat range, including lands within the jurisdictional boundaries of the Tribes and/or their treaty or aboriginal lands, including culturally and spiritually significant lands."

The Crow and Blackfeet tribes together have claims on virtually all the grizzly bear's historical habitat in Montana, documented on maps made by the US federal government. The present-day reality that title to those lands has been vested in the trust of ranchers, farmers, and city-dwellers of other races and cultures continues to be a point of courtroom dispute. Beyond the presence of sport hunters, grizzly bears must also contend with interstate highways, domesticated ungulates, and school playgrounds competing for their homeland. No legal decision will likely rewrite those deed books.

But the religious argument may transcend property rights. There's already precedent for Indian entitlement to the feathers of bald and golden eagles—federally protected species—that non-Indians may not possess. Were they to claim such entitlement to grizzly bears, which wander in and out of their reservations, that could extend to protection from any form of discretionary hunting. The 2018 district court brief forecast a potentially bloody clash could occur if an Indian stands between a hunter and a grizzly bear he or she considers sacred. That "will result in not only physical danger, but civil and criminal liability as well," the brief stated, "accordingly this conference of (state hunting) rights coerces plaintiffs into complicity with behaviors that contravene plaintiffs' sincere religious beliefs." In other words, does an Indian making a spiritual-rights claim by protecting a grizzly bear from a hunter actually commit hunter harassment, a criminal offense in Montana, Wyoming, and Idaho? Or would the protection be a treaty-backed, constitutional exercise in Freedom of Religion?

The tribes' participation opens up another interesting vector in the grizzly recovery process. The Endangered Species Act requires the Fish and Wildlife Service to make its decisions based on the best scientific and commercial data available. Indian attorneys question the legality of limiting the decision to only those value systems.

"It is the position of the FWS that they cannot consider the religious implications of their delisting decision because this would conflict with the ESA," the tribal attorneys wrote in *Crow Tribe v. Zinke*. "This position is in violation of RFRA [Religious Freedoms Restoration Act] and is arbitrary and capricious."

In a play for judicial efficiency, all the tribal religious arguments got left on the sideboard during the 2018 case. The judge decided the government flunked three more basic tests of its best scientific and commercial data regarding where the bears were, how they were counted, and whether they could safely travel between recovery areas.

Jimmy St. Goddard was in the courtroom, although his testimony never got debated. He came robed in a star-covered shawl, carrying a medicine bundle with a large eagle wing in one hand and a briefcase in the other.

"I hope that every American realizes he's like the bald eagle," St. Goddard said of the grizzly bear. "People would be outraged if you shot the bald eagle from the sky."

5

From a Single Hair

A POPULAR GAG POSTCARD IN MONTANA SOUVENIR SHOPS SHOWS a group portrait of bandaged and traumatized men outside a winter cabin: The Grizzly Bear Artificial Insemination Team.

I haven't found a picture of wildlife biologist Albert W. Erickson's research squad, but I'd bet they were the true-life models. Erickson pioneered tranquilizing grizzly bears for study, using a foot snare and an ether mask. Despite a field design that would give Wile E. Coyote pause, Erickson caught about one hundred grizzlies this way in 1952.

Five years later, twin brothers John and Frank Craighead picked up the task of introducing the human audience to the grizzly world. Their methods were scientific, although they borrowed heavily from popular culture in the way they crafted their stories. Inadvertently, they illustrated how scientific research depends as much on the audience as the investigation.

And they had an audience. In twenty-first-century terms, the Craigheads were multiplatform performers. As college sophomores before World War II, the Craigheads had bull-rushed *National Geographic Magazine* into publishing their stories of raising hawks. Their sister Jean Craighead George wrote the children's novel *My Side of the Mountain* about

Sam Gribley, a boy who survives alone raising falcons. It was based on her childhood experience with brothers Frank and John, who started raising falcons when they were just fourteen years old. She also wrote a girls' version, *Summer of the Falcon*.

During the war, the brothers taught military survival classes and cowrote *How to Survive on Land and Sea*. Its first edition came out in 1943. My copy of their fourth edition was published in 1984.

So when they decided to aim their curiosity at Yellowstone National Park's grizzly bears, they probably could have been sponsored by the TV-dinner industry. Their next ten years of adventures with bears made must-see Sunday evening watching on *Mutual of Omaha's Wild Kingdom* and National Geographic specials.

In 1957, Frank Craighead outlined a proposal to use dart guns with tranquilizers to work on grizzly bears in Yellowstone. He based the tactic on experiments the brothers performed in a Nevada wildlife refuge.

They set up a lab in Yellowstone's Canyon Village. A former Civilian Conservation Corps mess hall became base camp. They used its kitchen to feed the dozen or more biology students and professionals who came to work with them each summer. Ropes hung from rafters outside the mess hall. Before eating, each field hand had to first climb a rope; it was training for escaping drug-addled grizzly bears. Convenient trees weren't always available, however. Frank Craighead advised new biologists: "When releasing grizzlies, point them away from you."

The Internet Age has revived their exploits. An eighty-seven-second video clip posted on YouTube in 2014 of one famous Craighead grizzly darting garnered tens of thousands of replays. The movie footage shows the Craigheads getting chased into their station wagon by Bear No. 41, whom they'd nicknamed Ivan the Terrible. Their early-period drug dosages usually only worked for fifteen or twenty minutes. Ivan revived ahead of schedule as one brother attempted to attach an ear tag, and started demonstrating the second part of his nickname. The crew scattered as Ivan tore into the first strange thing in view: the tackle box containing the darts and drugs. He then charged headfirst into the station wagon's passenger door, before climbing onto the hood and roaring at the windshield. The Craigheads' film crew came with multiple cameras, so the final edit includes footage from inside the car as well as outside.

The Craighead team had captured and ear-tagged sixty-seven grizzlies by 1960. They used multi-colored streamers as ID marks, easily visible to researchers, tourists, and Yellowstone Park administrators. This antique methodology would soon undermine support for what was becoming the most Space Age advances in wildlife biology to date.

In 1954, Robert D. LeMunyan hung the world's first radio collar on a woodchuck. It only transmitted twenty-five yards. But the proof of concept reached Yellowstone. Frank spent two years working up a prototype that could withstand something more vigorous.

Assisted by their television fame, the Craigheads won cooperation from engineers at Philco Corporation as the company was pioneering America's home television and broadcasting markets. Philco executives saw the project as an advertising opportunity.

The original transmitters were based on ham radio technology. They had batteries dipped in rubber for waterproofing, and the whole module was sealed in resin-coated fiberglass. Almost as much effort went into the collar itself. The Craigheads tried twenty-seven different designs, including tape, copper and brass wire, and nylon filament like fishing line. They settled on coating the loop antenna with fiberglass.

The transmitter weighed about two ounces, backed up by two pounds of batteries. That gave the collar six months of power, broadcasting a signal ten to twenty miles to a long-range receiver or one mile to a handheld receiver, assuming the bear was upright (more on that in a minute).

Their inaugural bear turned out to be a well-known subject: a three-year-old female they'd captured, designated No 40, and ear-tagged with red and blue streamers the year before. On September 21, 1961, they caught No. 40 again and revolutionized wildlife biology.

But not before a near-comic misfire. The relatively docile sow had grown one hundred and twenty-five pounds since they'd handled her last. They bolted the transmitter around her twenty-eight-inch neck and turned on their receivers. They could hear their own heartbeats better than the radio signal.

Every idiot check came up negative. Batteries charged. Frequency correct. No. 40 started to revive from her double-dose of tranquilizing drugs, and there was no time for further tinkering. The crew prepared to embrace failure.

Until No. 40 got up and walked away. Suddenly, the receivers started getting seventy beeps a minute, loud and clear. When immobilized on the ground, her three-hundred-pound bulk had been blocking the transmission.

The Craigheads christened No. 40, Marian, after Philco Corp. president Dick Davies's wife. Marian disappeared in the snow, but was traceable by the radio signal. With regular battery replacement, the collar functioned for eight years.

When the Craigheads started using the radio receivers to follow their first radio-collared grizzly around the forests of Yellowstone Park, they once accidentally woke her up from a nap. Marian had been snoozing on the collar and blocking its signal—a problem Frank didn't realize until he was just forty feet from a startled three-hundred-pound predator. But instead of charging, Marian just looked at her human tracker and headed deeper into the woods.

"That day we realized there were two studies going on," Frank Craighead later wrote. "We were studying grizzlies. And they were studying us."

◃ ◃ ◃ · ▹ ▹ ▹

One immediately valuable result the radio collars produced was the revelation of where Marian and other tracked bears denned for the winter. That allowed research on hibernating bears, and gave insight on one of the biggest threats to their survival: their gall bladders.

Joel Varney was one of the Craigheads' electronics engineers, producing improved transmitters annually. Among his innovations was a thermistor, a temperature sensor that worked under an animal's skin. It was the size of a matchhead and could transmit by radio. By 1969, the Craigheads were using NASA Nimbus satellites to collect hibernation data, seven hundred miles up in space.

The thermistors revealed bears only drop about five or six degrees body temperature during their winter sleep. Compare that to rodents, which chill down to forty degrees Fahrenheit during their coma-like hibernation.

But confusingly, rodents frequently wake up and leave their burrows in midwinter. Why? To pee. They have to get rid of the toxic byproducts their digestive systems produce from their stored body fat.

Bears, on the other hand, typically don't wake up until spring. Yet they also don't sink into the deep sleep of true hibernation. And they don't have to pee.

Why? Because bears have a gall bladder of remarkable ability that neutralizes the waste produced from their wintertime self-consumption. Asian medical tradition picked up on this characteristic of bile from bears centuries ago, leading to a lively market for ursine gall bladders for traditional medicines. Modern Chinese facilities involve captive bears with drains surgically inserted in their abdomens to "milk" the bile those bladders produce. Demand for bladders and bile has led to the near extinction of most Asian bear species, and contributes to pressure on the huntable populations of bears in North America and Europe.

Western medical science doesn't offer much space on the pharmacist's shelf for bear gall bladder remedies. But bear biologists have first-hand observations of its potency for the original owners. Fish and Wildlife Service grizzly recovery biologist Wayne Kasworm radio-collared a grizzly shortly before it was gutshot by a careless black-bear hunter in the fall of 1984. Kasworm wasn't able to find the bear before it denned up for the winter, so he anticipated removing the collar from a dead carcass the next spring. Instead, the bear not only survived but thrived. When he caught it again the following summer, he confirmed the bear had been shot twice: once in the shoulder and once straight through the abdomen. Both wounds had completely healed. A human in similar circumstances would have died of peritonitis within days of the initial abdominal sepsis.

◄ ◄ ◄ · ► ► ►

Before the Craigheads institutionalized their "collar-and-follar" techniques, the previous big leap in wildlife biology was Galileo's refinement of the telescope. Until the availability of long-distance lenses, humans studied grizzly bears by following their prints in the mud, possibly assisted by an involuntarily conscripted horse we'd domesticated a few millennia earlier. We recorded our observations on paper, that two thousand-year-old invention. Besides Galileo's optical assistance, for the next four hundred years a field biologist's most technological asset was the slide rule and logarithmic handbook used to tally statistics.

Then in the span of a single generation we underwent the second great metamorphosis of human technology.

The first took place in the early 1800s. Napoleon fought the battle of Waterloo at the same speed as Alexander the Great in the Bronze Age: as fast as his horse cavalry could gallop. Forty years later, Ulysses S. Grant directed his armies by telegraph, moved them by steam locomotive, and armed them with machine guns.

The attempt to recover the grizzly bear from extinction in the Lower 48 states coincides with the second great metamorphosis. If you're reading this on an iPad, you hold in your hand more computing power than all of NASA had for the Apollo moon missions back when the Craigheads were debugging their grizzly collars. In the fifty years that *Ursus arctos horribilis* has gone from near extinction to near recovery, *Homo sapiens* has gone from digital watches that tell time to digital watches that fly drones while monitoring your blood sugar levels.

When Alston Chase wrote *Playing God in Yellowstone* in 1987, he tore into the hubris of Yellowstone National Park managers who assumed they could tinker with natural processes the same way teenaged mechanics souped up hot rods in the family garage. He totally missed the fact that teenagers like Steve Jobs and Bill Gates were using those garages to soup up computers and to reengineer society. Or as biologist E. O. Wilson put it, "During the 1980s and 1990s, before the world quite realized what was happening, it came of age."

All this scientific advancement ironically ignited conflict with an even more expansive assumption of human capacity—and led to the Craigheads' expulsion from Yellowstone. As those technological tools multiplied, so did the arguments over *who* got to play God.

Conservationists have built a towering pedestal of adoration for Aldo Leopold, who drafted the foundations of modern landscape ecology in his writings like *Sand County Almanac*. Not as many remember one of Aldo's offspring, Starker Leopold, although the son may have had more direct policy impact on America's wild places than the father.

In 1963, Starker Leopold produced an eponymous report for the Interior Department's Advisory Board on Wildlife Management in National Parks calling for natural management in the parks. They were not zoos, he argued, but real ecosystems.

"As a primary goal, we would recommend that the biotic associations within each park be maintained, or where necessary re-created, as nearly as possible in the condition that prevailed when the area was first visited by the white man," the Leopold Report authors stated. ". . . observable artificiality in any form must be minimized and obscured in every possible way."

Remember those ear tag streamers?

With Yellowstone Park's centennial approaching in 1972, park administrators bore down on the Craigheads' bear identification markings as a glaring example of artificiality. When their project started in 1959, part of their NPS-sanctioned mission was to provide bear management advice to park biologists. That request got rescinded in 1964. Non-NPS scientists were disinvited from the responsibility of wildlife control, although fieldwork in the park could continue.

Then came 1967.

That year, incoming Superintendent Jack Anderson appointed Glen Cole as Yellowstone's supervisory research biologist. Bringing the Craigheads to heel appeared to be Cole's top priority.

Also in 1967, Congress' Committee on Rare and Endangered Wildlife Species declared the grizzly bear an endangered species (although the designation lacked much authority until the passage of the Endangered Species Act of 1973). Fewer than six hundred grizzlies were assumed left in the Lower 48 states, mostly in Yellowstone National Park, and that number was presumed to be falling. Ironically, the Craigheads' 1967 census report to their Yellowstone overseers that summer showed grizzly populations were increasing by an average six bears a year.

A month after they submitted that analysis, the grizzly bears weighed in. In what Jack Olsen indelibly titled *Night of the Grizzlies*, two different bears killed campers in two separate Glacier National Park campgrounds on the same night. The deaths were the fourth and fifth grizzly-caused fatalities in the whole of National Park Service history.

Both grizzlies suspected in the killings were accustomed to feeding on garbage and attracted to trash and human food at the two campsites. That threw gasoline on the pyre Cole was lighting under the Craigheads. He wanted to remove bear-attracting garbage dumps from Yellowstone's visitor centers, as well as the identifying ear streamers and radio collars from Yellowstone's bears.

The Craigheads resisted on both fronts. Eliminating a major food supply (the dumps) would force bears to search new places for edibles they'd grown accustomed to—like campgrounds and backpacks. And erasing the identifications from their field bears would hamstring further research.

Not so, Cole insisted. Feeding at dumps would lead to grizzly population decline, he claimed, because adult boars would kill more cubs. As for the identification issue, Cole tried to flip the dumps to his advantage. Noting the Craigheads' tendency to trap and collar bears in the vicinity of dumps, he declared, "If you put garbage-dump data into the computer, you get garbage-dump data out." The Information Age was only in its infancy, but Cole was already picking up the lingo. Analysts still use the derisive acronym in computer science: GIGO—garbage in/garbage out.

Furthermore, Cole maintained the dump bears were a separate community from a presumed larger population of "backcountry" bears that had never tasted garbage. The starvation or elimination of dump-dependent grizzlies would conveniently open more habitat and resources for these more natural bears, he argued.

In hindsight, Cole was gambling on both counts. And his bluffs failed, at great cost to grizzlies. No research documented a hint of those backcountry bears. And no alternative natural food supplies made up for the calories grizzlies got from the dumps.

Nevertheless, the CCC mess hall the Craigheads used for their research headquarters got bulldozed in preparation for the Yellowstone centennial. Yellowstone supervisors denied them access to park bear management records, moved them into a US Fish and Wildlife Service house trailer, and forbade them from trapping or handling grizzlies. When Starker Leopold himself came to review the situation, the Craigheads refused to testify unless the NPS personnel first left the room.

And as the Craigheads had predicted, grizzlies started trying to replace their "unnatural" food supply by prowling campgrounds, leading to more conflicts with people. The Craigheads reported one hundred and sixty grizzly deaths between 1969 and 1972, an average thirty-two bears a year not counting undiscovered kills. In 1971, nineteen grizzlies were captured and relocated from the West Yellowstone dump. By the following spring, all but one of those relocated bears were dead.

In 1969, the year after Yellowstone's dumps were closed, Marian and her three yearling cubs entered Lake Campground in the park on October 10. Rangers trapped two of her cubs. Another ranger darted the third on October 13. Marian charged him, returned to her cub, and turned again. The ranger shot her in the head with a .44 Magnum pistol five times. Her three cubs were released, but all three were reported dead by 1972. Marian was still wearing her radio collar when she died.

A 1973 National Academy of Sciences report supported the Craigheads' methods and population estimates while criticizing the park service. It was a Pyrrhic endorsement. By the time scientific consensus had been reached, the Yellowstone park area had fewer than fifty breeding female grizzlies left alive.

◄ ◄ ◄ · ► ► ►

John Craighead kept captive golden eagles on the edge of the University of Montana campus, and Chris Servheen would exercise them on the slopes of Mount Sentinel while going to school there. I grew up bicycling past those eagles in Missoula. By Servheen's retirement in 2016, that campus had become a locus of molecular genetic analysis that would unlock grizzly bear secrets hidden in a single hair.

The science of genetics and the computers necessary to reveal it share a history as intertwined as a double helix of DNA. As the Craighead brothers were refining their grizzly tranquilizer cocktails, James Watson and Francis Crick were advancing their concept of the double-helix formation of deoxyribonucleic acid. Neither duo had much assistance from computers at the time.

Yet as the Craigheads combined wildlife biology with radio engineering to penetrate the grizzly environment, pioneers of physics and biochemistry were exposing the nature of information itself. The same inquiries that split the atom also unlocked the human genome, revealing the blueprints of each creature's construction encoded in their DNA molecules.

So what does this have to do with grizzly bears? What do you get from a handful of grizzly fur? A tiny bit of DNA. And with the blossoming of digital computers, we've unbraided those molecules to illuminate their lives literally across both space and time.

While I was working at the *Hungry Horse News* in the late 1980s, I interviewed a Glacier National Park biologist who was using a new gizmo. Known as a graphical interface, it looked like a box with a wire that he could slide across a map of the North Fork of the Flathead River and click specific locations. He had several other maps of the same river reach. One showed sites, known as redds, where bull trout had laid eggs. Another showed the redds of cutthroat trout. A third cataloged water temperature readings. He was compiling those separate studies to see what bigger patterns emerged; and instead of three spreadsheets full of numbers, he produced one map showing where everything was.

Today, we call that box with a tail the computer mouse.

It's hard to grasp how much computers changed the world within a few years of the grizzly bear's ESA listing, and then how rapidly computer technology advanced thereafter. The Apple 1 computer released in 1976 had no keyboard or screen. Eight years later, the Apple Macintosh and its mouse sold as many desktop computers as IBM's breakthrough PC1.

The "Mac" computer brought mice into millions of homes. Even though its original memory wasn't big enough to hold the software that drives a single app on a twenty-first century iPhone, the Mac nevertheless opened the world to the potential of digital manipulation. Steve Jobs claimed to realize the value of the mouse when a group of Xerox executives held a graphical interface demonstration for fellow (mostly male) engineers, and Jobs noticed all their wives talking about how much easier it would make printing PTA newsletters and church bulletins.

Adobe's Postscript was the original "killer app" for Apple computers, but it couldn't break into the big newspapers. They wallowed in the world of layout tables and pica poles and lead type. So Adobe sent sales crews to people like publisher Brian Kennedy, who could step out to the *Hungry Horse News* parking lot and see the future of journalism in the back of a car trunk. Little papers like the *Hungry Horse News* gave Apple and Adobe the financial momentum to overthrow IBM and its dependence on written code. Bill Gates and Microsoft saw the problem and turned the command lines of MS-DOS into Windows, essentially replicating the Apple drag-and-drop programming method. IBM and Xerox lay in the middle of the road, wondering what just ran over them.

By 1988, Apple Computer's defining feature was just starting to replace the scissors and library paste I literally used to "cut" and "paste" edited bits of my news stories together at the *Hungry Horse*. My younger colleagues get annoyed when I brag about snipping stories to ribbons and gluing them in new arrangements after I'd typed them on actual paper. For me personally, the single greatest benefit of the desktop computer was the delete key. My typing skills remain comic despite forty years as a professional writer—a career I never considered in my teens because I couldn't complete a typed sentence without soaking it in correction fluid.

◄ ◄ ◄ · ► ► ►

Kate Kendall epitomizes the transformation of wildlife science in the digital age. She began her career in the grizzly bear world right as the Craighead era closed. She remembered the Craighead brothers as "the most famous scientists in the country, with their *National Geographic* films and articles." Her research also charted another corner of the rift between science and politics.

One of Kendall's first encounters with a grizzly made her question the wisdom of her chosen subject animal. While pursuing her graduate work on a vegetation plot study in the Tom Miner Basin north of Yellowstone National Park, she and her field partner saw a sow grizzly and cub.

"She ran away, and we were thinking—cool, we saw a bear," Kendall recounted. "But she was just stashing her cub. Then she charged. I was by a tree I could have climbed, but there was no time. She came within an inch of my partner's toes, but didn't touch him. Then she whirled around and came within about ten feet of me, and then ran off.

"I started thinking about looking for other jobs, thinking it would be OK if I didn't study bears. Maybe I should study mice or something. But then I got the job in Glacier and I stayed with bears."

Kendall got assigned to National Park Service chief scientist Ted Studia in Washington, DC, in the middle of the Craighead controversy. After three years in the chief scientist's office, Kendall was sent to Yellowstone to work on her doctorate in 1974. The Park Service wanted to sponsor her in a graduate program as a way to expose the academic world to NPS philosophy. So it transferred her position and funding to the newly formed Interagency Grizzly Bear Study Team that was seeking a solution to the population crash. Throughout the '70s from March to December Kendall prowled the Yellowstone backcountry, setting up measures to start the recovery of the bears. The most grizzlies she ever saw in one year was six or seven. The rest she monitored by radio collar. By the early '80s, she heard about people driving the park's Washburn Road seeing two grizzlies chasing elk calves. Those recovery efforts were starting to pay off.

Yet Kendall told me she felt the National Park Service research division remained kind of a second-class citizen. Its supervisors lacked a good understanding of science-based management. Despite a big initiative in the late 1980s to expand technical resource guidance, it remained hard to get support for scientific activity, or make administrators understand the need for publishing the findings.

That started to change in 1993, when Interior Secretary Bruce Babbitt took all the research-grade scientists from the Department of Interior and created the National Biological Survey. He modeled the new agency on the US Geological Survey, with a mission to gather and share information about the nation's living natural resources. During the reshuffle, Kendall also moved to Glacier National Park.

And then came Representative Newt Gingrich and the Contract for America and the 1995 government shutdown. Kendall recalled how every month seemed to bring another new bill to eliminate this agency or cut that funding. After three years, the biological survey researchers moved back to the USGS.

"Glacier didn't want to lose its scientists, but that wasn't true of all the parks," Kendall said. "Yellowstone kicked theirs out." Glacier's administrators supported the independence of scientists from management, which kept the scientists free of political pressure.

"It was really refreshing," Kendall said. "We could attend science meetings, learn new stuff, and publish. That's hugely helpful, and it takes time and resources."

The move from Yellowstone to Glacier wasn't just a geographical shift for Kendall. Parks have different cultures. Glacier bans snow machines. West Yellowstone once billed itself the "Snowmobile Capital of the World." Grizzly density was twice as high in Glacier as Yellowstone. In her first hour-long reconnaissance flight over Glacier, Kendall saw forty-six bears. The Yellowstone grizzly study team had been all about trap-and-collar and radar telemetry. She found a very different scientific protocol in her new park.

"When I got to Glacier, there was a strong sentiment that we don't handle bears," Kendall said. "I put collars on a couple of bears that were trapped because they were habituated and moved, but otherwise management opposed radio collaring. So from my earliest days there, I tried to find other ways to study them. As soon as I heard there might be ways to study them through their genetics, through passive means, I was interested."

Love or hate the Craigheads, they had compiled the biggest single stack of grizzly bear research in the United States—possibly the biggest look at bears in the world. But they were all about one single ecosystem—Yellowstone. Depleted as they were, grizzlies persisted in a few more strongholds south of the Canadian border. The Greater Yellowstone Ecosystem was the most well-known, with Yellowstone National Park at its center. But the Northern Continental Divide Ecosystem, spanning 8.2 million acres from the Canadian border, through Glacier National Park and the Bob Marshall Wilderness Complex, to the edge of Missoula, Montana, had far more potential for grizzly recovery. The immediate problem was nobody knew how many grizzlies inhabited the NCDE. You can't tell if a population is recovering if you don't know whether it is growing or shrinking.

US Geological Survey biologist Kate Kendall pioneered methods of monitoring grizzly bear populations and movements by collecting fur on passive hair snares. Photo by Kurt Wilson. Courtesy *Missoulian* newspaper.

And until the Craigheads' radiotelemetry breakthroughs, all previous grizzly studies were based on direct observation, either by eye or ear. It was the best way at the time, but it wouldn't meet the needs of the 1990s. Then in 1995, a Parks Canada study in Revelstoke, British Columbia, pioneered a wildlife census technique known as the hair corral. Stick some bait where a bear will find it, surround it with a ring of barbed wire, and let the visiting grizzlies leave furry calling cards snagged on the barbs. Kendall heard about it the following year and wrote a proposal to the US Geological Survey for funding.

Flathead National Forest supervisor Kathy Barbelito and Montana Fish, Wildlife and Parks regional supervisor Mack Long met with Kendall. Barbelito said she couldn't move forward on grizzly bear recovery without a population estimate. Kendall pitched her idea for how to survey the population. And together they got to work finding resources. In particular, they got Montana's Republican senator Conrad Burns to push the Interior Appropriations Subcommittee to fund Kendall's study. Republican governor Judy Martz backed Burns up.

On the other hand, Arizona's Republican senator John McCain singled the project out as an example of "government pork" when he was campaigning for president in 1999. He brought it up in primary debates, wondering if the hair samples were for paternity tests or criminal background checks. The publicity and criticism made USGS leaders nervous. The same subcommittee that funded Kendall's grizzly bear sampling study funded their whole agency. Finally both Burns and Montana's senior senator Max Baucus, a Democrat, confronted the Congressional staff member who'd cooked up McCain's punchline. The staffer waffled between ridiculing the science or ridiculing the funding mechanism. Burns and Baucus maintained pressure. They showed Kendall's method got rock-solid, unassailable population estimates from that project. McCain eventually publicly apologized.

"I felt an enormous sense of responsibility," Kendall said. "They gave me a lot of money to collect this data. It was unprecedented in the world to work on such a huge scale. We had to figure out what the data is telling us with the newest, best models. Get it out and get it published."

Mid-1990s DNA analysis compares to current capabilities as an Apple II desktop computer compares to an iPhone XI. Likewise, mid-'90s grizzly monitoring required loads of equipment: a truck, a culvert trap, a road, powerful drugs, and expensive radio transmitters plus experts trained in their use. A hair snare needed a hiker with a backpack of test tubes, a spool of wire, and a bottle of bait—though that last odiferous item almost made Kendall opt for the old ways.

"I had a hundred fifty-five-gallon drums filled with fish and blood, aging a year," Kendall said. "Then we'd have to press the fish bodies out and mix what was left in a Sheetrock mixer. I'm done with that."

But the grizzly attractant did wonders, especially when combined with another insight Kendall brought to the methodology. The Canadian studies placed hair corrals by a grid map to get comprehensive geographic coverage. Kendall got the grizzlies to come to her, by coiling barbed wire around hundreds of "rub trees" that bears routinely use as ursine back-scratchers.

One way Kendall won over skeptics was to play video of grizzly bears doing a backwoods boogie on her rub trees. Now released into the fertile environment of social media, the dancing bears have been set to everything from disco to rap music.

"With all these remote cameras, you can see what the bears are doing when you're not there," Kendall said. "They're easy to set up. And they really develop a constituency for wildlife."

Kendall set up an even bigger hair snare project in 2003. Volunteers toted barbed wire and tiny bottles of bear attractant up to thirty miles from the nearest road. Then the forest fires started.

"I had sixty people in the field," Kendall said. "It was a nightmare for fire. We'd lay out directions, print the maps, hitch the horses, and a fire would start. We'd have to move someplace else."

Fortunately, the considerably wetter 2004 was the year of actual field work. Kendall deployed two hundred and forty people. That's the size of a compact Type I Incident Commander's fire camp, the kind of response assigned to fires threatening thousands of acres or city-limit borders.

"We were just a handful of biologists with eight million acres of roadless wilderness to cover," Kendall recounted. "It's incredibly cool thing as a biologist to work at that scale. Just one grizzly bear's home range is so large, hardly anybody gets to work at that scale."

In five years, Kendall's crew detected 1,539 grizzlies.

"We detected bears everywhere we sampled. Only the Rattlesnake unit (just north of Missoula) had no females. But they're occurring in the core and the periphery."

Further breakthroughs in DNA analysis made the hair-snare study more than a census. It produced a highly accurate population count without ever handling a grizzly. It also unveiled ursine family trees, diets, and movement patterns. At first, Kendall's DNA hair tests had difficulty distinguishing true grizzly bears from blond-phase black bears. By 2017, the tests could not only identify a specific bear, but they could tease out isotopes showing if that bear was eating more whitebark pine nuts or domestic corn from a farmer's field.

It also reveals family trees. For example, one male bear fathered at least seventeen offspring. He's been traced to the lineage of sixty-one descendants. In the southern end of the Bob Marshall Wilderness Complex, 68 percent of the grizzlies share ancestry with one boar and two sows.

Recheck the hair traps several times a season, and grizzly movement patterns become apparent. The system became known as genetic detection trend modeling.

The problem was that even as computer capabilities grew at Moore's Law, doubling in speed as they halved in price, Kendall kept coming up with new and tougher questions to ask.

"I was competing against myself to get sampling done," she said. "I swamped the lab. Nobody has tried running data sets as big as we have with the NCDE bears. We have such rich data, it takes months for each model to run. And we have dozens of models."

◄ ◄ ◄ · ► ► ►

A few blocks away from the Interagency Grizzly Bear Study Team's offices at Montana State University, George Keremedjiev has built the American Computer Museum in Bozeman. It displays the human attempt to manipulate information, from Babylonian clay tablets to a prototype of the quantum computer chip. One favorite display is the original IBM hard disk drive, which held five megabytes of data and weighed about five hundred pounds. Keremedjiev did the math and showed that the first Apple iPod would need one thousand compact pickup trucks to carry all its songs if dependent on that original design.

Keremedjiev's biggest challenge in the American Computer Museum is choosing within the warehouses of obsolete digital gear what milestones to put on display. His early history section is easy: artifacts like Isaac Newton's first-edition book of calculus has no competitors.

But after the transistor revolutionized digital computing in 1955, computer progress had all the permanence of last year's trendy Christmas toy. Optical fiber outperformed copper. Liquid crystal diodes usurped cathode ray screens. Solid-state memory replaced disc drives. Following Moore's Law, processing chips got faster and cheaper in a geometric progression.

Just over the Continental Divide, the nerds at the Rocky Mountain Environmental DNA lab in Missoula have blown my Flathead River bull trout mapper out of the galaxy. Michael Schwartz's crew specializes in teasing out the genetic signatures of species from massively complex sample sets. Give Schwartz a cup of water from a mountain stream, and he can parse out the environmental DNA (eDNA) that tells you if the stream has bull trout spawning in it or not.

Bull trout have federal protection under the Endangered Species Act, so special rules apply to physical activities, including research, in their critical habitat. But how can we tell which streams support bulls? eDNA to the rescue.

Before that breakthrough in 2014 fisheries biologists had to wade up miles of creek in fall, hoping to find the redds of piled-up gravel that bull trout use to nest their eggs. Bull trout live complex life cycles, spending their juvenile years in rivers, maturing to adulthood in large lakes, and then spawning in tiny creeks. Researchers often joke about finding three-foot trout in two-foot streams.

That was *so* 2014. Four years later Schwartz's lab took its game to a freakish new level.

The other productive way of detecting extremely rare animals is the remote camera. Set a bait site, or find a potential habitat, and let the robot brain's motion detector trip the shutter. Computer programs now can scan thousands of images looking for specific species in the file, such as distinguishing a couple of black-footed ferrets prowling among hundreds of similar-sized prairie dogs.

This worked great until a photo of a Canada lynx showed up on remote camera in Montana where no lynx had been recorded in decades. Presence of lynx triggers a federal critical habitat review—a very involved and controversial process. A complication is that Canada lynx look similar to bobcats, with tufted ears and a stumpy tail. A photo makes good evidence, but is not conclusive proof. For that, you need DNA.

So a biologist trekked into the site, while winter snow remained, where the camera had caught the image. He triangulated the spot where the animal was photographed, and took a core sample of the snow there. Back in the lab, he was able to date the layers of snowfall until he found the November slice when the photo was taken. He sent that sample to Schwartz's lab in Missoula, which detected Canada lynx DNA in the meltwater. Gold-standard proof came from a paw print in months-old snow.

Other DNA tricks can identify a specific grizzly bear, tell its relations to every other bear in its family tree, and detect if it's gotten into corn sugar (evidence of access to human food or garbage). Most mammals share about 90 percent of the same DNA coding in their double-helix blue-prints. A bizarrely small bit of the code separates us from ants. Even smaller tweaks determine the difference between black bears and griz-zlies. Cutting-edge geneticists have inserted the significant genomic plan for one animal into the generalized strand of another's DNA, and success-fully made a cow give birth to a sheep. They toy with the potential of doing the same thing with extinct animals, such as snipping the right bits among 4.7 billion DNA base pairs to let elephants raise woolly mammoths.

◄ ◄ ◄ · ► ► ►

The Craighead grizzlies may have been studying us, but their research programs haven't intruded into our lives like ours have intruded into theirs. What does the way we study grizzly bears reveal about ourselves? Consider to what other uses we've put the exact same technology.

One particularly consequential offspring of genetics and computer science is the gene drive, a segment of DNA that activates the plans encoded in other blueprint portions of the double helix. Precise manipula-tion of a gene drive can make an organism express or repress a trait. For example, it can adjust the glandular process of producing fertile sperm.

This has opened an opportunity in endangered species conservation with Pandoric potential. As Emma Marris reported in *WIRED* maga-zine, wildlife managers are considering triggering gene drives in invasive rats that would spread infertility through the population, eliminating the invasive species threat through its own sex drive.

Americans show interestingly squishy attitudes toward genetic engi-neering when it comes to manipulating animals. A Pew Charitable Trusts poll in mid-2018 found seven out of ten people were OK with tweaking mosquito reproductive genes to eliminate diseases like malaria. But nearly the same number opposed the same kind of manipulation to make an aquarium goldfish glow in the dark.

The split was much closer to a coin toss on more complicated questions. Just 41 percent approved of enhancing animals so they could grow organs for human transplant. But 55 percent liked the idea of tweaking animal genetics to make more nutritious meat.

Most pertinent for the grizzly bear's case, less than a third agreed with the concept of using genetic manipulation to bring back an extinct species. This idea has been widely floated as a solution, or a tempting challenge, to the question of endangered species recovery. If desirable animals teeter or fall over the cliff of extinction, we could rebuild them in a test tube and release them to some rewilded habitat prepared for their return.

This verges into the territory of moral hazard: Why worry about environmental screw-ups now if we can fix them later, at leisure? That last white rhino that died in 2018? We've got his sperm in a jar somewhere. Eventually after we've learned to quit paying huge sums to poachers for a few kilos of rhino horn for dagger hilts and erection assistance, we'll cook up a new herd and repopulate the savanna.

This isn't science fiction. The recipe for the woolly mammoth has already been published. We can use gene-editing technology to sequentially add the curved tusks, long fur, big muscle hump, and other characteristics to successive generations of altered Asian elephants, eventually breeding/building a mammoth like our prehistoric brethren hunted out of existence. If we've got the complete genome, as we do for the white rhino, we can insert its components into the sperm and egg of a complementary surrogate species and give birth to the whole critter.

As usual, some small print clutters the bottom of the contract. A phenomenon called microchimerism can laterally transfer some DNA from the contemporary host animal into the genome of the extinct target. So the home-brewed extinction victim might wind up with garbled crucial parts of the recipe. The revived anachronism would also face the "nurture" part of the nature/nurture conundrum. It would be raised by parents (and lab techs) lacking the species' inherent abilities. This could prove critical to some future grizzly bear revivification, as grizzly moms spend one to three years teaching their cubs where to find seasonal food, how to deal with humans and other dangers, and suchlike. Grizzly cubs of the year born now can't be released to the wild if their mother is killed— without her oversight their survival chances are nil. Even two- and three-year-old subadults have a very low survival rate without their mothers.

Interestingly, among the Pew poll takers who opposed using genetic manipulation to bring back extinct species, 14 percent objected because they "do not see a need or purpose to this, especially as it does not seem to bring any benefit to humans, or that resources should be focused else-where." In other words, it wasn't worth the trouble when the same lab techs might instead spend their time finding a tweak to cure diabetes or another threat to human health.

The persistence of a species we're driving to extinction should not depend on a safety net of our pulling off a test-tube moonshot of scientific breakthrough. Consider the list of what else we've asked science to do. Where's my flying car? How about the Babel Fish in the ear that solves the language translation problem? Even among the species on the endangered list, could the grizzly out-poll the masses who want to first rescue their tuna sashimi or their morning coffee or their chocolate? The line of plants and animals edging toward the company of woolly mammoths, passenger pigeons, and dodos grows longer with every passing year of increasing global temperatures and overuse of natural resources. Our philosophical and ethical capacities haven't yet undergone a commensurate revolution. Computer scientist Yonatan Zungar got his start as a physicist, and his first discipline's legacy of nuclear energy helped him produce a useful insight: "Computer science is a field that hasn't yet encountered consequences."

The technology of wildlife tracking has infected our human community in morally suspect ways as well. If you carry a cell phone, you've likely activated a tracking device that not only logs your every step but every purchase you make, every photo you take, and every connection you initiate or receive from all of your social acquaintances. Most of us will never see our individual daily lives displayed in such granular detail—those uploads get aggregated in massive "big data" analyses that marketers use to manipulate or forecast our commercial activity. But should you ever be perceived as a threat to the collectors of that data, you could share an existence as constrained as that of the grizzly bear.

For example, in China's northwestern Shenzhen Province, the Uighur ethnic group dominates the population. The Chinese federal government has imposed surveillance measures on Uighurs beyond anything George Orwell imagined. According to United States-based academics with long experience in Shenzhen, Uighurs in 2018 were required to report to their parents' home towns for documentation. As many adult Uighurs had moved to Shenzhen's larger cities for work, this served multiple purposes. Upon reporting to their natal police station, these adults next had to provide biometric data for identification. That included facial scans which could then be recognized on the video cameras that now mushroom on every street intersection in the cities. They also had to provide DNA samples for analysis.

Like the grizzly hair snares, those Uighur DNA profiles allow authorities to make exact matches of individuals based on traces of bodily material. And they reveal family history. In the Uighurs' case, that includes everything from review of the family's adherence to China's one-child policy to ensuring that relatives can be identified and drawn in as hostages to compel cooperation.

The forced return to home towns, followed by investigative identification means that anyone who has moved without a proper work or transit permit can be exposed to criminal conviction, removed from their city workplace, and effectively trapped in a rural area without resources.

If that seems to Americans like something only Chinese minorities need worry about, consider an investigation done by the *New York Times* in 2019. Its reporters got access to the cell phone tracking data of twelve million Americans, revealing "hints of faltering marriages, evidence of drug addiction, records of visits to psychological facilities" and who attended which parties during President Donald Trump's inaugural weekend festivities. The files showed who participated in protest rallies in Washington, DC, and who was going in and out of the Pentagon (and sometimes these were the same people, or their family members). The reporters didn't need government help—they got the records from a private company.

In the early years of the Endangered Species Act, a group of biologists in the US Fish and Wildlife Service tasked with nominating plant and wildlife candidates to the law's protection got nicknamed "The God Committee." Despite their heady authority, they never conceived of the brave new world where their colleagues could reach into an organism's intrinsics and rearrange its existence.

God willing, we may launch the ethical debate on the righteousness of such manipulation before we confront the possibility of a gene drive in overdrive—spilling unintended consequences beyond the bounds of some experimental terrarium. Otherwise, to quote E. O. Wilson again, "Science and technology, combined with a lack of self-understanding and a Paleolithic obstinacy, brought us to where we are today."

6

Ethyl's Ramble

THE ROOMFUL OF BIOLOGISTS HAD LOTS OF FUNNY IDEAS WHY
Ethyl the grizzly bear logged 2,800 miles arcing from Coeur d'Alene
past Florence and Missoula and eventually up to Eureka by way of Glacier
National Park.

Was she was looking for someone she couldn't find? Maybe she ate
a bad chicken and took a long time to walk off the indigestion. She had
Alzheimer's and couldn't trace her way back to her home range northeast
of Bigfork—one place she noticeably skipped in her three-year ramble
across Montana and Idaho.

"The one thing we can say is this was not representative of normal bear
movement, and certainly not female grizzly bear movement," said US Fish
and Wildlife Service grizzly bear recovery coordinator Chris Servheen in
2014. "She had some really bizarre travels."

Here's one more thing we can say about Ethyl. The twenty-year-old
sow demonstrated that grizzly bears can cross interstate highways, major
city boundaries, municipal landfills, and residential backyards without
getting in trouble with humans. She added hope that the big omnivores

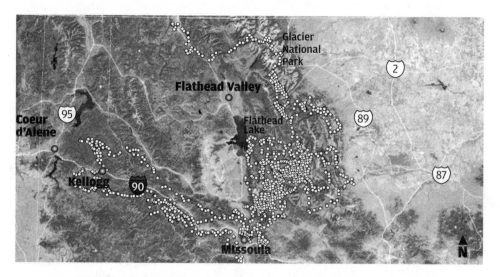

Ethyl's satellite tracking collar recorded a 2,800-mile ramble across huge swaths of Montana and Idaho—a very rare trek for a female bear. Courtesy Interagency Grizzly Bear Committee.

can coexist with people as their populations pooch out of their wilderness core habitat.

Ethyl spent most of her life around Montana's Lake Blaine, between the tourist town of Bigfork and the Swan Mountains. After game wardens captured her while raiding an apple orchard, she was relocated to the Wounded Buck Creek drainage along Hungry Horse Reservoir. She returned with a two-year-old cub in tow and got busted again in the apples in 2012. This time, Montana Fish, Wildlife and Parks bear specialist Rick Mace gave her a satellite-linked radio collar before hauling her and her cub to the more remote Puzzle Creek drainage, hard against the Continental Divide south of Marias Pass.

And then Ethyl took off.

She prowled around the Bob Marshall Wilderness Complex for a while, including a few peeks at the eastern Rocky Mountain Front between Lincoln and Augusta. Then she drifted down to the Mission Mountains and the Jocko Lakes area. Passing Arlee, she cleared Highway 93 and headed for the northern fringe of the Bitterroot Mountains.

That meant hopping the Interstate 90 corridor, the biggest single barrier to reunification of the two biggest grizzly ecosystems remaining in the Lower 48 states. Ethyl braved the four-lane freeway and headed west into Idaho.

She may have crossed I-90 several times as she explored the mountains around Kellogg and Wallace until she reached the city limits of Coeur d'Alene. A December 15 Kellogg newspaper article printed an Ethyl sighting about ten miles from the high school. She made a den somewhere in the Idaho Panhandle and hibernated through the 2012–13 winter.

If the story ended here, Ethyl would still warrant a chapter to herself in the bear biology books. Grizzly home ranges average seventy square miles for females and from two hundred to four hundred miles for males. Sow grizzlies rarely travel more than eight and a half miles into new country each year. One of Ethyl's fellow grizzly moms in the Mission Mountains alongside the Flathead Indian Reservation had a home range of three square miles, from mountainside den site down to a boggy basin where she foraged all summer.

Ethyl's collar went dormant to conserve battery power on November 25, 2012. It revived the following March, showing her moving back east along Interstate 90. She cruised past Superior, Montana, then straight up and over several steep drainages between I-90 and US Highway 12. She reached the southern fringe of Missoula on May 13. In a short day, she zipped through the Blue Mountain Recreation Area and then south a dozen miles to Lolo. She probed the foothills of the Bitterroot Mountains as far south as Florence.

"On May 20, she goes basically right through downtown Lolo and we didn't have any sightings," Servheen said. "She was minding her own business, walking around trying to figure out where she is."

Ten days later, she shot back into Idaho as far as Coeur d'Alene, as if she remembered she'd left something back at the den. Then she turned around, and safely crossed Interstate 90 again to return to Missoula. She went right past the city's landfill but only sniffed the garbage. She cruised some apple orchards in the meadows east of Evaro Hill. That fall, elk hunters spotted her eating the gut piles they left behind. Each night that fall, she'd pad four miles back to the Rattlesnake Wilderness north of Missoula to sleep.

Then she barged north up the Bob Marshall again, bypassing her Lake Blaine denning site, and headed for Glacier Park. After some time there, Ethyl moved west toward Eureka on the western edge of the NCDE. She lost her collar on October 17, 2014.

"That's a total distance of two thousand eight hundred miles," Serveen said. "The only place she didn't go in the Northern Continental Divide Ecosystem was the Blackfeet Indian Reservation."

‹ ‹ ‹ · › › ›

Ethyl's ramble capsulizes the problem grizzlies present to those who want to recover them. They won't—can't—stay still.

Let's start with food. While technically carnivores, grizzly bears come as close to vegetarian as anything with fangs. In some places, grizzlies subsist on almost 90 percent plant matter, supplemented by bugs and the occasional carrion buffet. Those five-inch claws and shoulder humps of muscle get a lot more use digging up roots and ant hills than dismembering elk.

To meet that need, grizzlies have learned to follow a green wave of plant regeneration through the growing season. As soon as they arise from their dens, they look for two things: a shot of protein from some winter-killed fellow mammal and a meadow full of new clover. They often find both in the runout zones of avalanche chutes.

As spring days lengthen, the bears start digging up the carbohydrate-loaded bases of plants like biscuit root, yampa, glacier lily, and wild onion. This serves until the plants reach flowering stage, whereupon the nutritional value of the roots fades. Bears move up and down in altitude, following the retreat of winter snowpack and the aspects of changing sunshine to fresh growth.

When summer sets in, bears look for berries and other fruit. Where possible, they sniff out middens of whitebark pine seeds buried by industrious but forgetful squirrels. In some remarkable spots in the Mission Mountains and the Beartooth Plateau, they climb near the summits of ten-thousand-foot mountain peaks to find the breeding sites of army cutworm moths and ladybugs. They shred rotten logs to dig out ant colonies, and yes, they do raid beehives for honey.

The claws and teeth do get put to more presumptive uses. In May and June, Yellowstone bears zigzag through meadow edges hoping to scare up elk calves (which are born virtually scentless, so bears hunt for them by sight). A rare bear may hunt and kill a bison, elk, or deer. More often, that offensive weaponry goes to chasing off wolves that have already brought down a big meal with their more effective pack-hunting methods. The reintroduction of wolves in the mid-1990s had a marked benefit on bear populations in Yellowstone Park.

Nevertheless, there's no one-stop shopping. What's the nutritional value of fighting for a berry patch before the berries have ripened? Male grizzlies in particular do not share, and will attack virtually anything that impinges on their meal of the moment. But they're moving through that habitat like we cruise the farmer's market, picking up fast-sprouting lettuce at one stall in April and ignoring another until the good tomatoes appear in August.

When she dropped her satellite-connected Argos collar in 2014, Ethyl disappeared from active research. However, the lopsided 'W' she traced across the maps of Montana and Idaho continues to tantalize her human overseers. If she'd gone twenty miles farther west of Eureka, Ethyl would have tagged three recovery ecosystems. And if she settled in the Cabinet-Yaak Ecosystem, fireworks would have gone off in Fish and Wildlife Service headquarters.

◄ ◄ ◄ · ► ► ►

Forty years previous, that office braced for more of an implosion. As Dick Knight, the original leader of the Interagency Grizzly Bear Study Team put it, "Every grizzly bear carries our society inside him like a bomb, a ticking bomb, already well advanced toward blowing him off the face of the earth, and continuing relentlessly to tick toward ignition unless we intervene to disarm it."

Before Knight took the job in 1973, perhaps six hundred grizzlies remained alive south of the Canadian border. The 1975 ESA designation listed all grizzlies in the Lower 48 states—a single population destined to subdivide into a legal quagmire.

Lewis and Clark's Voyage of Discovery journals repeat a detail that regularly confounds modern grizzly discussions. The white explorers reported grizzlies almost exclusively on the open grasslands. Once they headed into the mountains flanking the Continental Divide, where most of today's grizzlies reside, bear reports virtually vanish from the logs. Although *Ursus arctos horribilis* inhabited the mountain regions all the way to the Pacific Coast, the journals report no grizzly encounters until they return to the grassy valleys of eastern Idaho.

One reason might be that things are just harder to see in the forest. Meriwether Lewis got shot in the leg by one of his own nearsighted men who mistook him for a deer in heavy brush on a hunting foray. When Interior Secretary David Bernhardt attended a grizzly management conference on the Rocky Mountain Front in 2019, he noted "I find it very ironic we didn't see any bears in the conservation area, but as soon as we turned around, we saw them along the highway."

Grizzly researcher David Mattson theorizes grizzlies of central North America evolved in tandem with prairie buffalo herds. He offers two main reasons for the coevolved relationship of grizzly to bison, one quantitative and one strategic.

First, quantitative: there were millions of bison. Early United States military surveys ballparked figures of fifty million to two hundred million in the early 1800s. That's a lot of meat on the hoof—enough to underpin the nomadic economies of Sioux, Cheyenne, Blackfeet, Crow, and other Plains Indian nations.

Second, and more intriguing, Mattson argues the sheer size of a dead bison makes it an ideal grizzly co-evolutionary. Grizzlies can eat a lot of meat, but they aren't well-designed hunters. Their claws and teeth lack the refined lethality of the mountain lion. Their solitary nature sacrifices the pack-attack strategy of the wolf. So the grizzly learned to play defense instead of offense.

Covering the landscape with herds of bison means leaving lots of dead bison laying around. Mattson shows archaeological evidence that grizzlies were particularly prominent in river bottoms (rivers kill bison in high spring runoff flows, ice breakthroughs, and general water-related mishaps).

Why fight a one-ton horned and hooved opponent that can run as fast as you can (and jump higher: a mature bison has a six-foot vertical leap), if a river will serve up dead ones without a struggle?

And here's where the size matters. A hundred-pound dead mule deer lasts about a day amid the scavengers. A six-hundred-pound elk carcass might take three days to be stripped clean. But a dead bison, two thousand pounds of stinking flesh, can occupy a grizzly for a week. All it has to do is use its powerful muscles to swat away trespassers and occasionally roll the body over to feed on the other side. It's sumo wrestler versus karate master. If the big guy doesn't have to move much, the speedy little guy's advantages go for naught.

Yet none of the grizzly recovery zones developed by the Interagency Grizzly Bear Committee include the evolutionary habitat that produced *Ursus arctos horribilis*. On the contrary, the conservation strategy for the NCDE designates a wide swath of prairie east of the Rocky Mountain Front wilderness fringe as Management Zone 3, where grizzlies get little social tolerance.

This sets up a tantalizing situation. In recent years, young male grizzlies have started roaming the grasslands of central Montana. At least seven were killed by game wardens or ranchers after they got too inquisitive around ranch operations near Great Falls in 2020.

But if they could make it just fifty miles farther, those dispersing bears would reach the Missouri Breaks country where most of Lewis and Clark's dramatic bear encounters took place. The watershed of the Missouri River already features nearly 1.5 million acres of public land in the C. M. Russell National Wildlife Refuge and the Missouri Breaks National Monument. As of 2020, it also includes nearly 400,000 acres of privately managed land under the American Prairie Reserve (APR), a nonprofit organization intent on restoring the American bison. Adding a keystone predator to that landscape would actually benefit the restoration effort. As it is, APR has to sell permits to harvest some of its bison to human hunters to mimic natural predation.

APR's published literature mentions it would like to see grizzlies return to the Breaks. But it de-emphasizes predator restoration as something beyond its authority. In fact, much of the ranching community along the Missouri Breaks region has lined up in opposition to bison restoration. They argue the wild bovines carry a risk of exposing their domestic cattle to brucellosis, a disease that makes ungulates abort their calves and can cause milk fever or mastitis in humans. While the science on brucellosis vector points more to elk than bison, the resistance remains strong and politically entrenched.

At the same time, the Blackfeet, Cree, Chippewa, Lakota, Dakota, Gros Ventre, and Assiniboine nations have also pursued bison restoration on their reservations along Montana's Hi-Line region north of the Missouri River. The Blackfeet already have grizzlies. The other tribes have also quietly expressed willingness to add grizzlies back to their lands. The question is how can they get there?

◄ ◄ ◄ · ► ► ►

The federal Endangered Species Act's stated goals are to conserve at-risk plants and animals (protecting them from extinction) *and* to use "all methods and procedures which are necessary to bring any endangered species or threatened species to the point at which measures provided pursuant to this chapter are no longer necessary." Getting on the ESA list of endangered or threatened species affords the troubled creature protection. Those protections, in turn, are supposed to recover that creature's survivability to the point it can get off the list—get "delisted."

After grizzly bears in the Lower 48 states were listed as a threatened species in 1975, wildlife managers had two tasks. First, they had to define their problem: How many grizzlies were left, what threatened their survival, and what might help their recovery. Second, they had to implement those recovery actions and confirm they got the desired result: A recovered and self-sustaining population of grizzly bears in their natural habitat. It wouldn't do to create a captive breeding program, produce thousands of bears, and distribute them to zoos. Once a recovery plan is adopted and deemed successful, the Department of Interior issues a delisting rule declaring the species free of the need for ESA oversight and moving management restrictions to more routine levels. Should the species backslide under those relaxed rules, federal protections can be reimposed through the ESA.

The US Fish and Wildlife Service proposed a recovery plan for grizzly bears in 1993 that got shot down in court. The service came back with a formal delisting rule in 2007 specifically for grizzlies in the Greater Yellowstone Ecosystem, which also failed its court challenge. Delisting opponents convinced the US Ninth Circuit Court of Appeals that a recent and sudden disappearance of Yellowstone's whitebark pine nuts and cutthroat trout, known grizzly food sources, was inadequately accounted for in the GYE conservation strategy.

Whitebark pine nuts have so much energy that biologists measure middens by quarter-pounder units or "QPUs"—a joking reference to the thousand calories in a McDonald's Quarter Pounder hamburger. A single squirrel stash may hold two or three QPUs worth of fat and protein.

Unfortunately, whitebark pine trees grow only on high mountainsides and need decades before they're mature enough to produce seed cones. An invasive blister rust fungus killed most of the whitebark stands in Glacier National Park in the early part of the twentieth century. Yellowstone National Park's groves hung on until the early 2000s, when a warming climate allowed mountain pine beetles to advance to the pines' wintery elevations and kill about 75 percent of the surviving trees.

Cutthroat trout fell victim to another invader—lake trout introduced illegally into Yellowstone Lake. Cutthroats spawn in shallow, moving water, and for much of the park's history attracted swarms of bald eagles and grizzly bears (and tourists) to places like Fishing Bridge. The predacious lakers, which eat cutthroat and other fish, spawn along deep underwater rock shelves, safe even from most dedicated gill-net fishing boats. Within a few years of the lake trout's appearance in Yellowstone Lake, cutthroat numbers throughout the park fell by 90 percent.

Servheen and the IGBC deployed squads of biologists to get the court an answer that could re-justify the delisting proposed by the agency. In 2013 they released their "Response of Yellowstone Grizzly Bears to Changes in Food Resources: A Synthesis." In short, the fifty-four-page report said bears could find other things to eat. "Based on extensive demographic analyses completed to date, we have not observed a decline in the Yellowstone grizzly bear population but only a slowing of population growth since the early 2000s, possibly indicating the population is nearing carrying capacity."

That conclusion implied two things, which will eventually bring us back to Ethyl. The first concerns that "carrying capacity" statement. As Yellowstone grizzly populations roughly tripled between the 1970s and 2000s, the need for home ranges appears to have encouraged some bears to wander out of their Park Service stronghold into new country.

And the no-decline statement included the observation that grizzlies continued to appear fat and healthy despite the loss of several of their high-energy, traditional food sources. In particular, the study found grizzlies were getting more meat from "scavenging ungulates that died from other causes, usurping kills from other carnivores and use of remains from hunter kills" especially in the fall.

For grizzly delisting opponents, these two things added up to a big problem. The way they solved the equation went: Bears leaving the park + bears eating more meat = bears getting in trouble with people = dead bears.

Even so, with a response to the appeals court's food supply question in hand, the US Fish and Wildlife Service released another proposed delisting rule for GYE grizzlies in 2017. That too wound up in court.

◄ ◄ ◄ · ► ► ►

One of the measures of success for species recovery is genetic interchange: Are there enough individuals in communion with each other to keep the population genetically healthy? Grizzly delisting critics say that by subdividing the entire contiguous United States grizzly listing into six recovery areas, the Fish and Wildlife Service introduced a fatal flaw in its delisting plan.

In 2020 a federal appeals court remanded the GYE delisting rule for failing to explain what happens if some bear populations get declared "recovered" while others remain endangered. This gets at a bigger issue for overall grizzly recovery: Can big, productive ecosystems like the Greater Yellowstone and Northern Continental Divide link their populations to provide for natural migration of bears into struggling areas like the Cabinet-Yaak or Bitterroot recovery areas?

Why does linking matter? That question has bedeviled every court challenge to grizzly Endangered Species Act status. Isn't it enough that a recovery area acquires enough bears to be considered recovered?

The simplest answer is inbreeding: Grizzly populations could collapse for lack of genetic diversity. In 1994 in the Serengeti, a canine distemper virus variant killed a third of the lion population in less than a year—more than a thousand animals in one of Africa's healthiest wildlife communities. Biologists feared that if a similar outbreak hit a more constrained population such as the Gir lions of India, those big cats could vanish from the Indian subcontinent.

But what's a genetically effective or solid population number? The conservation biology rule of thumb for wild predators calls for "effective populations" of at least five hundred mature breeding females to ensure genetic diversity for more than one hundred years. Within any population, only a fraction will be mature breeding females. Conservation biologists assume it may comprise a quarter of the whole. So if you have a thousand grizzlies in the NCDE, the effective population of sows capable of raising cubs is around two hundred and fifty.

Fred Allendorf trained so many young biologists in the basics of conservation genetics at the University of Montana that an auditorium of admirers dubbed themselves "Allendorfians" during a presentation held in 2015 to honor him with a lifetime achievement award for molecular ecology. In formal objections to the IGBC's conservation strategy, Allendorf stated a single isolated population needed at least five thousand members to be genetically viable. He added there was no quick fix to the challenge.

"Repeated simulations of grizzly bear populations have shown a low probability of going extinct within one hundred years," Allendorf wrote in 2019, "but also show extinction probability rising sharply after one hundred years, with many populations going extinct within two hundred to three hundred years." He recommended unifying the multiple recovery areas into a single protected habitat, aiming at a minimum meta-population of two thousand to three thousand grizzly bears.

However, the principles of conservation biology don't earn automatic respect in the courtroom. While the genetic math works out cleanly on the blackboard, state wildlife agencies mount an equally forceful argument about how many animals a specific landscape can support. The IGBC maintains the Greater Yellowstone Ecosystem has reached carrying capacity at 750 grizzly bears, to the point they are dispersing in search of new territory dozens of miles beyond their recovery zone. There they mingle with ranchers, outfitters, and rural residents who see them chiefly as a liability or a threat. How could the area hold a thousand additional bears for the sake of genetic diversity, if it's exceeded its social carrying capacity?

Take the opinions of David Yoder, the leader of a Hutterite colony near Valier, about thirty miles east of the Rocky Mountain Front. The Front, as its adherents call it, guards the eastern trailheads to the Bob Marshall Wilderness Complex—a landscape so scenic the Forest Service protected it as a "primitive area" thirty years before the passage of the Wilderness Act of 1964. Those trails pass through a series of strike valleys created by the tectonic forces that raised the Rocky Mountains. At the edge of the continental plate impact, sedimentary layers got thrust skyward at intense angles. Their softer layers eroded away, leaving long straight ridges. From the air, they look remarkably like the scars a grizzly bear's claws leave in aspen bark.

Yoder likes to boast to all the PhDs at grizzly meetings that his sixth-grade education makes it easier to see what a needless threat grizzlies pose to his farm and children. Why, he asks, should he skip the profits of growing corn and keep his children cowering behind electric fences so that grizzlies can give his colony nightmares? His parents never had to deal with that, and neither did he until about 2014 when grizzlies started prowling the prairie. The fact that those grizzlies are reappearing, to prospect the grasslands they used to dominate before Lewis and Clark started the great white bear eradication in 1805, doesn't factor into Yoder's business model.

Hutterite colonies comprise some of the most successful farms and ranches along the Rocky Mountain Front. More technologically comfortable than the Amish, Hutterites have adopted cell phones and credit cards while maintaining a strictly traditional religious community structure. Children start working in the fields before they can read. Yoder occasionally calls one over when leading tours through the colony's corn fields, emphasizing the tall stalks and the short child. Would *you* like to move irrigation pipe in here, he asks me, knowing that a grizzly sow and three

Montana state biologists examine a nine-hundred-pound grizzly bear that hid in a storage shed on a Hutterite farming complex in Montana. The bear was removed without injuring anyone in the colony. Courtesy Montana Fish, Wildlife and Parks Department.

yearlings might have carved out a daybed as big as a backyard swimming pool inside and stocked it with pilfered corn?

Even Front residents who profess to love grizzlies don't like living with them. They recall the bear-free fishing holes they used to frequent when they were kids, which they're now terrified of entering as adults. They hate the spasm of pain that comes from accidentally brushing an electric fence. One sheep rancher told me he never realized how many twin lambs his ewes birthed until he got that fence, and the grizzly predations at lambing time stopped. But he also dreads the dark when he remembers he forgot to energize that fence before the sun went down, reducing the line of defense to the walls of his living room.

Ranchers and hunters in Wyoming and Idaho made similar objections. They were finding grizzlies in places they'd never had to deal with them before, had to mount defenses that cut into their profits and security, and saw no reason why they had to curtsy before what they deem a federally protected menace: especially one their own federal government argued was recovered and doing fine in the places where people liked seeing them—the national parks and remote wilderness areas.

The carrying capacity argument has two big weaknesses, both scientific and social. First, no scientific consensus exists on the "biological carrying capacity" of grizzly bear habitat. The first page of the *NCDE Habitat-based Recovery Criteria for Grizzly Bear Population in the Northern Continental Divide Ecosystem* acknowledges "There is no published method to deductively calculate minimum habitat values required for a healthy and recovered population." Instead, the criteria focus on measurable numbers of roads, livestock grazing allotments, and recreation sites in 2011 and sets the population of bears at that time as its baseline. If the census trend goes up, it's assumed the habitat is allowing bears to thrive.

By using grizzly census numbers as a proxy for habitat quality, grizzly managers have denied themselves any secondary measuring stick to show how many bears a given habitat might hold. They can't say a spot on the map has enough huckleberries to support a given number of grizzlies, because they've only counted the grizzlies and not the berry bushes.

So while some scientific studies claim grizzlies are moving out of their core habitat of the Greater Yellowstone Ecosystem because the interior has filled up, other researchers reject the idea of seeing the park like an overfilled terrarium with grizzlies spilling over the walls. Instead, they point to two different forces. One is the age class of grizzlies in the outer fringes. They tend to be younger animals, who typically get displaced by older boars that command two or three times the average territory of a young grizzly. And second, the new places grizzlies have been found also contain lots of corn, alfalfa, livestock, garbage, deer, and elk—the bountiful byproducts of the dominant species (humans). Why wouldn't a hungry bear go somewhere with more food and less competition?

As for social carrying capacity, no one has a strong definition for "social capacity" nor a way to measure it, despite the phrase's prevalence in conservation strategies, legal briefs, and public statements. That's not to say Yoder's goals, values, and culture have no currency; just that we have no exchange rate.

"This is the real challenge for grizzly bears as we're moving into the state management phase," said Gregg Losinski, spokesman for the Interagency Grizzly Bear Committee. "They aren't just in the backcountry any more. They're going to expand into places that are biologically suitable, which for grizzly bears is just about anywhere. But the expansion also has to be socially acceptable. It's not what bears are going to do, but what we allow them to do."

As cattle rancher Wayne Slaght noted earlier, the American public would never notice the loss of a few hundred cow-calf operations in the Rocky Mountain West. It wouldn't add a penny to the price of a Quarter Pounder. National surveys show overwhelming support for the Endangered Species Act and for protecting its subjects—support that crosses party lines, income groups, and other ideological divides. Should a popularity poll swamp the interests of the iconic American cowboy? The mascot representing the constitutional tension between the tyranny of majority rule and the bottleneck of minority rights is the grizzly bear.

◄ ◄ ◄ · ► ► ►

The Endangered Species Act's Section 7 requires the designation of "critical habitat" to ensure the survival of listed plants and animals. By law, destroying critical habitat is tantamount to destroying the protected species. Whatever landscape has what the species needs to survive gets marked on the map, and any public agency proposing activity that might hurt its survival must first consult with the Fish and Wildlife Service for possible mitigation or prohibition. Controversially, critical habitat can also include private property, as well as water used by irrigators or hydropower producers.

That principle worked well for animals dependent on particular foods, geographical conditions, or similar limitations. But the omnivorous grizzly bear can live practically anywhere it can find enough calories.

For its grizzly critical habitat plans, the Fish and Wildlife Service faced a Hobbesian choice. It couldn't impose consultation authority over the Lower 48 states grizzlies' historic range, because that covered nearly half the contiguous nation. It couldn't restore the remaining grizzlies to their evolutionary habitat, because those prairies and river bottoms were now domesticated cropland and pasture. And even the mountain strongholds where the last few hundred grizzlies outside national parks denned were counter-claimed by humans unwilling to compromise their pursuit of profitable resources (trees, oil, natural gas, ski slopes).

The year after the grizzly was designated a threatened species in 1975, the service proposed declaring about twenty thousand square miles of Montana, Wyoming, and Idaho as its critical habitat, right when the region's major timber companies embarked on a massive logging effort in the old-growth forests of Montana and Idaho. Subsequent industry protests stalled the designation.

In 1993, the Fish and Wildlife Service proposed a concept called distinct population segments (DPS) for grizzly recovery. The six recovery areas (conveniently remote and predominantly national parks or wilderness areas) would be tended to separately until the bear numbers reached an agreed upon carrying capacity. Then a specific recovery area could be declared a DPS and delisted from federal protection.

The resulting conservation strategy maps for each recovery area look like a bullseye, with remote and secure habitat (usually national parks and wilderness areas) in the center, a tolerance area around that core, and a management area beyond that. People living in the tolerance area are expected to adapt to the grizzly where possible by doing things like securing their livestock feed and enduring the occasional visit. Those in the management zones have more precedence, with the bear likely to get moved or destroyed if it becomes tempted by human resources. Some recovery zones are tantalizingly close together, by a grizzly's standard of travel, but few bears have survived passage through those management rings.

This strategy works on a social level, as defined by local political support, and was the prime justification for declaring success in grizzly recovery when the federal government proposed delisting Greater Yellowstone's DPS in 2007. But as noted earlier, it fell apart in court when the government couldn't show the habitat had the food alternatives needed to replace lost whitebark pine seeds and cutthroat trout.

The 2013 habitat analysis answered that question, but a 2018 court ruling pointed out a biological Catch-22. Before the government could declare the Greater Yellowstone grizzlies a recovered DPS and delist them, it had to show that removing protections from one recovery area wouldn't harm the remaining ones. Failure to prove this risked "Balkanizing" the weaker recovery areas like the Cabinet-Yaak that need to recruit bears from the bigger areas.

Recovery also meant genetic stability. Yellowstone grizzlies have the most serious case of genetic isolation in the Lower 48, and the NCDE grizzlies aren't much better off. In the 2018 courtroom, the judge repeatedly asked the Department of Justice lawyers to show him the page of the strategy assuring there would be linkages or transfers to the other recovery areas, and got no response. The catch is if the recovery areas are genetically linked together, how can we say they are distinct, independent populations?

◁ ◁ ◁ · ▷ ▷ ▷

A year after the 2018 court defeat of the Greater Yellowstone grizzly delisting rule, members of the Interagency Grizzly Bear Committee wondered how they'd handled the linkage-area question in a memorandum of understanding drafted in 2000. The committee's administrative secretary said she couldn't find it in the archives.

From the audience, Mike Bader raised his hand: "I have a copy." The pre-computer history of grizzly bear recovery lives in his garage. "It's not digitized," he sighs. "You can't search it unless you go through the box."

Bader himself has become a reluctant citizen of the Internet Age. He cofounded the Alliance for the Wild Rockies in 1985—one of several groups frequently called "radical environmentalist litigants" by Montana's Republican congressional delegates. He cofounded the even more awkwardly named Flathead-Lolo-Bitterroot Citizen Task Force. On resumés, he refers to himself as an independent natural resource consultant. What Bader mainly does is show up and remember.

"A lot of people forget how many people Chuck Jonkel taught," Bader told me. "I watched him do calculus by hand with a pad and pencil."

He grew up watching the Craighead brothers on *Mutual of Omaha's Wild Kingdom* Sunday-night TV show. His father once woke him up early on a family camping trip to show him a pawprint in the dust: "Son, that's a bear track. Don't panic everyone else."

He joined Save Our Wildlife when he was twelve. On a school outing along the Cedar River in Iowa, his teacher pointed out a factory's discharge pipe pouring waste straight into the river. The teacher reported the sighting, and Bader realized "you can stop bad things by exposing them."

While studying for a forestry degree at the University of Montana in the 1980s, Bader became a Savage: the nickname for summer employees in Yellowstone National Park. He hiked for miles in the summer, occasionally coming across a grizzly track.

"Back then, if you saw one in the wild, it was a big deal," Bader said. "I'd walk around the edge of [Yellowstone] Lake in August and there'd be a skiff of snow and you'd see these enormous grizzly bear tracks. You'd see fish bones and skin and tracks. You knew they were right out there in the trees. You didn't hang around."

After a couple winters selling gas to snowmobilers in the park, Bader saved enough money to enroll in the national park ranger school in Santa Rosa Junior College. He returned to Yellowstone and spent two winters on ski patrol, going on search-and-rescue missions in between details shoveling snow off hotel roofs. When he made the summer staff, he'd go on carcass patrol, checking popular trails for bear danger.

"You'd go out with a pistol and a shotgun," he said. "You'd watch the sky for the crows, and know if there was a dead animal up ahead. That would stop you from walking into an ambush. You could hear an ant fart—you were so attuned to the presence of danger. But everything that was happening was so awesome."

In his second year as ranger, he got assigned to a bear patrol with Chuck Jonkel's son, Jamie. Other rangers in lookout towers with binoculars would watch them, occasionally warning of a grizzly on the other side of a thicket they were entering. He remembers running into Doug

Peacock then, and advising him that if Peacock got attacked by a grizzly, no one was coming to rescue him.

"I saw a sow once in geyserite soil, in this island of trees in a thermal area," he recalled. "This huge grizzly. She comes out and starts excavating a big hole. Then she pulls out a front quarter of some animal—a huge chunk of meat she'd buried there for harder times. She came back and got it."

Bader and Alliance for the Wild Rockies (AWR) soon turned their attention to grizzly bears. While the Interagency Grizzly Bear Committee got to work on rewriting its 1993 recovery plan, Recovery Coordinator Chris Servheen was simultaneously developing plans to reintroduce grizzlies into the North Cascades and Bitterroot ecosystems. Washington state opponents rallied against the North Cascades proposal, but a coalition of conservation groups and timber companies got behind the Bitterroot initiative. In what became known as ROOTS, or Resource Organization On Timber Supply, the two sides envisioned a deal. Defining a place where grizzlies could have priority would also give certainty to the places where loggers could log. Removing long-term market uncertainty from the forest inventory was enough incentive for the sawmill owners to forsake some country for the bears.

But the deal depended on reintroducing five or six grizzlies a year for five years on an experimental basis. By "experimental," the Fish and Wildlife Service meant those grizzlies wouldn't be considered protected under the full Endangered Species Act. Instead, they'd be classified under the Act's 10-J provision, which allowed killing them, for a variety of reasons, with relaxed federal oversight.

The proposal ignited a political firestorm among both conservative politicians in Idaho and grizzly recovery advocates in Montana. Bader and other supporters of AWR attacked the plan from the environmentalists' corner, pulling support away from the Defenders of Wildlife and National Wildlife Federation, which both backed the ROOTS coalition. They counterproposed a more far-reaching "conservation biology alternative" with dedicated habitat improvements to encourage natural grizzly migration instead of artificial transplants. They also called for a nearly fourteen-million-acre recovery zone compared to the roughly four million acres covered by the ROOTS plan. Eventually the proposal got blocked by President George W. Bush's interior secretary, Gail Norton.

As coordinator for the entire grizzly recovery effort in the continental United States, Servheen had gambled heavily on the Bitterroot grizzly reintroduction and lost. The bet included most of the resources for a simultaneous effort to restore bears to the North Cascades Ecosystem in Washington, which then completely stalled.

Seventeen years later, that North Cascades reintroduction plan was revived by President Donald Trump's interior secretary, Ryan Zinke. But scandal-plagued Zinke resigned in 2019 and was replaced by his deputy, David Bernhardt. Although an independent analysis found the public supported the North Cascades reintroduction by a ratio of 62:1, Bernhardt claimed "overwhelming opposition" to the plan justified its termination in 2020. Interior officials ignored my repeated requests to back up this claim. Nevertheless, Servheen savors the irony attached to the actions of reintroduction opponents in the Bitterroot. If the reintroduction plan had gone forward, those grizzlies would have been an experimental population with a local civilian management board authorized to kill any grizzly that exceeded local, social tolerance. Instead, emigrating grizzlies—as long as they still have it—bring their full protection of the Endangered Species Act with them. And Norton never formally rejected the plan. As of 2018, it still sat on a shelf in Washington, DC, with a "just add grizzlies" label.

7

The Bear on the Bicycle

"OH GOD, BEAR!"

Brad Treat's penultimate words were his cousin's only warning. The two men were on a mountain bike ride on the Green Gate Trail, just across Highway 2 from Coram, sandwiched between Glacier National Park and the Bob Marshall Wilderness Complex. Treat led, pedaling with competitive effort, about sixty feet ahead. He whizzed around a blind corner. Then came a thud, followed by an animal's roar of pain or surprise.

Two seconds later the cousin came around the same corner and saw a large grizzly bear standing over Treat's body. Treat called his cousin's name twice—his final words (which weren't included in the coroner's report, leaving the cousin unidentified). The second man stopped his bike about thirty feet away from the crash, uncertain what to do. He described the bear as brownish-black, very big, with bristled-up fur. The bear focused on Treat's body, never looking at the companion. After about thirty seconds, the cousin decided he had no chance of pushing the bear off the scene, so he turned around and rode for help. When he could hear the highway, he dismounted and carried his bike through the brush to flag down a passing car. It took roughly an hour for him to reach a phone and call 9-1-1. It was June 29, 2016.

The Interagency Grizzly Bear Committee Board of Review analyzed the impact scene in clinical detail. Treat's demise took just sweeps of a second hand. The investigators estimated he was pedaling about twenty-five miles per hour when he saw the grizzly. The tire tracks on the trail showed no signs of braking. Treat plowed into the bear so hard, he made a horizontal bruise on his chest where he hit the handlebars. His biking shoes were clipped into the pedals, so his momentum flipped both him and his bike over the bear's body. Treat flew into the ground hard enough to break both wrists and shatter his right shoulder blade.

The grizzly responded with its paws and claws, mauling Treat's head and shoulders and shattering his bike helmet. It also bit him, but the postmortem reported only "mouthing bites or test bites to see if the victim was still a threat." The bear didn't do anything else to Treat's body—didn't move it, didn't cover it like the grizzly did with Lance Crosby's remains in Yellowstone National Park—didn't do any of the things bears do with food they plan on caching to eat later. It vanished.

Montana state game wardens set two culvert traps and a network of remote cameras to learn if the grizzly remained in the area. Over the next forty-eight hours, they got nothing. Except for one neighbor's report of seeing a large black grizzly near her driveway a mile and a half away from the incident, the suspect was never seen again.

Which stands to reason, given what we know about that bear. Thanks to the genetic analysis breakthroughs discussed in chapter 5, that's a surprisingly large amount.

The crash left twelve samples of bear DNA on Treat's bike and body, mainly hair and saliva. Forensic analysis revealed the matching grizzly had been trapped in Glacier National Park's Camas Creek drainage in 2006. Because it was a male and the biologists were looking for females, they did not collar it but only recorded its biometrics and let it go. At the time, it was estimated to be eight to ten years old and weighed three hundred and seventy pounds.

Its DNA signature showed up in hair traces found in grizzly census efforts five more times around the Coram vicinity over the years. But the bear itself stayed out of the log books. It didn't threaten livestock. It didn't cruise garbage dumps. It didn't challenge hunters for kills.

It did get spotted occasionally, including a probable encounter just half an hour before it killed Treat. A Swan River Outfitters guide was leading a string of dudes on horseback about eight hundred yards away from the crash site when they saw a large brownish-black grizzly bear ahead of them. The grizzly charged to within six feet of the group before veering off, making noises and snapping its teeth.

Between 1998 and 2011, DNA hair snares revealed at least six male and three female grizzly bears using an area within a three-mile radius of the crash site. Radio-collar records showed another five males and five females traveling the same area. Grizzly bears like this one live eighteen or twenty years only by strict adherence to ursine self-discipline and by good fortune. The sheer number of temptations and threats—bird feeders, freight trains, picnic baskets, five-lane freeways, hunting camps, and research labs—packed into the southwest corner of Glacier National Park give a bear little chance of avoiding some kind of human interaction.

Chris Servheen had barely retired from his career-long post as grizzly recovery coordinator for the US Fish and Wildlife Service when he got asked to lead the board of review into Treat's death. It was Servheen's eighth such postmortem since he took the job of coordinator in 1981. He released his report on March 3, 2017.

"With something like mountain biking, the high speed and quiet nature of riding increases the probability of encounters with bears when you're coming around blind curves," Servheen told me. In the case of Treat's collision, he said, "here's a bear that's twenty years old, who's lived in a high-density human area his entire life. He's pretty skilled at staying away from trouble. We think he was just as surprised as Mr. Treat was. The two of them probably had only one or two seconds before they encountered one another."

After the initial forty-eight-hour search and trap deployment, state game wardens stopped trying to catch the suspect grizzly. They concluded the bear didn't threaten human safety, despite having just killed a human.

US Fish and Wildlife Service biologist Wayne Kasworm had just replaced Servheen as interim leader of the grizzly recovery effort. Treat's death crystallized one of his top tasks: Getting people to agree on how much safety they all must give up to coexist with bears.

"They're wild animals, and we are not controlling them," Kasworm said. "What we attempt to do is provide information so people can make reasoned judgments about what is safe activity or not safe activity. We're trying to get some conversation going, to get people thinking about what is going on out there in the woods."

To deal with objective dangers in the outdoors, people already self-limit their recreation in many ways. Boaters avoid rivers during spring runoff, or accept the consequences of lost gear, wrecked boats, and possible death. Golfers voluntarily leave the links when a thunderstorm brings lightning over their metal clubs and spiked shoes. Snowmobilers and backcountry skiers check avalanche forecasts and weigh the risks of the day's adventure.

"We're trying to get folks to recognize and take on responsibility for their own safety when they walk into known grizzly bear habitat, when grizzly bear habitat is taking over more and more of Montana," Kasworm told me. "When a bear results in a human safety issue, or it's killing livestock repeatedly, we remove the bear. But if you're tooling around on your mountain bike and you bump into the bear and you're scared, that's not necessarily a reason to remove the bear."

◄ ◄ ◄ · ► ► ►

Is it a reason to remove the bikes? And what about everything else humans like to do in bear country? Whose interests rule?

Three years to the day after Treat's death, Flathead National Forest supervisor Chip Weber declared his disagreement with Servheen's report. New controversy had arisen over a commercial ultramarathon and a backcountry bike shuttle service in the national forest land around Whitefish, Montana, about twenty miles from Coram.

"I want to start by strongly repudiating the notion that as an agency, we ought not promote, foster or permit activities because engagement in those activities presents risk to the participants," Weber told the Interagency Grizzly Bear Committee's summer 2019 gathering in Missoula. "The issues around this are much broader than trail use, and grizzly bears and both people and wildlife may suffer if the discussion isn't expanded."

As to Board of Review report, Weber told me he had great personal respect for Servheen but "his (Servheen's) focus is grizzly bear recovery and solely grizzly bear recovery. Mine is serving the American public and the needs they want in the context of many wildlife species and an overall conservation mission that's very, very broad."

Individual sporting events like the Whitefish ultramarathon have such minimal impact on grizzly bears, Weber said, they fall under a categorical exclusion from in-depth environmental review. At the same time, those events endear increasing numbers of people to their public lands as the number of users grows year after year.

"There's a broad public out there with needs to be served and not just the needs of the few," Weber said. "We think that greater good for the greatest number will be served. That fosters connectivity with wildlands and a united group of people that can support conservation. And the best conservation for bears is served by figuring out how to have these human activities in ways that are as safe as they can be, understanding you can never make anything perfectly safe."

The US Forest Service's founding chief, Gifford Pinchot, stamped that utilitarian philosophy into his corps at the beginning of the twentieth century. At one time, national forest signs all bore the legend "Land of Many Uses." The new agency motto is "Caring for the Land, Serving People." More and more, those people want to risk rafting the rapids of Wild and Scenic Rivers, paragliding off ridgetops, highmarking snowmobiles in avalanche basins, and picking huckleberries in bear country.

But what about caring for the land? Does some theory of limits exist that can set thresholds for how much people-serving is too much? By tradition or taboo, there remain places in cathedrals and palaces where people don't go, or at least don't get free rein to pursue their ambitions. It's possible to free-climb the Eiffel Tower, but Parisian police will await the victory rappel.

I once sneaked a photo of the Crown Jewels of England, but I got escorted out of the Tower of London when I tried to snap a second.

An old farmer's quip goes "Whiskey's for drinkin', water's for fightin'." Public land and water management debates in the West sometimes result in armed sieges, like the takeover of Oregon's Malheur National Wildlife Refuge in 2016. In the 1980s, some opponents of old-growth logging revived an old lumberjack trick and started driving metal spikes into tree trunks, which would cause a high-speed bandsaw in a lumber mill to explode like a land mine. The US Forest Service's ecology mascot Woodsey Owl had to stay out of Fourth of July parades in Washington due to death threats when the Interagency Grizzly Bear Committee considered transplanting grizzly bears into the Bitterroot Ecosystem of Montana and Idaho in the 1990s.

◄ ◄ ◄ · ► ► ►

Will Rogers supposedly said "Buy land—they ain't making any more of the stuff." Humans seem to have an inexhaustible supply of both intentions for that land and the wherewithal to act. Nature doesn't adapt so fast.

For example, Treat was thirty-eight years old when he encountered his last grizzly bear. The off-road bicycles available when he was born weighed fifty pounds, had no disc brakes, no shoe clips, no suspension. The first slickrock trails in places like Moab, Utah, were just getting mapped and were known only to desert-rat thrill seekers when he was learning to pedal.

By 2019, these thrillists, as they've come to be called, can use apps on their smart phones to race against one another in the virtual world by recording their trails and times to an online community of fellow riders. Global positioning satellites track their progress and chart the results against all other riders who've attempted the same route. No need for race day.

In 2016, some 2,500 people attended Brad Treat's memorial service—the same number of people now bike Glacier National Park's Going-to-the-Sun Road every spring before it opens to automobile traffic. The only bikes that weigh fifty pounds have electric motors assisting their riders.

Glacier National Park prohibits bicycling on its trails but allows it on automobile roads and a small forest route near Apgar. And bikers on those routes before the driving season starts often find bears don't poop in the woods: They poop on plowed roadways where it's easier to travel.

Spend a lot of time in the backcountry, and you get really familiar with feces. Deer drop round brownish-black pellets about the size of Raisinettes, inspiring generations of practical jokes played on tenderfoot Boy Scouts and other novices. Elk droppings look similar but are more oval and as big as generous caramel candies. Wolf turds look like bent cigars, with lots of hair poking out. Mountain lions defecate similarly, but cats skin their kills before eating so there's no hair in the scat. Grizzlies, being both omnivorous and inefficient digesters, tend to take a dump. They leave what looks like shovelfuls of compost, with berries and leaves still identifiable. Only when they've been eating meat do their scats become distinctly sausage-like.

Glacier Park policy presumes that bikes, because of their faster speed, have a bigger impact on wildlife than hikers. However, the National Park Service officially restricts bike use because it treats Glacier backcountry as wilderness under the 1964 Wilderness Act (which prohibits wheeled equipment)—not because of any potential wildlife or safety concern. One variation to that is Glacier's policy of not plowing the Going-to-the-Sun Road before April 1. That's to give bears arising from hibernation some time to roam and feed with minimal human interaction. The rule also incidentally limits the chance of collisions between people and wildlife.

The Forest Service, which manages most of the federal wilderness in the United States, considers bicycles "mechanized transport," which is prohibited by the Wilderness Act. Many people confuse the law's stance on "mechanized" and "motorized" transportation. However, the words have distinct shades of meaning. Motorized means engines; mechanized means wheels.

Fire gave *Homo sapiens* the nutritional leverage to evolve bigger brains, by transforming raw food into easily digestible calories. Wheels gave us the physical leverage to move all the cargo those brains conceived. Archaeologists still spill pitchers of beer over which was more essential to the dawn of civilization (when they're not arguing over the primacy of beer or bread as the first civilized food).

Wheels occupy such an intrinsic role in modern life, conceiving culture without them seems absurd. They hide in the rails that guide our dresser drawers, clunk under our grocery carts, spin our Lazy Susans. We build them into our picnic coolers, and marvel at how our parents must have struggled hauling the old Colemans by those squeaky handles.

I abandoned a great kid-friendly camping idea in frustration when I learned a canoe cart violated the Wilderness Act, meaning I couldn't roll my paddle-powered watercraft across two miles of trail separating Kintla from Upper Kintla Lakes in Glacier Park. No gears, no pedals, just a couple wheels and an axle. OK? Nope: The wheels make it mechanized. You want your gear in wilderness, you haul it on your back. Or bring a horse.

The no-wheels policy seems like some sort of self-flagellation. Until you visit a place like Nepal's Namche Bazaar in the Himalayas, where the town clings to mountainsides so steep that anything mounted on wheels would instantly roll away and crush someone below. Anyone who's marched the trail to Everest Base Camp (or experienced the Solu Khumbu for its many other scenic and cultural qualities) discovers that every tube of Pringles and solar-powered disco light made it there on someone's back, without a wheel in sight.

So humans do impose limits for arbitrary reasons. United States law prohibits *mechanized* transport in federally designated wilderness areas. The National Park Service (in Glacier Park anyway) and the US Forest Service interpret that to mean no wheels. That means no bikes in the best bear country.

To confuse matters, Treat's encounter occurred in a slice of Flathead National Forest land between a national park and a wilderness area, where the mechanized rule *did not* apply. Nothing about the landscape, other than boundary signs, indicates *here* but not *there* in any way an animal might comprehend. Humans also struggle with the distinction.

The post-mortem writers sought to use the incident as a teachable moment, and included a five-page set of recommendations and lessons for recreating in grizzly country.

"The unfortunate death of Mr. Brad Treat from a grizzly bear attack that was precipitated by a high-speed mountain bike collision between Mr. Treat and a bear necessitates increased attention to the dangers associated with mountain biking in black bear and grizzly bear habitat," the recommendations began. "There is a long record of human-bear conflicts associated with mountain biking in bear habitat including the serious injuries and deaths suffered by bike riders."

The Board of Review expanded upon established hiker advice to be vigilant, carry bear spray, make noise, don't run from encounters, and don't hike alone. For mountain bikers, it produced an eight-suggestion list focused on the different ways bikes and bears interact. Those included calls to ride slowly because bears encountered at high speed will likely react defensively and injure bikers.

The "make noise" suggestion was amplified by the observation that "mountain biking is a quiet and fast activity that may cause you to get much too close to a bear before either you or the bear knows it, resulting in a surprise encounter and a defensive attack by a surprised bear." One contributor suggested sticking playing cards in the wheel spokes.

A University of Calgary study refined the problem even further, finding the audible signal of a mountain bike in the woods disappears beyond fifty-five yards. Alaska Department of Fish and Game biologist Rick Sinnott noted that's coincidentally the same radius within which a grizzly bear is likely to react aggressively to a surprise encounter.

The Treat advisory warned against riding at dusk or dawn, because of the reduced ability to be aware of surroundings at times when bears are most active; and at any time to avoid thinking, "It won't happen to me."

"That kind of attitude is what can get you in serious trouble whether you are mountain-biking or doing any other potentially dangerous activity," the recommendation stated. "Be prepared and be safe. That way you can enjoy your activity and you and the bears will be safe." The list concluded with the reminder that humans have tourist status in the places bears consider home.

Neither Treat nor his cousin carried bear spray on their ride. But Treat was far from a "won't happen to me" individual. He was a twelve-year veteran Flathead National Forest law enforcement officer who regularly jogged and biked on the Green Gate Trail network. He also served on local search-and-rescue, swiftwater-rescue, and avalanche-rescue teams, himself having to recover "won't happen to me" hikers and boaters when things "happened."

⊰ ⊰ ⊰ · ⊱ ⊱ ⊱

Swan View Coalition director Keith Hammer lives a few miles south of the Green Gate Trail, and has spent most of his life trying to protect grizzly bears. Most of that time has been spent fighting people like Servheen and Kasworm, who Hammer considers too intent on scoring a delisting win for the Endangered Species Act to consider what he thinks the bear really needs. Protection from mountain bikes is high on Hammer's list.

"I've hiked my whole life," he told me. "I mountain-bike. I've never been charged by a black bear or grizzly while hiking. But I've been charged twice on a mountain bike. The first was by a black bear with two cubs. She was in front of me and she charged. Then she went back and got her cubs out of the trees and that was the end of it."

"But last summer . . . ," he trailed off for a moment.

> You run into bears near streams. It's good habitat, plus they can't hear you coming. I'm biking and its quiet, and the next thing I hear a woof and a growl, and those lungs huffing in and out. I've heard lots of bears, usually going away from me. This was following me. Nothing feels more stupid than having both hands on the handle bars where you can't grab your bear spray. The only way to deploy it is to stop, and you can't stop. It's different on a road. You have good lines of sight. It's riding on trails that's the problem. I've worked played and camped in bear habitat. If I want to live longer, I need to quit mountain biking. It ain't rocket science.

Somer Treat, Brad's wife, took a very different approach on the third anniversary of her husband's death. In a public letter she "fought against any association or focus with an agenda, clear or subtle, that would attempt to limit recreation or grizzly bears on public land." Two weeks after Brad's death, Somer Treat started running the same trail where the accident happened. She said she's done so every day since.

"I run in the woods—with the bears—because I still can," Somer Treat wrote. "I saw a grizzly bear last week on my morning run; I felt the fantastic tingle inside my soul, the feeling of knowing I still get to experience *THIS*. Let me be clear, this magic tingle feeling was the core of Brad's existence. It defined his professional life, and how he spent his personal time on public lands. The final perfect moments of Brad's life were spent doing exactly what he believed in."

Glacier National Park routinely closes trails frequented by grizzlies, often for entire tourist seasons. Yellowstone National Park has seventeen bear management areas covering nearly 20 percent of the interior, with shifting rules based on grizzly seasonal movements. The popular Firehole area just north of Old Faithful is closed to use from March 10 to just before Memorial Day weekend. The Washburn area west of Tower Junction is accessible by special permit only from March 10 to July 31, and then closed for the rest of the summer and fall. Grant Village, where park officials once considered building a major hotel complex, is off-limits to any camping before June 20 or whenever the grizzlies finish feeding at trout spawning streams. Many other areas limit backcountry use to trail travel and established campsites only—no off-trail exploring allowed.

National parks have the prerogative to impose such rules on visitors. Tourists expect that level of oversight within park boundaries. But the national forest and private lands just across the line follow much looser rules. Brad Treat died just a couple miles south of the Glacier Park boundary. Just across the Flathead River, his bike ride would have been prohibited as a federal crime.

Hammer's Swan View Coalition led a federal lawsuit in 1999 that forced the Flathead National Forest to add a strict review of grizzly bear needs to any human development in the bear's core habitat. Modern pressure to open roads and trails into those areas for off-highway vehicles and bikes has eroded allegiance to those standards, he fears.

In particular, the coalition testified against the agency's growing tendency to overlook decommissioned roads when calculating the miles of development in those remote places. Such roads may be blockaded to stop large vehicles, but they remain passable to hikers and bikers: "[T]hat spells disaster in the face of rapidly increasing, high-speed trail running and mountain biking that is resulting in deaths to both people and bears."

Servheen's report essentially agreed with that premise. A second part of the recommendations addressed human convenience: "Before new trails are opened to mountain biking in bear habitat, particularly grizzly habitat, there should be careful evaluation of the safety and reasonableness of enhancing mountain bike access in these areas where bear density is high." That included consideration of sight distances in thick brush and the risk of routing trails through feeding areas like huckleberry fields or avalanche chutes, plus consideration of seasonal closures to biking during grizzly bear feeding times.

◄ ◄ ◄ · ► ► ►

In another study Servheen coauthored, his colleagues found one of the most effective ways to prevent human–bear conflicts was keeping human food away from bears. That's so simple, it's been boiled down to a seven-word slogan: A fed bear is a dead bear.

The math is pretty simple too. A pound of huckleberries, which when ripe make up a huge slice of the grizzly bear dietary pie chart, contributes 166 calories. A hyperphagic grizzly preparing for hibernation needs between 20,000 and 40,000 calories a day.

Meanwhile, a pound of sunflower seeds for a backyard bird feeder has 2,585 calories. A hummingbird feeder with thirty-two ounces of sugar water has 3,200 calories. Game wardens call them bear crack vials.

Hence the emphasis on keeping human "pic-a-nic baskets" out of Yogi Bear's reach. Sounds simple, until Yellowstone Park bear habitat coordinator Dan Tyer collected all the food storage rules aimed at federally protected grizzly bears on a single spreadsheet. The printed result came out six and a half feet long, in type the same size as this book font. It reflected twenty-one separate agencies and jurisdictions, with entries ranging from whether it's safe to keep toothpaste in a tent to how to dispose of a dead pack mule on the trail.

"We have too many interpretations on how we should interpret the orders," Tyer told me. "You can move across the Yellowstone Ecosystem

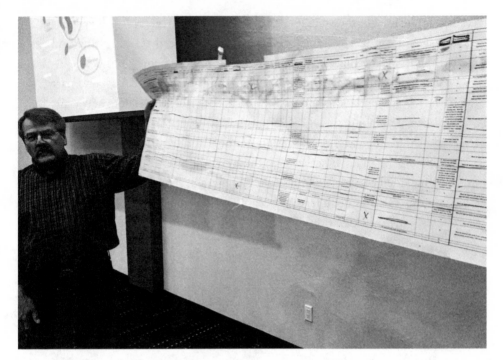

Yellowstone bear habitat coordinator Dan Tyer holds up a spreadsheet nearly seven feet long listing different food protection orders for national parks, national forests, state wildlife refuges, and other jurisdictions. Photograph by the author.

on a pack trip, step across a line and have an order that's fundamentally different from the neighboring order."

In the Greater Yellowstone Ecosystem backcountry, all food must be hung out of bears' reach. But in the Northern Continental Divide, food can be left on the ground if it's attended. Tyer said that's resulted in horse wranglers sleeping on grain sacks during pack trips in the Bob Marshall Wilderness Complex.

‹ ‹ ‹ · › › ›

The Bob Marshall Wilderness Complex encloses about two million acres—twice the size of adjacent Glacier National Park. But the boundaries have a subtle difference. Glacier uses the North and Middle Forks of the Flathead River for two sides, and a relatively arbitrary survey line across the prairie for its eastern edge. The forty-ninth parallel of the Canadian border makes the northern limit. All of Glacier National Park's core mountains and valley habitat lie inside those lines.

In contrast, most of the Bob's original perimeter ran along the crest of its watersheds, connecting dots of mountain peaks. Inside the line was "big W" wilderness. Outside was regular national forest. That divides mountains in half by administrative principle that no grizzly bear can see or smell. Logging projects can and did march right up to the wilderness boundary and stop, clear-cutting precise, square sections alongside virgin forest.

Lolo National Forest analysts had labeled about eighty thousand acres of those fringes "recommended wilderness" in the 1980s. The recommendation meant the Forest Service should preserve the wilderness character of those lands until Congress determined if they belong in the federal wilderness system or not (only Congress can designate wilderness areas). Specifically, in these wilderness study areas, that meant no permanent human development, no roads, no logging, and no mechanized access.

Over the next human generation, snowmobiles grew more powerful and mountain bikes more capable. User groups started lobbying Congress for their own admission to special places, such as the Spread Mountain and Otatsy Basin areas along the Bob Marshall's southwest edge.

Smoke Elser spent six decades leading dudes and hunters on horse trains into those places. The dean of Montana's outfitting heritage agreed to share his favorite place in the world with his least-favorite pastime, and it nearly broke his heart.

Inside Elser's cobblestone office/stable on the edge of Missoula, a tangle of elk antlers in the corner holds an even more jumbled collection of hats, bugle tubes, bear spray cans, and fishing pole cases. The prickly array mirrors the uneasy pack string of collaborators pulling for new wilderness designations around the Bob Marshall. He held a list of supporters containing eighty signers, ranging from Backcountry Hunters and Anglers and the Blue Ribbon Coalition to Paws Up Resort and Zoo Town Surfers. Pyramid Mountain Lumber and the Seeley-Swan ATV Club shared space with The Wilderness Society and the Associated Students of the University of Montana.

"I'm opposed to having mountain bikes in wilderness," Elser told me. "I don't think they belong there. But I know our biggest challenge is Congress is looking at allowing mountain bikes in all wilderness. Some members of the steering committee felt we could not get any more wilderness on the south end of the Bob without including the snowmobilers and mountain bikes. I will support what we've done. I'm the only one who voted against it. But everyone else agreed. And I want Grizzly Basin. I want that Monture drainage. So I had to compromise. But I'm not going to compromise anymore."

Grizzly Basin and the Monture are two more of those fringe areas below the mountain crest boundary of the original Bob Marshall adjacent to Spread Mountain and Otatsy Basin. Grizzly bears regularly roam all four areas. So do trophy elk and rare herds of mountain goats. The tiny headwater creeks on the mountainside attract massive bull trout to pristine spawning gravels.

In return for endorsing full federal wilderness protection of eighty thousand acres in a 2016 congressional bill, the International Mountain Bicycling Association (IMBA) and two Montana mountain biking groups laid claim to Spread Mountain for future cycling trails. That's next to a proposed 2,200-acre recreation management area designated for snowmobile use.

That irked environmentalist coalitions like Mike Bader's Flathead-Lolo-Bitterroot Citizen Task Force, which also includes the Montana Sierra Club, Wilderness Watch, and Swan View Coalition. Elser feels hemmed in, much the same way his century-old ranch in the upper Rattlesnake Valley has been surrounded by Missoula's suburban houses.

"IMBA came to me," he went on.

I have their book right up there, with all kinds of red lines through it. The steering committee—I talk to them eyeball to eyeball. Mountain bikers and snowmobilers are going after a different sort of recreational benefit than what I'm going after or hikers are going after. We're seeking the hush of the land. Solitude. Every turn of the trail is a new experience to enjoy at our own pace. Mountain bikers are out to challenge the resource. It's about how fast you can go and how many miles you can put on. Snowmobilers are after the highest mark on the hillside, the highest speed across the meadow.

I won't step over the line again. But we've got to get that piece through. To get eighty thousand acres of additional wilderness, we're going to have to compromise some.

In a Missoula office a short bike ride from Elser's stable, Zack Porter has the job of justifying those value trade-offs. Barely half Elser's age, the Montana Wilderness Association (MWA) field director argues he's struggling with the same conundrums his mentors have faced for the past fifty years.

"We're not putting bikes on the landscape—they're already there," Porter said. "The Forest Service, for all they've done well protecting these recommended additions, has not managed those areas in light of shifts in recreational use over the decades. If the Forest Service had taken proactive steps according to the 1986 Lolo National Forest Plan, we wouldn't be having this argument. And we'll only run into more of these problems if the Forest Service doesn't lead."

Porter proved prophetic. In 2018, Montana's and Wyoming's Republican congressional members authored bills to strip wilderness study area status from more than a million acres proposed for wilderness designation in the 1980s. Several of the areas get regular use by grizzly bears moving between core habitats.

Porter also brings up what happened in 2009, when the Beaverhead-Deerlodge National Forest plan eliminated thousands of acres of recommended wilderness around Montana's Big Hole Valley because of growing snowmobile use.

"That was perfectly legal," Porter said. "That's why we can't wait—why we can't hang on to the status quo of study areas and recommended wilderness. The Forest Service can undo its recommendation when it revises the forest plan. And it hasn't shown any desire to rise to the occasion and manage these conflict areas."

Mountain biking advocates aren't waiting either. That same week Porter celebrated the introduction of a Senate wilderness bill protecting the Bob Marshall fringe (along with some compromise bike- and snowmobile-use areas), the National Sustainable Trails Coalition hailed the introduction of a House bill allowing the use of bikes and other wheeled equipment in federal wilderness areas.

That coalition supports a nationwide change allowing local wilderness managers to set their own rules on bike access. The House bill "puts mountain bikers on the same footing as campers, hikers, hunters, and equestrians by restoring federal agency authority to set conditions on cyclists' use of trails in wilderness," according to the group's press release. It was reintroduced in 2019.

Coalition executive director Ted Stroll aimed the legislation directly at that Forest Service "non-mechanized" definition. He maintains the Forest Service overstepped its bounds when it clarified wilderness management rules in 1984, determining bikes were "mechanized transport," as defined in the Wilderness Act. Stroll argues that's not only a legal error, it unfairly overlooks the damage due to other kinds of wilderness activity.

"There's a strange divide in federal land where ten feet from the boundary (of wilderness) you can do all sorts of things, but inside, nothing's permitted except horses and walking," Stroll told me. "You can have massive (horse) pack trains with all the disturbance that causes. Dogs? No problem at all. But a single mountain biker is excluded 100 percent of the time. We need to think about this more deeply than 'hooves good/wheels bad.' We should be looking at what is the optimal interaction of humans and wildlife, and regulate accordingly."

Desire to protect the last prime slices of wild public land has evoked two distinct responses from environmentalists. Some have sued the Forest Service over its travel plans and enforcement. Others have collaborated with the agency and industry on legislation to change the land designation. The tactics define what Porter calls the elephant at the conservation campfire.

"Some people believe in the collaboration process, where everyone gives a little to get a lot," Porter said. "Some prefer a lawsuit where the judge says, 'This is how it will be.' That may hold ground, but it isn't building a movement. That isolates you in a corner."

Porter agreed with Elser and the majority of MWA's more than five thousand members that bikes don't belong in federal wilderness. But until that wilderness gets designated, there's room to negotiate. That's how a bike trail penetrated fourteen miles into Missoula's backyard Rattlesnake Wilderness (created by Congress in 1980), and how the Cabin Creek Special Management Area wound up preserving a snowmobile race route between Bozeman and Yellowstone National Park in the middle of the 1983 Lee Metcalf Wilderness Area.

"There's what's allowed inside the boundary, and there's where you draw the boundary," Porter said. "If we can build a bigger tent by redrawing the boundary, that might be a successful way forward."

In other words, if memorializing a place already well-known to snowmobilers and adding another drainage for bike recreation attracts the support of a Senator willing to introduce legislation, who's got a better offer?

"I would love to see every inch of roadless area protected," Porter said. "But that won't move the [Congressional] delegation into action. If we wait for some magic alignment of stars for every last acre of roadless to be protected, we'll have nothing, and I'm unwilling to see pragmatic ideas passed on while we wait for some magic scenario to come about. Our agreement is stronger for having the involvement and endorsement of these groups and constituencies."

Flathead National Forest supervisor Chip Weber put the debate in even starker terms. "Sadly the public discussion around these events and improvements has been too often in support of a narrowly-focused, discriminatory and exclusionary agenda lacking in intellectual and philosophical integrity," Weber said, adding "You're being asked to weigh in strongly in favor of an agenda I think needlessly creates a chasm between a strongly conservation-oriented hiking community and the community of bikers and runners that is equally dedicated to wildlife conservation. Both society and bears would be better off if they become united in bringing about conservation objectives."

◄ ◄ ◄ · ► ► ►

What about the animals? Do humans owe wildlife some space or restraint? A growing body of research shows that human activity interferes with wildlife nesting, feeding, resting, and breeding.

A 2009 *Journal of Wildlife Management* study by Oregon researchers Leslie Naylor, Michael Wisdom, and Robert Anthony found that elk are most disturbed from their feeding and resting behavior by the passage of all-terrain vehicles, followed by mountain biking, hiking, and horseback riding, in descending order. The study took place in 2003 and 2004 at the Starkey Experimental Forest and Range, an enclosed forest with a resident elk herd near La Grande, Oregon.

In their management recommendations, the researchers noted that "particularly ATV riding and mountain biking . . . caused the largest reduction in feeding time and increases in travel time." They added that "resource allocation trade-offs between management of elk and off-road recreation will become increasingly important as off-road recreation continues to increase on public lands."

Whether animals have rights or not, they do have predictable behaviors. Predators pursue prey, especially when it runs away. The faster it moves, the more likely a mountain lion or bear will act on instinct and give chase. That makes mountain bikers especially vulnerable.

Two weeks before Treat died, a black bear mauled triathlete Karen Williams when she was six hours into an ultramarathon race in the Valles Caldera National Preserve, New Mexico. The fifty-three-year-old was in thirtieth place out of fifty runners, but the only one to encounter the female bear and its cubs. The sow knocked her over and started clawing and biting her head and neck. She survived. Wardens with the New Mexico Department of Game and Fish later found and killed the bear.

Montana Fish, Wildlife and Parks Region One bear biologist Tim Manley (a close friend of Brad Treat's) wrote about the incident on his personal Facebook page. His comments got included in an IGBC official transcript.

"There are more and more foot and bike races in mountainous areas and this is something I have been worried about happening in NW Montana," Manley posted. "I just don't think it is a good idea to run down trails in areas with bears or mountain lions around . . . especially the races that occur overnight like they had a few years ago along the Swan Divide."

That 2010 Swan Crest 100 endurance race from Swan Lake to Columbia Falls attracted about fifty participants for the hundred-mile event. Hammer's Swan View Coalition threatened to sue the Forest Service for permitting a commercial event in grizzly bear habitat without any analysis of risks. The organizers nearly canceled, but instead refunded participants' $250 entrance fees and ran it as an informal gathering, thus avoiding the "commercial" trigger in the Forest Service rulebook.

"We're promoting some of these recreational uses that put people more at risk in bear and [mountain] lion country," Manley told me. "There's a major mountain bike race that goes through the Whitefish Range, along Trail Creek and Red Meadow, that's all in prime bear country. Your reaction time is just different when you're on a mountain bike coming around corners. Some of these events don't make sense as a smart thing to do in bear country."

Alaskan biologist Sinnott did a records check in 2017 and found twenty-two collisions between bears and bikers since 2000 in North America.

"Only four of the bikers carried bear spray or rode with someone who did," Sinnott wrote in the *Anchorage Daily News*. "In three instances the bear spray was at hand and appeared to deter or curtail the attack. In the fourth case bear spray in the biker's pack was released in the bear's face when it bit the pack. Counting on a bear biting into your bear deterrent is not a recommended procedure."

A hiker moving slowly on foot also has more opportunity to learn from the ground. Flipped-over rocks, torn-up tree stumps, and fresh scat all offer clues to the presence of others in the woods. Bikers, especially at speed, have to concentrate on the trail rolling beneath their handlebars. Even with our pathetically small sinus cavities, we humans can often smell warnings. That's particularly true of a rotting carcass which has become a bear banquet, and which that grizzly will instinctively defend to the death.

◄ ◄ ◄ · ► ► ►

Meanwhile, the mountain bikes keep getting lighter and tougher, with special gears for climbing and improved brakes for the descent. The original gas-powered moped cycles met no one's idea of an improvement: loud, smoky, lawn mower engines bolted to a bike frame, ideal for singeing one's inner thighs while annoying the neighbors.

Electric bicycles first hit the market in the early 1900s, shortly after Orville and Wilbur Wright turned their bike shop into an airplane research lab. It took another century before battery technology became light and compact enough to realize the dream. By 2015, drive systems barely bigger than a couple of water bottles had made transnational cycling tours an option again even for seventy-year-olds.

E-bike makers were forecast to sell about forty million of their creations worldwide in 2020. That doesn't include things like the Copenhagen Wheel—an add-on electric motor that can retrofit a traditional bicycle for about $1,500.

Such innovations present a new enforcement headache. The electric motors make no more noise than the pedals, and they're too small to give away a rider's intention to flout the National Park Service's non-motorized regulations. If you can't tell the sheep from the goats, you fence them all out.

And then there's human performance. In the 1930s, the namesake Robert Marshall of the Bob Marshall Wilderness Complex was notorious for hiking solo for weeks at a time, often logging thirty-five miles a day through trackless mountain ranges. The idea that dozens or even hundreds of people might someday run those routes as a competitive sport did not occur to Marshall or anyone else when he ran the Forest Service's office of recreation management for President Franklin Roosevelt.

On my last trip to Chaney Glacier, and the one time I actually drew my bear spray, it was my own kind that scared me most. Halfway into my thirty-mile, three-day adventure, something was coming at me on the trail. For a long while, I could hear loping foot-pads but couldn't see anything. I pulled the Velcro holster strap loose.

Around the corner appeared two men wearing T-shirts and jogging shorts and bandoliers racked with energy drinks. I mention the outfits because I was wearing my fleece jacket and carrying thirty-five pounds of gear four miles short of any official campground. These guys were dressed for a jog in Central Park, with no juice bar or gym locker room for miles in any direction. And they were headed away from the closest composting toilet at a serious clip, perhaps ninety minutes before sunset.

That was my first encounter with long-endurance trail runners. I suspect they intended to tag Fifty Mountain campsite, turn around, and make the Going to the Sun Road before the moon came out.

Such runners routinely race fifty miles across the Bob Marshall core in a day, on a route that professional outfitters like Smoke Elser spend a week leading dudes on horseback through the most productive grizzly habitat in the Lower 48. Few can afford the thousands of dollars such guided adventures cost. Fewer still have the stamina to "Bag the Bob" in a twenty-four-hour ultramarathon. Yet both groups claim a vested interest in the heart of the biggest bit of landscape in the contiguous United States that grizzly bears still call home.

Who am I to tell those runners to stay home? I was out there too, packing a three-ounce titanium cooking pot instead of an outfitter's cast-iron skillet. I enjoy the assistance of modern technology in ways that don't involve wheels.

The Endangered Species Act asks people to think about what adjustments we're willing to make for other forms of life. National surveys show most people support such sacrifices. That breaks the debate down to two questions. First, do we want to keep having wild grizzly bears? If no, then the Endangered Species Act "problem" goes away with them.

But if we say yes, we want grizzlies, then the debate becomes all about limits and sacrifices. Not only loggers and miners, but bikers and hikers must leave something on the table for the bear.

8

Roadkill

THE BITTERROOT VALLEY SOUTH OF MISSOULA RUNS STRAIGHT north–south for seventy miles. On the valley's west side, the five-thousand-vertical-foot front of the Bitterroot Mountains marks one edge of the most extensive wilderness complex in the Lower 48 states (the place we could hide the state of West Virginia). The Bitterroot River runs along the valley bottom, flanked by multi-million-dollar vacation homes the locals call "trout palaces" nestled along its Blue Ribbon fly-fishing waters. The more mundane humps of the Sapphire Mountains form the east rim of the valley.

In October 2018, a groundskeeper at the Whitetail Golf Course north of Stevensville noticed something had been digging for earthworms in the putting greens. The invader also had a predilection for snapping off the flagpoles in the holes. Montana Fish, Wildlife and Parks bear specialist Jamie Jonkel set a culvert trap, expecting to nab a black bear. But when the groundskeeper checked it the next morning, he reported something much bigger—a young male grizzly bear. Jonkel hauled it back north across Interstate 90 to the southern fringe of the Northern Continental Divide Ecosystem (NCDE) and released it.

The Selway-Bitterroot Recovery Area poses a tantalizing goal for grizzly watchers. It used to have grizzly bears: its last officially recognized resident was killed in 1932 (although reliable accounts recorded tracks and spoor into the 1950s). In the 1990s Doug Peacock and other volunteers scoured the place for contemporary signs of grizzly occupation, backcountry treks that included a harrowing climb of a snow-packed mountain face to take hair samples from a bear den spotted during an aerial survey. The hair turned out to be *Ursus americanus*—a black bear.

A black-bear hunter mistakenly shot a male grizzly bear in the Bitterroot Wilderness's Kelly Creek drainage in 2007, marking the first confirmed presence of *Ursus arctos horribilis* in half a century. It had apparently traveled south along the rugged Montana-Idaho border from the Cabinet-Yaak Recovery Area.

The Stevensville golf course grizzly essentially sneaked in a back door. While the official recovery zone attention focused on the Selway-Bitterroot Wilderness and its glaciated peaks to the west, this bear traveled via the much easier (and more urbanized) terrain through the rolling Sapphires to the east.

And here was a grizzly that had found its own way to the undiscovered country, and got ejected. The reason, according to the IGBC Bitterroot Subcommittee leaders, was they had no plan in place to release a captured grizzly in the Bitterroot Recovery Area, despite having spent most of a decade in the 1990s preparing to transplant grizzlies there.

To get between ecosystems, grizzlies must find paths they can travel without getting in trouble. As part of the NCDE conservation strategy, Montana Fish, Wildlife and Parks biologist Cecily Costello built a computer program that predicts the routes grizzlies might use to travel between the southern edge of the Bob Marshall Wilderness Complex and the Greater Yellowstone Ecosystem. The first thing she had to do was get into the mind of a wandering bear.

Costello did that by stockpiling the same kinds of radiotelemetry maps Ethyl's ramble had produced, only for one hundred and twenty-four male grizzlies at least two years old.

"You had to model the effect of not knowing where you're going," Costello said. Wherever a bear changed direction, she'd catalog the possible reasons why. Creek crossing? House nearby? Road or trail fork? Cliff wall?

"We'd compare the random choices with what the bear picked, to see if landforms made a difference," Costello said. "The only places they consistently avoided were big open valleys."

Once she'd built up an inventory of preferences, Costello overlaid them on the terrain between the Northern Continental Divide Ecosystem and the Greater Yellowstone Ecosystem (GYE). About fifty miles separate the two regions. More importantly, bears would have to maneuver around Helena, Butte, Dillon, Interstates 90 and 15, and hundreds of ranches, farms, and subdivisions. While roughly 87 percent of the Northern Continental Divide Ecosystem belongs to the public, only half of the landscape between there and the GYE has similar protection. The rest is private, developed property.

"We tend to focus on remote and public and protected as the place where bears live," Costello said. "We need to get away from that. Bears are going to live where they decide to live. They don't look at a place and ask 'is this a wilderness?' They live close to people, and we have to figure out how that works in the future."

Costello's color-coded maps projected two kinds of routes. One, shaded in purple, charted the most direct paths between the two ecosystems, bearwise. The other, in yellow tones, predicted the most secure connections where bears were less likely to run into people. While less efficient, mileage-wise, Costello said those yellow zones had high potential to attract a wandering bear who is exploring new country while avoiding conflict.

So instead of punching southeast on the mountain fringes above Lincoln, Helena, and Bozeman to reach the wilderness areas north of Yellowstone Park, an NCDE grizzly might find it less stressful to make a long sweep southwest through the Bitterroot and Sapphire Mountains, around the Big Hole Valley and into the Centennial Mountains on Yellowstone's western edge.

Costello's next step was to play her model like a video game, with a digital bear avatar acting on the tendencies she'd compiled. She ran this game twenty thousand times, and came up with two frustrating results.

First, no digital bear made it from the NCDE to the GYE.

And second, the model grizzlies did move straight east out of the Rocky Mountain Front into Montana's central plains. This replicated the movements of actual NCDE bears, the ones probing the city limits of Great Falls and Lewistown.

By 2017, grizzly bears started appearing still farther south in Montana's Big Hole Valley for the first time in a century, probably following the Sapphires. A Montana Fish, Wildlife and Parks study indicated the bears might be exploring the roundabout connection between the ecosystems that Costello's model predicted. Along the way, those bears might naturally colonize into the Bitterroot Recovery Area.

The golf-course grizzly also probably took advantage of some wide spaces where it could follow Clark Fork River shorelines to cross under Interstate 90 bridges instead of having to make an over-the-asphalt sprint like Ethyl likely did farther west of Missoula.

That highway passage matters because the Americans who kill the most grizzly bears already possess the most effective government document needed: a driver's license.

Interstate 90 defines the northern boundary of the Bitterroot Recovery Area with concrete Jersey barriers. The ride from Lookout Pass on the Montana-Idaho border has been brightly signed and walled to reduce the disturbing number of wrecks that occur on its steep curves. Some stretches go for six or seven miles without a break in the three-foot-high medians.

Three feet may not seem much of a hurdle. But visit any modern zoo and discover what the keepers have learned: Most wild animals won't jump something if they can't see their landing spot. That's how they can keep the gazelles penned with low hedges just wide enough to obscure what's on the other side. Both state and federal transportation engineers have been scrambling to design effective tunnels and occasionally overpasses that wildlife will willingly use to cross highways.

"The berry load in FWP Region 2 is a driving force for some of these fatalities," Jamie Jonkel told me. "There's so much chokecherry and serviceberry to eat, but they've got to cross these highways to access those food sources. The best habitat is intersected with four-door bullets speeding by every five minutes. That's why it's so important to get these wildlife crossings in."

The dictionary defines "mortality" as both death and loss. For grizzly bears along the Northern Continental Divide, both definitions come into play around roadways. The death of a mother sow means the loss of her cubs, even if they survived the wreck. And losing an adult female of breeding age hits hard on that conservation-biology effective population, so the long-term loss could rise even higher.

On July 28, 2018, a driver on Highway 93 ran into a sow grizzly and two of her cubs about three miles south of Ronan. The bear family apparently came out of the barrow pit where Post Creek enters a culvert under the highway and tried to cross together about 11 p.m. All three bears died at the scene. The driver and one passenger were injured and the car had to be towed away.

Bear biologists with the Confederated Salish and Kootenai Tribal Wildlife Department found a third cub from the family in a tree near the scene the next day. The thirty-four-pound cub was taken to a tribal holding facility and killed after biologists determined it was too young to survive without its mother.

"The entire family group is functionally removed from the ecosystem," said Stacy Courville, tribal bear biologist. This was the second litter of cubs that female had produced that biologists knew of. Courville said she had another group of three cubs when he collared her in 2015. One of those cubs died that fall trying to cross Highway 93 at Crow Creek, almost the same spot where its mother died three years later.

"Compared to the rest of the highways in the NCDE, Highway 93 has more deaths per mile than any other highway including Highway 2," Courville said. "We killed ten bears on thirteen miles of 93, between St. Ignatius and Ronan, between 2004 and 2017. And now we have five more this year alone."

The average NCDE grizzly bear vehicle death toll is three a year. In 2015, there were six, and the previous high was seven in 2007. The year 2018 saw thirteen NCDE grizzly road-related mortalities before August. Four of those "mortalities" were one dead female bear who left behind living bear cubs too young to return to the wild. They were luckier than the Post Creek survivor; a Canadian zoo adopted the triplets. But all four might as well have been dead for NCDE population counts.

The 2018 roadkill statistic carries a special irony because the fatal stretch lies just north of one of the most extensive wildlife highway crossing structure networks in the United States. CSKT, the Montana Department of Transportation and the US Department of Transportation spent millions of dollars installing underpasses and one massive overpass along fifty-six miles of Highway 93 from Evaro Hill north of Missoula to St. Ignatius. The project ended just south of Post Creek, one of several drainages bears travel between the forested Mission Mountains and the farms and ranches of the Mission Valley. Plans exist to extend the crossings farther north, but no budget was in place for that work through 2020.

Courville recovered the radio collar of another sow he'd captured in 2016. It showed she'd spent most of her time between Post Creek and the National Bison Range.

"She crossed the highway thirty-nine times," Courville said. "We never got a picture of her using a crossing structure. She's probably crossing at grade [over the asphalt roadway]. The Bison Range did get a picture of her inside the range, with her two-year-old cub. They're in there on the creek where they find bison carcasses. That's a huge attractant."

Likewise, Ethyl made it across Interstate 90, apparently several times. Quantifying the characteristics that make a grizzly comfortable with a road crossing has become a holy grail for bear biologists and conservationists. The grizzly bear preservation group Vital Ground spends much of its energy and dollars acquiring such critical spots—often just a handful of acres at each. The nonprofit land trust estimates it could connect all the major recovery areas in Montana by acquiring about 188,000 acres of linkage spots, most in parcels of 200 to 5,000 acres apiece.

It will be a scramble. The Bozeman-based group Headwaters Economics found that between 1990 and 2016, more than 300,000 acres of open space in the nine counties surrounding the NCDE got converted into housing, adding about 30,000 new homes. That happened mostly on the west side of the ecosystem, right in the places where Vital Ground has been trying to span the gaps to the Bitterroot and Cabinet-Yaak Recovery Areas.

North of the Canadian border in British Columbia, grizzly biologists refer to Canadian Highway A3 as "The Meatmaker" for its terrific toll in wildlife roadkill. That said, a Canadian grizzly popularly known as Winston crossed six highways and four railroad lines, swam the Fraser River twice and visited the United States during an epic decade of collar-and-follar. Winston was captured first in 1991 and fitted with a radio collar. He got picked up again a year later, and then started his international trek. The third time came in 1999; although the bear in the trap no longer had a collar or ear tag confirming its identity, it was thought to be Winston.

◄ ◄ ◄ · ► ► ►

Roads limit grizzlies in another fashion. If bears were to consider us a disease, fatal on contact, roads are the circulatory system that spreads the infection.

Four days before the motorist ran into the three grizzlies on Highway 93, Montana Fish, Wildlife and Parks workers found a dead sow grizzly near the southern end of Hungry Horse Reservoir in the Spotted Bear Ranger District. The sixteen-year-old female's radio collar sent out a mortality signal, indicating it had stopped moving. The carcass was too decomposed to immediately reveal the cause of death. She joined fourteen NCDE grizzlies killed by something other than vehicle collisions by mid-summer 2018. But along with the Highway 93 sow, the ecosystem lost two of its rarest commodities: mature breeding grizzly mothers.

"There is a difference in how I look at the impact of highways versus impact of road access in grizzly bear habitat," said Frank van Manan, research biologist with the Interagency Grizzly Bear Study Team in Bozeman. "When we talk about highways, it's direct mortality from vehicle collisions and barriers to movement. When we talk about access on forest roads into grizzly habitat, the density of those forest roads have an indirect effect. They make grizzlies more vulnerable to various sources of mortality like poaching or conflicts with campers. There's a strong correlation between forest road density and grizzly survival, but it's not necessarily from vehicle collisions."

A 2018 British Columbian research study concluded that across west-central North America, we humans are the biggest threat to grizzly bears over age two, "and almost all are killed near roads." While we run over a fair share, we shoot most of them. The road simply gave the hunter or picnicker (indirectly) an opportunity to pick a fight and win on the bear's turf. In twenty years of radio-collar grizzly studies from British Columbia, Canada, every one of the bears killed by people died within a hundred meters of an all-weather road.

Concurrently, the biggest predictor of a bear population's success was the density of roads in that terrain. Specifically, places with less than six-tenths of a kilometer (four-tenths of a mile) of road per square kilometer had the best survival rates for breeding female grizzlies and their cubs. Conversely, the report found "A landscape saturated with roads would not be conductive to productive grizzly bear populations, *even if they were closed* [emphasis added]."

The roads increase much faster than grizzly bears. In British Columbia, which already has 750,000 kilometers (466,000 miles) of backcountry dirt roads, new ones were added at the rate of 10,000 kilometers a year. The road-dense Flathead Valley just across the border from Glacier National Park reported the same number of female grizzlies killed in self-defense by fall elk hunters as were legally taken by spring grizzly hunters (this before British Columbia banned grizzly trophy hunting in 2018).

Both the GYE and NCDE conservation strategies acknowledge the habitat threat that roads aim at grizzlies (beyond the highway roadkill problem). Both propose to deal with it by capping development of new roads, trails, and other human conveniences to create what's called "secure grizzly habitat" at 2011 thresholds. The Flathead National Forest's new grizzly bear management policies will be shared by five national forests and other state and federal agencies.

That means keeping the remaining roadless or lightly roaded parts of the national forests undeveloped, so the grizzlies have places to avoid people. Yet the new rules allow new roads to be built or old roads to be reopened, for things like timber sales or firefighting or recreation projects.

"What the new decision would do is say where we are now is sufficient—there's no need to go further with road closures or decommissioning," said

Nancy Warren, a private consultant developing the bear road policies for the Flathead Forest. "The [grizzly] population has done well with current conditions. We will have no net increase in roads and no net losses of secure core. If you're going to build a brand new road in some subunit, you have to take one off by decommissioning it or making it impassible."

However, the agency will analyze forest and state-managed roads in grizzly primary conservation areas, Warren said, but not federal highways. The Forest Service keeps tabs on state and federal highway projects, but considers them separate from forest management questions.

"It is one of the central challenges for managing for grizzly bears—they cross all those jurisdictional boundaries," said Warren. "The Forest Service has jurisdiction on the national forests, but no jurisdiction on Highway 93."

That agency attitude and jurisdictional variability drives delisting opponent Mike Bader of Missoula crazy. He argues the whole Forest Service approach to roads—which says no additional roads can be added without removing an equal amount somewhere else—will condemn bears to extinction because the amount of facilitated human access never goes down. "Removal" can mean putting a gate or piling an earthen berm at the head of a roadbed that's otherwise left intact. Bikers and OHV riders have shown that ingenuity or plain brute force can get around those barriers. And research has shown that even closed roads contribute to grizzly bear deaths, because they ease human entry into remote spots.

"They're saying we can have more recreation, more highways, more mountain bikes, more motorized access and ignore climate change, and still have as many bears as we want," Bader said. "That's why they don't include paved highways in their road calculations. If they did, they would have to include more areas in their security habitat to offset the highway threat. They want to build more roads and walk away from the ones they promised to close."

‹ ‹ ‹ · › › ›

Grizzly growth models forecast the NCDE population to climb between 2 and 3 percent a year. The model accounts for roughly twenty-five grizzlies getting killed by people annually, through hunting mistakes, self-defense, management removals, or vehicle collisions. So when 2018's tally reached fifty-one, Flathead Forest supervisor Chip Weber called that evidence that a healthy population of bears was spilling out of the core.

Keith Hammer counters that more human activity pushing into that core is what's driving grizzly bears out. He grew up around Bigfork on the edge of Montana's Swan Mountain Range, a few miles from the homes of both Brad Treat and Kate Kendall. His father managed the Creston Fish Hatchery. The household was a regular meeting place for federal employees and field biologists.

A neighbor had a Christmas tree farm. Hammer had his first grizzly bear encounter there, coming across tracks in the November snow while harvesting trees in the early 1970s. His first bear in the flesh showed up draped over the tailgate of a pickup, legally shot by an East Coast hunter in the Bob Marshall Wilderness Complex on a guided trip.

In college, Hammer worked summers on US Forest Service trail crews. The workers spent ten days in the woods, followed by four-day weekends. Glacier Park hotel employees learned quickly to yield the pool table when the trail crew rolled into the bar.

"I realized I wasn't going to climb the career ladder teaching kids to run chainsaws," Hammer said. "A trail crew partner had a friend who owned a small logging company. So I went to work for him. We did all the small jobs the big companies wouldn't touch, with a small bulldozer and draft horses."

It was there he concluded that protecting virgin timber from development helped grizzly bears, and protecting grizzly bears was a way to protect those virgin forests. So when the Forest Service proposed logging the Swan Face in 1984, neighbors turned to Hammer for help organizing the protest. The plan called for clear-cuts twenty and thirty acres in size in the Krause Basin just east of Hammer's home—some of the most productive grizzly bear habitat in the Swan Mountains. He helped form the Swan View Coalition to fight the project, and has been its president ever since.

"My peers were tree planters and loggers," Hammer said. "They didn't have degrees in environmental studies or journalism like the activists today. They came from a different place. Most of the activists today don't have first-hand experience in the woods working."

Hammer now works out of a converted greenhouse crammed with documents. The closet in his bathroom doubles as a backcountry gear depot, including five cans of bear spray. On a January morning, his desk was just visible under three thousand pages of drafts and appendices from the Flathead National Forest's new management plan.

"They've spent about $800,000 a year every year since 2012 doing this," Hammer said, looking at the stacks of Forest Service documents. "It's Headache Central."

While that fight helped forge a set of grizzly habitat protections on the Flathead National Forest known as Amendment 19, Hammer said it also revealed how the federal government has abandoned policing its own actions.

"The Fish and Wildlife Service was supposed to keep an eye on everyone," Hammer said. "They were supposed to have veto power over the Forest Service. But under [President Bill] Clinton's Northwest Forest Plan, everyone's supposed to agree to get along with each other. That took away all the checks and balances between agencies. How many times have private individuals or groups had to step in to make agencies do what the agency thought should be done, yet felt constrained not to do? Try and stop a grizzly bear hunt without the Endangered Species Act. Agencies weren't able to restrain each other. They were only made to quit hunting, or to close roads, in response to court orders."

Van Manan and Costello work from a few years' and occasionally decades' worth of data. Conservation biology critics poke at their results, arguing the trends don't extend nearly far enough to absorb the possible mistakes or unanticipated extremes. After all, this research has taken place over less than the span of a single human's professional career. A significant number of the grizzly's regular researchers, advocates, and critics have been at this work since the bear was put on the Endangered Species List in 1975.

In 2018 at least fifty-one grizzly bear deaths were confirmed in the NCDE. The bear biologists' rule of thumb is that at least one more bear died for every one we know about. That means the true probable butcher bill came to around one hundred grizzlies that year.

The NCDE conservation strategy sets a threshold of 800 grizzlies in the ecosystem as its minimum. If there were between 750 and 850 NCDE grizzlies in 2004 according to Kate Kendall's hair corral studies, that growth rate should put the census at 1,050 to 1,350 by 2018.

In written challenges to the Interagency Grizzly Bear Committee, Bader pointed out those growth trends depend on several unrelated research projects working together. If they don't mesh, and Bader offers several reasons why they wouldn't, then the 2004 grizzly number might have been as low as seven hundred. That would mean 2018's population hadn't met the minimum eight hundred threshold, let alone reached a surplus.

"It's a mistake to say more mortality means more bears," Bader said. "More mortality means more dead bears."

Bader's outburst echoes a more formal assessment made by British Columbia Auditor General Carol Bellringer, who found it nearly impossible to calculate Canadian grizzly hunting mortality levels due to "excessive dependence on extrapolation methods" rather than on-the-ground population inventory and monitoring.

As a result, Canadian bear managers in the Akamina area north of Glacier National Park failed to detect a population decline of what turned out to be between 40 and 50 percent between 2006 and 2013. Bellringer concluded that managers depended more on their "expert opinion" of population density than on actual monitoring; missed a major change in food supplies while not collecting any food data; and didn't recognize how big a toll "non-hunting-related human-caused mortality" was taking on the grizzly bear population.

In Bader's calculations, a mortality threat to grizzlies from one direction should be offset by more protections in another. If the risk of killing bears on highways along the fringe of the core habitat rises, then those core areas should be made safer. And that means fewer forest roads.

"These expansions to four-lane highways make it harder for all wildlife," Bader said after the Flathead Reservation sow death was reported. "Bears parallel the roadsides, looking for roadkill [to eat]. We've had twenty-six mortalities just in the NCDE. We're exceeding recent averages and we haven't even hit August. And these are the best bears. They're the ones getting around the barriers, finding the best habitat."

Then we have the links themselves, the bears. Grizzly bears aren't tourists. A Glacier Park grizzly has no inclination to see Old Faithful and get a Yellowstone Park T-shirt. The place is already crawling with belligerent resident bears who aren't interested in sharing their already oversubscribed food supplies. As for the Bitterroot Recovery Area between the Northern Continental Divide and Greater Yellowstone Ecosystems? A main reason that area had big pre-Manifest Destiny grizzly populations was a massive seasonal influx of Pacific salmon spawning there every fall. A twentieth-century dam-building spree on the Columbia River watershed choked off that resource. In 1994, exactly one red-skinned sockeye salmon made it through the fish ladders on the Columbia and Snake Rivers to reach the spawning beds of the eponymous Salmon River and Red Fish Lake in Idaho.

There remains sex tourism. Where grizzlies are concerned, that's not being facetious. Male bears in particular cruise for days looking for mates. One instructive fact of Ethyl's ramble was the places she didn't remain and what she didn't find. She obviously found enough food along 2,800 miles of Rocky Mountain forest to stay healthy for three years. But she didn't find a mate.

She didn't find anyone to fight either. Montana Fish, Wildlife and Parks biologist Mace joked that Ethyl seemed to be traveling with a "Be People-Aware" brochure and a can of people-spray on her journey. Apparently she'd learned her lesson after getting caught and collared in 2006 and again in 2012.

The Flathead National Forest's new forest plan got formally adopted in January 2019, during a government shutdown with little public notice. Its grizzly bear habitat standards became the template for five other national forests sharing jurisdiction over the bears in the Northern Continental Divide Ecosystem. That encompasses a demographic monitoring area bigger than Massachusetts and Connecticut combined. Where once grizzly bears ruled oceans of open prairie, Ethyl and the golf-course grizzly island hop through a sea of humanity.

9

Grisly Hunting

HUNTING STORIES CLAIM STRANGE SPACE ON THE BOOKSHELF. They burst with compulsion from the teller, like evangelical testimony. Oddly enough, they often feature a thick strand of humility. More than not, the story ends with the one that got away, the almost-but-not-quite, the lesson learned rather than the trophy taken. Like photographers, hunters know pulling the trigger takes up a millisecond of an experience that extends for hours or days on either side.

They're also an acquired taste. In *The Omnivore's Dilemma*, food activist and author Michael Pollan essentially betrayed himself describing his first hunt for wild boar in California.

"Approaching his prey, the hunter instinctively becomes more like the animal, straining to make himself less visible, less audible, more exquisitely alert. Predator and prey alike move according to their own maps of this ground, their own forms of attention, and their own systems of instinct, systems that evolved expressly to hasten or avert precisely this encounter."

After three pages of breathless stalking and an encounter with the quarry, he veers into self-reproach.

"Wait a minute. Did I really write that last paragraph? Without irony? That's embarrassing. I'm actually writing about the hunter's 'instinct,' suggesting that the hunt represents some sort of primordial union between two kinds of animals, one of which is me? This seems a bit much. I recognize this kind of prose: hunter porn."

Pollan professes to roll his eyes whenever he reads "Ortega y Gasset and Hemingway and all those hard-bitten, big-bearded American wilderness writers who still pine for the Pleistocene." The old pornographers would probably laugh and shove him closer to the campfire. The cave painters of Chauvet, the hieroglyphic carvers on the tomb walls of Egypt, the amulet makers of Assyria weren't depicting big predators and their human pursuers as some sort of agrarian peace offering. They commemorated Man's Bid for Significance against the overwhelming dominance of the wild (the goddess of the hunt, Artemis, is a rare exception to this masculine rule). A successful (generally male) hunter presents his kill to the tribe and declares "I am worthy" not just amongst men but within the animal kingdom. In the *Nibelungenlied*, the hero Siegfried kills the dragon and drinks its blood to learn the song of nature and speak with other animals. Someone in the Chauvet cavern left a cave-bear skull carefully positioned on a boulder, which explorers found thirty-seven thousand years later.

◄ ◄ ◄ · ► ► ►

So where does hunting play a role in the human relationship with grizzly bears? After looking at how Indigenous and settler cultures thought about killing grizzlies, and how grizzlies and humans use the landscape they share, what might we say about the ultimate interaction: Combat?

Fair-chase hunters, myself included, maintain there exists no better way to commune with the wild than to become a predator. Unlike photographers, bird watchers, or long-distance runners, only a hunter applies every sensory ability in concert. Sight, hearing, scent, touch, stamina, and intellect all convene to the service of taste (and appetite), in the immediate *now* of a snapping twig in a dark forest. Pollan himself concluded his tale observing "I enjoyed shooting a pig a whole lot more than I ever thought I should have."

"Fair chase" refers to a set of ethical rules for killing wild game animals. Its first principle requires a hunter to eschew any improper advantage over his or her quarry. In Montana, where I'm most familiar with the laws, that means I can use a powerful rifle with telescopic sights to make up for my puny fingernails and short canine teeth. But I can't use lasers to refine those sights, or radios to coordinate with fellow hunters, or bait to lure game into range, or a variety of other tricks (many of which are legal in other states).

Montana law also requires me to recover every edible part of the animal I kill except the offal. I must bring out the genitals for proof of sex, but I'm not required to bring the head or antlers. As many consider the antlers of a deer or elk the "trophy," that rule might seem strange. It does illustrate the split personality hunting presents. Are modern hunters gathering groceries, or playing at sport?

To produce a set of antlers, a bull elk must dedicate nearly half its metabolism every spring and summer to growing a new rack by fall mating season. Even so, a tiny fraction of dominant bulls impregnate more than 90 percent of each year's available cows, leaving the rest of the males all dressed up with no one to love.

No recipe exists to turn an antler into dinner, although a few recipes claim to stimulate male virility. A hunting companion of mine suffered a serious leg wound when he slid down a steep slope as the dead deer he was dragging stabbed him in the calf.

In other words, antlers are a hassle. And yet humans go to ridiculous lengths to acquire them. The pastime of "shed-hunting"—collecting the antlers shed each spring—is often called "Easter-egg hunting for adults." Until it was rescheduled for safety concerns, miles of Montanans would line their trucks and ATVs at the gates of the Blackfoot-Clearwater Game Range on the night of May 14, waiting to be let in at midnight for first crack at fallen antlers. The fact shed-hunters frequently ran into grizzly bears in the dark was one of the reasons starting in 2014 that the state moved the official season opening to noon on May 15.

The trophies a grizzly bear offers include three- to five-inch claws, teeth, skulls, and pelts. Their gall bladders, paw pads, and other organs have value in some illegal markets. But their biggest prize may be the story a bear hunter gets to tell: I killed something not only far bigger and stronger than me, but something known to fight back. Well, maybe.

◄ ◄ ◄ · ► ► ►

During his pre-presidential days, Theodore Roosevelt found it took a lot of lead to put a grizzly down. His account of the 1889 hunt, with all the inherent contradictions, burnishes his manly image.

In *Wilderness Hunter*, Roosevelt wrote of parting ways with a hunting guide he found "an exceedingly disagreeable companion" named Griffith or Griffin ("I cannot tell which"). He headed across southwest Montana's Big Hole Valley with a favorite little mare, a buffalo sleeping bag, a fur coat, and a washing kit—with a couple spare pairs of socks and some handkerchiefs. His grub sack held a frying pan, some salt, flour, baking powder, a small chunk of salt pork, and a hatchet.

Making camp on the second day after departure, Roosevelt went looking for a grouse for supper. He found a "grisly" bear instead (Roosevelt deliberately changed the spelling, claiming it was better to reflect the bear's fearsome nature than its "grizzled" or silver-gray color).

The *grisly* was heading away from the future president, so Teddy shot it in the rear. It retreated into a thicket of laurel trees. Roosevelt ran to the edge and heard it "utter a peculiar savage kind of whine."

Roosevelt moved in and the bear moved out the opposite side of the brush, and then turned broadside to its assailant. Roosevelt reported "scarlet strings of froth flung from his lips; his eyes burned like embers in the gloom."

Roosevelt shot again, learning later he'd hit the bear in the heart. It even so charged straight at him, and Roosevelt hit him with a third head-on shot that went clear through the body. It kept coming, swiping at the man with a paw as its charge carried it past him. The bear made three more bounds and collapsed, rolling "over and over like a shot rabbit."

Simultaneously touting his own courage and the worthiness of his quarry, Roosevelt concluded "The most thrilling moments of an American hunter's life are those in which, with every sense on the alert and with nerves strung to the highest point, he is following alone . . . the fresh and bloody footprints of an angered grisly."

Roosevelt remains a frustratingly contrary figure in wildlife management, as with so many other aspects of his political career. On one hand, biographer Douglas Brinkley argued in *The Wilderness Warrior* that Roosevelt simply "enjoyed shooting the birds and animals he loved the most . . . for he considered himself privileged as a Darwinian well-schooled in tooth-and-claw violence." The famous origin story of the "Teddy Bear" that Roosevelt refused to kill has a much more gruesome backstory. Brinkley reports that Roosevelt's hunting guide had captured and tied a Louisiana black bear to a tree for Roosevelt to shoot after several days of unsuccessful hunting. True to the toy-maker's tale, Roosevelt declined to do the deed. He ordered the guide to kill the bear with a knife instead.

Yet this same man persuaded the nation to share his care for wild things, presciently writing:

> Defenders of the short-sighted men who in their greed and selfishness will, if permitted, rob our country of half its charm by their reckless extermination of all useful and beautiful wild things sometimes seek to champion them by saying that 'the game belongs to the people.' So it does; and not merely to the people now alive, but to the unborn people. The 'greatest good for the greatest number' applies to the number within the womb of time, compared to which those now alive are but an insignificant fraction. . . . The movement for the conservation of wildlife and the larger movement for the conservation of all our natural resources are essentially democratic in spirit, purpose and method.

Back in 1916, Roosevelt addressed ninety-two million Americans when he wrote that—a quarter-fraction of today's citizenry who have inherited the public trust he championed. A significantly larger percentage were hunters then as well.

◃ ◃ ◃ · ▹ ▹ ▹

The lure of abundant big game drew many adventurers to the West in the frontier days of the mid- and late-1800s. Artist George Catlin sent back paintings of herds of wild bison grazing along Montana's Missouri River

Breaks. Army engineer John Mullen reported "exceedingly abundant" herds of big game during his road-surveying expedition through the state in 1859.

Plentiful jobs in the mines and forests also attracted trainloads of immigrants, who brought their appetites along with their ambitions. Those miners and loggers had to be fed, and cattle were expensive. So "market hunters" went after those elk and deer that Lewis and Clark raved about. The toll had become so obvious that one of the legislated reasons for designating Yellowstone National Park in 1872 was to create a sanctuary for the big game that was disappearing elsewhere. Ironically, the new park's first concessionaire, the Park Improvement Company, cut costs by serving its employees elk, bison, deer, and bighorn sheep.

The double irony was that Yellowstone's high-elevation plateau was defined by mapmakers for its geothermal wonders, not its biological habitat; its square borders amputated the richer valley bottoms where wildlife migrated in winter. Once Lewis and Clark left those valleys and entered the mountains along the present Montana-Idaho border, they nearly starved for lack of game. In 1882, General Philip Sheridan reported to Congress on the lack of winter range, and proposed doubling the size of the park to include Montana's Yellowstone River and Wyoming's Jackson Hole drainages.

So began a grand-scale attempt to manipulate wildlife populations by human intervention. Yellowstone's first survey and exploration expeditions consistently reported its dearth of animals. Mountain man Jim Bridger reportedly warned Captain William Raynolds against crossing the plateau in 1856, saying "a bird can't fly over that without taking a supply of grub along." The 1870 Langford Expedition could barely sustain itself on its four-week trek. The subsequent Hayden Expedition in 1871 reported just a single mule deer. The Fourth Earl of Dunraven, Windham Thomas Wyndham-Quin, explored the Hayden Valley in 1874 and journaled, "Not a fresh track, and nothing whatever eatable to be seen." And geologist Theodore Comstock in 1873 found such a paucity of wildlife that he recommended the area be managed as a game refuge with transplanted animals.

Meanwhile, the meadows and prairies of Montana, Idaho, and Wyoming where those fabled wild herds roamed were getting transformed into domestic pasture. The Sioux leaders Sitting Bull and Crazy Horse and their warriors defeated Colonel George Custer at the Battle of Little Big Horn on June 25, 1876, spoiling the headlines of the United States' first centennial celebration two weeks later. But what the winners called the Battle of the Greasy Grass was the last significant victory in what the dominant American society called "the Indian Wars." And with the elimination of military threat, settlers' cattle production in Wyoming, Montana, and Idaho went from negligible in 1870 to two million head by 1885. Sheep got a later start but finished strong, rocketing from zero to fifteen million between 1880 and 1900.

To reduce grazing competition (and destroy the economic basis of Indian tribes), white gunmen commenced a systematic slaughter of bison starting in the 1870s. Increasing drives of cattle from the south also brought in bovine diseases like Texas tick fever, which devastated the buffalo herds just as smallpox and measles eviscerated the Indian nations.

Yellowstone's remnant bison population was supposed to be the nation's reserve, but it had shrunk to about two dozen members by 1900. Federal authorities had to import captive bison from private herds in Texas and on the Flathead Indian Reservation to bolster the survivors.

Poaching was such a problem inside Yellowstone that the US Cavalry relieved the civilian management staff in 1886. It sent scouting parties to drive big game herds *into* the park, and sowed the northern valleys with domestic grasses to improve grazing. It also deployed bounty hunters to eradicate the wolves, mountain lions, and coyotes presumed to prey on the immigrant elk and deer.

Amazingly, Alston Chase in *Playing God in Yellowstone* reports the military also "put out garbage for the bears," which even then were considered a tourist attraction rather than a wildlife menace. A superintendent's report in 1895 mentioned "bears had increased notably" thanks to the assistance.

We did such a thorough job killing the native predator populations, ecosystem management left us little choice but to take on the predator's job of population control. We applied some pretty blunt tools. Yellowstone became an elk factory. Most of the park's grazing land occupies a plateau half a vertical mile higher than the surrounding valleys, where few mammals can make a living in winter. Instead, they migrate to those lower valleys—where humans had built fences and piled haystacks for domestic cattle and sheep. Rifle hunters took advantage of choke points like the Gardiner Canyon to slaughter thousands of elk trying to reach the meadows of what ranchers along the Yellowstone River had dubbed "Paradise Valley."

Those elk that learned to be wary of the winter firing lines faced near-starvation conditions inside the park. Even so, they managed to breed themselves into crisis. Rangers herded them into corrals and shipped them to game ranges elsewhere in the nation. Colorado got 350 Yellowstone elk delivered in 1913.

By 1934, the giveaway program wasn't keeping up. Yellowstone authorities started shooting thousands of elk inside the park, in addition to what private hunters killed outside the boundaries.

The problem wasn't isolated to Yellowstone. A decade later, rangers in Colorado's Rocky Mountain National Park began shooting their overstocked elk herds as well. A 1951 study in Yellowstone found the Rockies' Northern Range could only support 5,000 elk. A 1955 survey found 10,000 elk there. Rangers that winter rounded up 6,535 of them. They shot 1,974 on the spot.

This pattern of radical swings in population continued throughout the twentieth century. When wolves got reintroduced to the Greater Yellowstone area in 1996, some hunting advocates claimed the effort turned the park into a "predator sink" and pointed to the plunge from 17,000 elk pre-wolf to 7,000 a decade later. That ignored the predator-free rollercoaster of the mid-century, when Park Service employees killed 26,000 elk between 1930 and 1968, while hunters outside the park tagged another 45,000. The park's internal elk census went from a pre-cull average of 12,000 to around 4,000 when the program stopped in 1969.

◁ ◁ ◁ · ▷ ▷ ▷

Elk reproduce rapidly. Grizzly bears do not. The difficulties behind keeping elk inventories at a steady simmer, instead of boiling or freezing, hasn't inspired confidence among grizzly protection advocates. They argue putting a hunting season on a predator that took nearly fifty years to recover from its last overhunting mistake seems irrationally risky.

Montana authorized a grizzly bear hunting season in 1975, the same year the grizzly made the Endangered Species List as a threatened animal. The hunt continued until 1991, when the Fish and Wildlife Service failed to prove in court that Montana had enough "surplus" bears to justify hunting a species it was ordered to recover. Montana wildlife officials claimed a hunt would actually ensure the grizzly's recovery, stating "the only feasible way to maintain the grizzly bear's natural human avoidance behaviors is to allow low-level hunter harvests." Population estimates at the time assumed between 459 and 813 grizzlies lived in northwest Montana.

In 2007, the federal government's first Greater Yellowstone grizzly delisting proposal claimed the addition of trophy hunting would increase public tolerance for grizzly bear recovery. But it had to add "there is no scientific literature documenting that delisting would or could build . . . tolerance for grizzly bears." On the contrary, analyses of predator management tended to conclude as in one University of Wisconsin 2015 study that "The shortage of evidence for the effectiveness of killing predators to protect property or human safety should induce hesitancy among trustees to provide for this use. . . . If one cannot demonstrate a broad public interest in killing predators, then predator killing becomes a competing, private use without priority."

Nevertheless, that's what the representatives of Wyoming, Idaho, and Montana's wildlife agencies insisted on when the US Fish and Wildlife Service finalized its second attempt to delist Greater Yellowstone Ecosystem grizzly bears from the Endangered Species Act in 2017.

Days after the rule was published in the Federal Register, the three state agencies released a tri-state memorandum of understanding divvying up the available bears for a hunting season in 2018. The allowable mortality, divided by percentage of state land in the GYE, allotted Wyoming twenty-two huntable grizzlies, Idaho one, and Montana six. Because breeding-age females have disproportionate impact on population growth, each state assumed it would close its grizzly season if one sow was shot (Wyoming claimed it could afford to lose two sows).

Yellowstone National Park's arbitrary boundaries give Montana three tourist entrances (Gardiner, West Yellowstone, and Cooke City/Silver Gate) to Wyoming's one (East Entrance) and Idaho's essentially none. The resort town of Jackson Hole funnels Idaho and southern Wyoming travelers into Yellowstone, but they have to pass through Grand Teton National Park first.

That obscures the fact that 95 percent of Yellowstone Park, and its core grizzly bear habitat, lies inside Wyoming. So does much of the most productive demographic monitoring area outside the park: the hunting country grizzlies have tended to disperse into.

In 2017, the Greater Yellowstone demographic monitoring area held an estimated 718 grizzlies in a 19,000-square-mile region about the size of Vermont and New Hampshire combined. Pope and Young's archery expedition excepted, bears inside Yellowstone National Park and adjacent Grand Teton National Park have always been off-limits to big-game hunting. However, the states' post-delisting conservation strategy for grizzlies there specifically prescribed hunting to "manage grizzly bears as a game animal." Anticipating a court challenge to the delisting rule, Montana's Fish and Wildlife Commission balked at setting a 2018 grizzly hunting season. But the same commissions in Wyoming and Idaho decided to press ahead. Wyoming put twenty-two permits in a lottery system. Ten chosen hunters would get access to prime grizzly habitat near the park, with each allotted up to ten days to kill a bear. As hunters either tagged out or expended their ten days, the next tag holder would be allowed in. The season would run for sixty days or until one female grizzly was shot. A second district with less productive grizzly habitat would allow all twelve permit holders to hunt simultaneously, until the season expired or someone killed a sow.

Idaho offered one tag, also by lottery. Its lone grizzly hunter would be accompanied by a state game warden to ensure no sows got shot.

Wyoming's format got played to its ironic extreme when the state Game and Fish officials sorted through some seven thousand applications for the inaugural hunt and awarded one of the ten most coveted permits to Tom Mangelson, a wildlife photographer known particularly for chronicling the many cub litters of Sow 399 in Grand Teton National Park. Fresh off the publication of his coffee-table picture book *Grizzlies of Yellowstone*, Mangelson loudly paid his $600 and announced he'd work as hard as he could to shoot a grizzly in his usual fashion—with a camera.

An organization of Jackson Hole residents called Shoot 'Em with a Camera also crashed the party. Founding member Kelly Mayor won another tag in the most restricted zone.

"We will have twenty of the sixty days where no bears can be killed," Shoot 'Em co-founder Deidre Bainbridge told me during a Missoula protest rally. "And buying the tags makes us consumptive users. That gives us more say at the table where wildlife is managed."

◄ ◄ ◄ · ► ► ►

Missoula hunting book author Susan Reneau says she doesn't care if she doesn't see a grizzly bear—she can't wait for its hunting season.

"As someone with back and neck problems, I am probably not capable of hunting a grizzly bear," Reneau told me on her way to visit a back specialist in Butte. "But if I'm not physically able to hunt, I'm still personally going to buy a hunting license simply to help wildlife. One reason we have wildlife hunting is to provide revenue for wildlife management. It's hunters and fishermen who provide the revenue for wildlife, not the bird watcher or the hiker. Whether you harvest a grizzly bear is beside the point."

Reneau can back up her counterintuitive claim. Montana Fish, Wildlife and Parks depends on hunting and fishing license sales for two-thirds of its annual budget. Most of the remainder comes from federal sales taxes on the sale of bullets, hooks, and other recreational equipment. The department gets no state general fund tax support.

The dictionary may have defined "unabashed" on an image of Susan Reneau. Her wardrobe of red-white-and-blue hats and shirts, a collection of hoop skirts, and her outsized personality make Reneau a common focal point at Fourth of July celebrations and historic remembrances. She makes sure no Veteran's Day or Memorial Day event goes unnoticed, and organizes gatherings for national anniversaries like September 11. She also closes most of her email about wildlife with a footnote, "In the spirit of Theodore Roosevelt, Ding Darling, Horace Albright, George Bird Grinnell, and the men of the late 1800s and early 1900s that created the federal land systems and all the state game and fish agencies and game laws, I say, the wildlife and its habitat cannot speak, so I must and so must we all."

"From my standpoint as a hunter, there's a value to having grizzlies delisted as a declaration to the world that this population has come back," Reneau said. "That's a wonderful success story, like how the bald eagle has come back or the wolf has come back. I buy a license for wolf hunting every year, and I've never seen one during hunting season."

Safari Club International mounted two justifications in its 2018 *amicus curia* brief for hunting grizzly bears. One was the threat Yellowstone-area grizzlies posed to SCI member outfitters and hunters who had contended with grizzlies while in the field. Allowing a hunt would control and reduce this hazard for outfitters and their clients, SCI claimed.

The second was simply that big-game hunters like to kill big game, and the grizzly qualifies as a trophy. The bear population has recovered, they maintain, and the states should offer them as game animals. Allow hunters a chance to partake in what Spanish hunting writer Ortega y Gasset declared: "the greatest and most moral homage we can pay to certain animals on certain occasions is to kill them."

Neither claim has much scientific foundation. Alaska has an estimated thirty thousand grizzly bears, concentrated in a few highly productive parts of a region bigger than nineteen other US states combined (ranging from Rhode Island to Oklahoma). Starting in 2010, Alaska greatly liberalized its grizzly bear hunting regulations, resulting in kill rates on the Kenai Peninsula twenty-five times higher than previous years. Even so, no studies have found the increased grizzly killing accomplished the stated goal of increasing moose and caribou populations.

"It's hard to get worked up about Wyoming's hunting season with all the shit that's going on in Alaska," said grizzly bear researcher Sterling Miller, who spent the bulk of his career studying those Alaskan bears. "They're a prime example of how to do everything wrong in large carnivore management. Alaska is trying to kill as many grizzlies, wolves and black bears as they can, mandated by state law. It's the most unscientific bear management you could have."

As to the hunter safety matter, dozens of hunters die every year in car wrecks or weather mishaps, being struck by heart attacks in the field, and occasionally getting accidentally shot by comrades. Only two of those hunters in the first twenty years of the twenty-first century did so by losing a challenge to a bigger predator for the ungulate the human tried to claim. Another common factor in conflicts where the grizzly dies stem from bears who, having been wounded in previous hunting encounters, then seek easier-to-catch food like livestock. For all involved, hunting is a high-risk endeavor. The day Wyoming's 2018 grizzly hunt was to start (before a court ruling blocked it), a professional hunting guide named Mark Uptain died when a grizzly attacked him while he was cleaning his client's elk near Jackson Hole. Among other oddities, Uptain's death triggered a workplace safety review by the Wyoming Occupational Safety and Health Administration.

Retired University of Calgary biologist Stephen Herrero wrote what many consider the foundational book on the subject, *Bear Attacks: Their Causes and Avoidance*. In a 2018 interview with the Canadian Broadcasting Company, he said using grizzly hunting to achieve human safety was "ridiculous."

"If you want to remove them, you have to remove the whole ecosystem," Herrero said. "If you want to try to hunt bears to the point that we are eliminating danger to people, you'd be in for a blitzkrieg, an orgy of killing that wouldn't solve the problem but sure would create a lot of havoc."

Viable reasons also exist for using public hunters to limit animal populations. They voluntarily pay for the opportunity that otherwise would require state-employed gunners to fulfill. Letting *somebody*, hunter or game warden, kill grizzlies makes local residents feel safer and valued by the government they pay for. Those reasons have little basis in biology, but they carry heavy economic and social weight. Even so, some biologists like Miller endorse hunting as a way of controlling grizzly numbers.

"The truth is," Miller told me, "hunting of grizzly bears is biologically not very much of a problem. What's really important in the demographics is the mortality of adult females. You can shoot a hell of a lot of males without demographic consequences. If you keep the female mortality low, 4 to 5 percent depending on population, then your population will not decline."

◄ ◄ ◄ · ► ► ►

About three thousand brown bears inhabit Sweden, a country slightly larger than California. About two thousand grizzlies live in the three-state area around the Northern Rocky Mountains, where their population increases about 3 percent a year. The Swedish brown bears, in comparison, grow by about 15 percent a year.

In a variation of "women and children first," Scandinavian biologists found that female brown bears there were keeping their cubs close a year longer than usual as defense from hunters.

"The young are like a shield, a protection, that increases the survival of the mother," said Jon Swenson, a professor at the Norwegian University of Life Sciences in As, Norway. "If that's inheritable, and it might be, then it's an example of hunter-induced evolution. Animals respond to selection pressures, and a lot of hunting is selective."

Sweden has decades of experience hunting brown bears genetically similar to Montana's grizzlies. Swenson has a tight Montana connection, too: He grew up in Shepherd, in Yellowstone County, and once worked for the Montana Department of Fish, Wildlife and Parks.

Sweden sets no annual limit on killing brown bears, although it does have regional quotas that end the public hunting season once reached. Swedish brown bears like to hunt reindeer calves in the nation's northern regions. This angers the Indigenous Sami communities who herd reindeer. Swenson said the Swedish government in 2017 issued so many bear kill permits for livestock protection that it couldn't offer a public hunting season in one region: The quota had already been filled and the bear population shrunk by 10 percent.

Swedish hunters who buy an annual permit (similar to a Montana conservation license) and pass an annual rifle-handling course may shoot almost any solo bear they find during the hunting season, Swenson said. They may not shoot bears in family groups, however.

"It used to be only Swedish hunters hunting bears for meat and rugs," Swenson said. "But now we have foreign hunters and a lot of money involved. That's something that's changed in the last ten years."

Female brown bears in Scandinavia tend to be about 10 percent smaller than their American grizzly cousins, and they reach breeding age sooner. For a long time, having cubs at a younger age and raising them for only one and a half years was a feature of the population. Recent increases in hunting interest and kill quotas in Sweden appear to have modified that family behavior.

This presents a tricky tradeoff for the bears. Spending just one and a half years raising cubs means a female can mate more often, adding more cubs to the population. But spending two and a half years as mom means more cubs survive to adulthood. Male bears often kill cubs in spring and summer to restart a sow's breeding cycle. People kill mature bears during hunting season. Which strategy gives a cub the best odds of reaching reproductive age? Swenson's study showed solitary female bears were nearly four times more likely to die from hunting than those that hung around with their offspring. So sticking with the family helped both cubs and mature females live longer in Sweden.

"As managers, we were interested to know how much has this change affected the population growth rate," Swenson said. "The lower reproductive rate was offset by a higher survival rate of the female. And we see that keeping the young for that extra year increases the survival of the young."

Wildlife managers in the Rocky Mountains have the same interests as they consider hunting quotas for delisted grizzly bears, according to Montana Fish, Wildlife and Parks bear biologist Cecily Costello. However, American grizzly moms already keep their cubs for two and a half years, without hunting pressure. That could be due to the Rocky Mountain grizzlies' more constrained living space, where they face internal competition from territorial mature bears.

Would US grizzlies persevere before such hunting pressure? Sweden's experience indicates they might. But Scandinavian brown bears' faster growth rate implies they have access to much more food and secure territory than their American cousins.

"Any season we would have, at least right now, is going to involve a pretty small number of individuals," Costello said. "And any hunting mortality has to fit into what's left over after we account for other sources of mortality [such as poaching, roadkill, management removals]. It wouldn't have the kind of effects that it has in Sweden where they have a lot more hunting pressure."

◄ ◄ ◄ · ► ► ►

All American wild animals, including those protected by the Endangered Species Act, are wards of the federal estate. The United States has a rare tradition among nations in placing its wildlife in public trust. Most of Robin Hood's Merry Men were hiding in Sherwood Forest for killing "the king's deer," violating the legal principle that the aristocracy owned everything in an estate (including the peasants). But according to the US Constitution, every American citizen gets to vote on the president, who picks the secretary of interior, who oversees wildlife management and endangered species decisions.

However, this egalitarian concept has some exclusive national side effects. For example, care of public wildlife in the United States has largely and controversially devolved to individual states. The US Forest Service and Bureau of Land Management oversee millions of acres of federal public land, but state wildlife agencies dominate all decisions regarding the wildlife roaming those acres. In 2019, that led to a lawsuit by the Center for Biological Diversity accusing the US Fish and Wildlife Service of neglecting its duty to enforce USFS food storage regulations in parts of Idaho's grizzly recovery areas where that state's Fish and Game Commission allowed black-bear hunters to attract their quarry with bait—typically the same odoriferous donuts and bacon grease that draw grizzly bears into human food habituation and trouble. The suit asked who was in charge—the federal land manager or the state wildlife manager—when a federal public trust animal is threatened by a state policy.

The commissioners of those agencies typically represent the less than 5 percent of the population who buy hunting licenses. They have shown scant welcome to "nonconsumptive users"—the bird-watchers, river float-ers, and backpackers who buy cameras and canoes instead of hooks or bullets. State wildlife agency budgets for non-game species rarely break single-digit shares. Many hunting-centric states have passed laws or even constitutional amendments enshrining hunting heritage and raising bar-riers to "ballot-box biology" from non-hunting factions.

And historically, residents of those states have viewed grizzly bears as predators and pests to be shot on sight. As wolf biologist David Mech put it, "It is ironic that this simple majority-rule type of wildlife management is basically the same approach that extirpated carnivores many years ago. Although there were no actual referendums at that time, there were bureaucrats acting contrary to scientific opinion but bending to the public will. . . . The lesson to be learned is that public sentiment is fickle. If major carnivore management decisions are determined by public mood rather than by the knowledge of professionals, we could end up with California full of carnivores and North Dakota with none."

A 2016 nationwide study by the Ohio State University Department of Animal Sciences found Americans' opinions about wild predators had grown more friendly than they were in 1978. The authors concluded "increasing levels of urbanization, income and education within societies are changing the way societies value and utilize wildlife." They acknowl-edged that other studies of rural areas reported greater hostility toward predators over the same timeframe, especially toward wolves. But "any increased negativity in wolf-occupied areas may be 'drowned out' because the areas wolves occupy in the United States are generally remote and the human densities in these areas are extremely low."

◄ ◄ ◄ · ► ► ►

Hunters look to the North American Model of Wildlife Conservation to make their case. This theory was originally promulgated by Saxton Pope and Arthur Young, Aldo Leopold, Theodore Roosevelt, and other found-ers of the conservation movement in the United States, and codified by biologist Valerius Geist in the 1990s. It posits that hunters are the best caretakers of public wildlife.

The model has seven principles:

1. *Wildlife is a public trust resource.* Legal scholars trace this all the way back to the Roman Emperor Justinian in AD 529 and on through the Magna Carta. The US Supreme Court codified it in 1842.
2. *There is no place for markets for wildlife.* The extinction of passenger pigeons (the most common bird in the United States until it was shot from the skies as a pest and for food) and bison from the prairies, along with near-elimination of deer and elk from forests during the early twentieth century, galvanized hunting organizations to take control of wildlife management.
3. *Allocation of wildlife by law.* Elected governments, not property owners, get to decide what to do with surplus wildlife, through permits and licenses.
4. *Wildlife can only be killed for legitimate purpose.* This can include food, fur, self-defense, and protection of property. It also wraps in principles of "fair chase" hunting that frown on using unfair advantages or wasting meat.
5. *Wildlife are considered an international resource.* The Migratory Bird Treaty Act of 1916 made this essential, as biological research confirmed that wild animals don't respect national borders.
6. *Science is the proper tool for discharge of wildlife policy.* Aldo Leopold and Teddy Roosevelt pushed the use of scientific research as a policy requirement to offset the economic and property rights claims of land managers.
7. *Democracy of hunting.* The public's wildlife belongs to the public, not some privileged class or special interest. Anyone who can buy a license can hunt on public land.

State wildlife agencies claim their fidelity to the North American Model of Wildlife Conservation has been instrumental in the restoration of wild turkeys, whitetail deer, pronghorn antelope, wood ducks, beaver, Canada geese, black bears, elk, desert bighorn sheep, bobcats, and mountain lions—all species that nearly disappeared from the landscape before there was an Endangered Species Act to protect them.

Those animals were saved by the focused efforts of hunters and sportsmen who contributed billions of dollars through the twenty-first century to buy habitat, fund game wardens, endow research programs, and educate the public about the value of America's wild kingdom. It wasn't the Center for Biological Diversity but the Boone and Crockett Club that threw down for the restoration of those herds popularized by Meriwether Lewis and William Clark and George Catlin.

Exceptions exist. The Nature Conservancy paid to save the Pine Butte Swamp at the foot of the Bob Marshall Wilderness Complex specifically to help grizzly bears. Contributors to the Alliance for the Wild Rockies and Sierra Club have supported pivotal lawsuits that strengthened the nation's environmental laws, including ESA cases regarding the grizzly bear. Americans of all political stripes and levels of woodcraft have pioneered the techniques of preserving wild habitat from human encroachment. The rest of the world comes to the United States to learn from the masters.

Most of those masters work for state wildlife agencies, paid by those hunting and fishing revenues. Most of the remainder comes from federal sales taxes set by the Pittman-Robinson Act and the Dingell-Johnson Act on the sale of ammunition, fishing tackle, and other hunting-related recreational equipment.

This raises big problems. The first is that bird-watchers, grizzly photographers, and other "nonconsumptive" nature users have no avenue to contribute to management of their non-game species of preference, and hence they share little voice in the agency decisions that control all the wild critters. That violates the first, second, third, fourth, and seventh principles of the conservation model.

Numerous economic studies show nonconsumptive activities like tourism and wildlife watching bring to local economies two to ten times as much money as hunting and fishing. These studies also reflect the 95 percent of the US citizenry that doesn't hunt. Most state wildlife agencies exactly reverse that ratio in their budgets, allocating about 5 percent or less to non-game species.

One practical result of delisting grizzlies from Endangered Species Act protection would be the withdrawal of federal presence from bear management. The Interagency Grizzly Bear Committee has overseen millions of dollars in grizzly collaring, monitoring, data gathering, and analysis. Its biologists catch dozens of bears a year, archive the demographic studies, and commission the reviews when grizzlies kill or maul humans. When that goes away, state wildlife agencies face the choice of filling the void. However much of the load they pick up, those departments will do so on the backs of those who buy hunting and fishing licenses and equipment that fund management budgets.

The leaders and appointed commissioners of those agencies come almost exclusively from occupations that have a vested economic interest in the wildlife they manage, whether they be hunting outfitters, ranchers, farmers, or politically connected landowners. That cuts contrary to public trust legal doctrine, which presumes special interests don't get undue influence over what belongs to the all trustees (all American citizens).

Alaska further clouded the ethical water in 2010 when it started allowing grizzly hunters to sell hides and skulls of the bears they killed. That directly violates the second principle by creating a market for wildlife. A grizzly claw necklace I found at a Missoula gun show retailed for $1,000.

Critics of the North American Model of Wildlife Conservation argue it sanctified an institution that can't uphold its own principles, because the principles themselves don't add up. The University of Montana's Bolle Center director Martin Nie points out that only the first tenet—that wildlife is a public trust resource—actually has a foothold in federal jurisprudence. The rest stand ambiguous and full of exceptions.

"The model provides no principle or guidance about how to address the complicated tensions between federal, state and tribal governments in the management of wildlife on federal lands," Nie wrote. "In fact, the model fails to include a principle related to habitat at all, nor does it mention the role played by federal lands (and federal environmental law) in American wildlife conservation."

In 2018, at the request of the federal Aldo Leopold Wilderness Research Institute, Nie and colleagues looked into who wields authority over wildlife on federal lands: the states or the federal government. They found the federal government was shirking its duty.

"Federal land management agencies, including the U.S. Forest Service, have an obligation, and not just the discretion, to manage and conserve fish and wildlife on federal lands," the research team wrote, "contrary to the myth that the states manage wildlife and federal land agencies only manage wildlife habitat. We traced the origins of this myth and explain why it is both wrong from a legal standpoint and is limited from a biological one."

The Forest Service, which oversees the Leopold center and funded Nie's study, disavowed its conclusions. In a bizarre series of emails, Forest Service officials offered three contradictory reasons why the study was unacceptable. When I confronted the agency with those disparate emails, I got no response.

A year 2000 inventory found 2,497 vertebrate species endemic to the United States. Of those, more than a thousand mammals, birds, and fish currently have Endangered Species Act protection as threatened or endangered species and several hundred more fall in the "warranted but precluded" status. That led Yale University carnivore researcher Susan Clark to observe the trend "could be viewed as a growing failure of the state fish and game organizations as well as the overall institution of wildlife management and the [North American Wildlife] model itself."

◄ ◄ ◄ · ► ► ►

Look across the Canadian border at what happened in British Columbia in 2017. There, the provincial government banned trophy hunting for grizzly bears in response to a substantial public campaign in favor of the bears. Hunting grizzlies was still allowed, but the hunters had to surrender the hide, skull, and paws (the trophies) to provincial authorities.

Some pro-hunting bloggers protested this was a misreading of public opinion, where the Parliament got swayed by urban residents who only ever saw bears in zoos. British Columbia has one of the bulkiest single populations of grizzlies under a single governing body. It has shown the ability to sustain 4 to 6 percent mortality from hunting while maintaining many substantial grizzly populations.

Non-resident hunters paid British Columbia guides between $17,000 and $25,000 to hunt a grizzly, according to a 2018 lawsuit filed by a Canadian outfitter attempting to overturn the ban. The complaint alleged that without a trophy hunt more than 2,000 workers at 245 guide companies were out of a job, which they'd booked out to at least 2021 before the ban was approved.

Others like Canadian hunting writer Paul McCarney pointed out that hunters make up 2.7 percent of British Columbia's 4.6 million residents (and that percentage of the whole is falling).

"It doesn't do hunters any favors to act with a sense of entitlement or righteous attitude towards wildlife policy discussions with the non-hunting public," McCarney wrote. "There is no science that said the bears must be hunted. The choice to hunt was simply a social choice. As long as society condoned a hunt, science was the tool used to help set a sustainable harvest level."

Unlike the bald eagle (inadvertently poisoned by the pesticide DDT aimed at mosquitoes) or the snail darter (its waterways threatened by hydroelectric dams), the near extinction of grizzly bears in the United States was personal. The listing notice under the Endangered Species Act states the bear suffered from deliberate, often government-directed, extermination efforts involving shooting, trapping, and poisoning. The pre-ESA hunting regulations of Montana, Idaho, and Wyoming all classified grizzly bears as non-game predators, killable without a license or season.

In their 2018 defense briefs, the delisting attorneys pointed out the social change that's taken place since the grizzly bear was listed. All three states now classify grizzlies as big-game species, and have set up detailed regulations limiting where and how many bears can be killed, even as their actual grizzly hunting seasons remain under legal injunction.

Making the grizzly bear a game animal is a political choice. The historical record shows that hunting grizzlies does not contribute to human safety nor does it benefit secondary species like moose. Under Endangered Species Act listing, problem grizzlies can still be killed to defend human life, to protect livestock, and during the course of resource or management activity. State wildlife managers could impose the same rules without a hunting season. With only two thousand grizzly bears roaming the Lower 48 states, certainly no one can say they're needed for food. Given the challenges of effectively managing wildlife populations like elk, which are abundant, do we want to apply the same public hunting tools to a far-more complicated species in short supply?

One compromise could be the British Columbia model, where public hunting is allowed but trophy-taking is prohibited. That would continue the role of private hunters in wildlife management but remove the profit motive commodifying a rare, charismatic predator. Prohibiting hunting over bait for all bears, grizzly and black, would further help reduce the availability of human food in bears' diets. If Americans want to keep wild bears, and keep them out of driveways, they must recognize the relationship requires discipline on the human side.

United States Department of Interior surveys show hunter numbers have fallen steeply in the US while national opinion polls show the public's support for the Endangered Species Act remains high. In 2015, an American dentist killed an internationally known lion named Cecil on a guided hunt in Zimbabwe. The fact he had a legal permit for the hunt didn't override Cecil's status as a tourist attraction studied by the University of Oxford. International outrage resulted in the dentist's loss of hunting privileges in Zimbabwe and the US Fish and Wildlife Service adding lions to the Endangered Species List, limiting the ability of hunters to import their lion "trophies" into the United States. If hunters think their pastime suffered when Cecil became a trophy, just wait until someone mounts Sow 399 or another Instagram-famous road bear from Grand Teton National Park on the rec-room wall.

10

Grizzly at Law

COMPARED TO ENCOUNTERING GRIZZLY BEARS ON A BIKE, THROUGH a rifle scope, during a ceremony, or at a rub tree, meeting one in a courtroom sags in the drama department.

Yet the sterile confines of a judicial opinion hold the closest encounter most Americans will ever have with a grizzly. There they actually have, as the gamblers say, skin in the game with tax dollars, votes, and personal freedom on the line. That shows up nowhere as clear as in the bifurcated world below a judge's bench.

Missoula's Russell Smith Courthouse has seen its share of Endangered Species Act cases, including recent jousts over the wolverine, arctic grayling, and Canada lynx. During a 2010 hearing on gray wolf delisting, its front-door sidewalk was jammed with dueling protesters. Some clutched stuffed wolf toys. Others wore hunter's orange vests. While I sat through the wolf delisting testimony, my email inbox bulged with editorial advice from wolf-lovers and wolf-haters.

One anti-wolf story verged on urban-myth status, ostensibly about a guide who nearly lost his client to a pack of killer wolves while on an elk hunt in the Bitterroot Mountains. I received four versions of the story, all attested to by the sender as coming from a reliable relative or friend of a friend, and all with slightly fumbled details. One account described a solo hunter instead of a duo. Another emptied his rifle at the pack, while still other accounts had shooters using up their pistol ammo. The number of surrounding wolves was as consistent as the length of the fish that got away. The wolves may also have massacred a tiny herd of terrified elk on a frozen lake. (For the record, the year wolves did become a big-game species in Montana, wildlife biologists found mountain lions outscored human hunters four to two on wolf kills in the Bitterroots.)

From the other side of the litigation came an email from a writer in California who implored me to view the attached pictures and understand the true essence of the debate. What followed was a series of buckskin-clad Indian maidens with Swedish facial features, bathing their infant children under the gaze of a protective wolf spirit illuminated by the Northern Lights.

Eight years later as I waited to enter the Yellowstone grizzly delisting courtroom, only bear protection advocates marched on the sidewalk. Where were the grizzly hunters, I asked aloud.

"It's the difference between protecting Little Red Riding Hood and shooting Teddy Bear," quipped a lawyer in line behind me.

Another big difference between the grizzly and wolf court fights was the social status of the subject animal. The photo app Instagram debuted in October 2010, the same month as the wolf delisting hearings. Eight years later, Sow 399 had her own Instagram hashtag along with tens of thousands of Facebook admirers. Through digital channels, images and stories of grizzly bears had penetrated far deeper into American society than had any previous courtroom critter.

Political theorist Hannah Arendt called storytelling a way of rehearsing personal feelings in public without direct confrontation. Little Red Riding Hood makes a hero of the hunter who shoots the wolf. Teddy Bear wants to be hugged and nurtured. They signal values that stop short of pro-hunters and no-hunters accusing one another directly of cruelty, greed, ignorance, or arrogance.

In a courtroom, those stories have to put up or shut up. The August 30, 2018, hearing was so packed with attorneys representing more than thirty parties and intervenors, bailiffs had to open a second chamber for spectators who watched by video monitor.

The plaintiffs asking to keep the Yellowstone grizzlies listed as a protected species launched at least twenty different legal reasons why the government had failed in its job to justify its delisting rule on sufficient scientific or administrative grounds. That didn't include the huge folder of American Indian Religious Freedom Act complaints to present if those challenges failed. The US Department of Justice attorneys had an equal number of reasons detailing why the Yellowstone grizzlies had recovered and no longer needed federal protection. They were backed up by half a dozen state wildlife agencies, livestock associations, and hunting organizations all insisting the people living in grizzly country deserved assurance the bear would not threaten their ways of life.

The whole pile boiled down to a single word: Delist. Had the government met or not met the requirements to delist Greater Yellowstone Ecosystem grizzly bears from the Endangered Species Act? The reduction simplified the judge's decision, but complicated the problem.

⊰ ⊰ ⊰ · ⊱ ⊱ ⊱

Since inception, the Endangered Species Act has kept 99 percent of its listed species from going extinct. That's an unqualified success.

The recovery score—the number of species removed from federal protection—looks exactly opposite: 2 percent. Representative Paul Gosar, R-Arizona, said, "A 2-percent success rate? Nobody can say that's a success story. And throwing more money at it doesn't help."

The Yellowstone grizzly bear was the eighth animal ever to make the Fish and Wildlife Service's endangered species list and forty-ninth out of fifty-four species to reach the recovery list. Eleven species have gone extinct since listing. At current count 1,464 animals remain threatened or endangered. Let's leave plants out of the discussion for the moment.

What animals shall we rally around? Listing every tenth critter in the current catalog of threatened and endangered species, let's see a show of hands for the constituencies interested in:

Cecek minnows?

Sakhalin sturgeons?

Nihoa millerbirds?

Acropora rudis coral?

Dusky sea snakes?

Thyolo alethe?

St. Vincent's parrot?

Ash Meadows naucorid?

Florida grasshopper sparrow?

Yosemite toad?

I'm not questioning the value or impact of any of these species. But I'm also not seeing any billboards appealing for their salvation. When you picked up this book, how many competing titles covered the plight of the dusky gopher frog of Louisiana? That endangered amphibian was working its way through the federal courts in 2020, crystallizing an issue that could prove critical to grizzly bear delisting: How much authority can the government exert over potential frog habitat that doesn't have any endangered frogs at the moment? How many people fear or idolize the dusky gopher frog?

The frog ruling could affect grizzly reintroduction in its two biggest ecosystems, the Bitterroot and North Cascades—neither of which had resident grizzlies in 2020. If the ESA has no authority over places that the species in question doesn't presently inhabit, even if those places are part of its historic range, the reintroduction tool falls out of the toolbox.

The same week the Yellowstone grizzlies went to court, Duke University conservation biologist Stuart Pimm released an international study showing how preserving tiny bits of quality habitat had more urgency than preserving large swaths of territory for endangered species protection. And the sheer scope of needs for all those species has the conservation movement stretched thin.

"Not all species are like the grizzly," Pimm told me. "A lot of species have relatively small geographic ranges. If we just worry about protecting huge swaths of the western United States, we're not going to worry about the myriad of small fish, butterflies and lizards that occur in the Southeast United States."

On the other hand, Pimm noted grizzlies need to be managed on a continental scale.

"So if the question is do you want to protect large areas or small areas, the answer is yes—I want both," Pimm said. "We need large areas for grizzly bears, and tiny places for building bridges or tunnels for endangered species to use."

This illuminates the split nature of public interest in the Endangered Species Act itself. Any one of those threatened or endangered critters has the potential to leverage significant economic and social change in the effort to keep it from going extinct. But the grizzly bear had people up before dawn in August 2018, lining up for seats and a chance to listen to lawyers argue for four hours. If that's not the definition of a charismatic megafauna, show me a better one.

◄ ◄ ◄ · ► ► ►

Most animals on the Endangered Species List get defined by critical habitat: a combination of the acres of landscape where they're known to exist and the landscape that has the resources they need to exist. Those two criteria don't always overlap, on a map or a courtroom.

This framework spawns a list of built-in problems. The Greater Yellowstone Ecosystem alone incorporates five national forests, two national parks, three states, and twenty county governments—and that's just the public institutions. Four decades into its existence, the Interagency Grizzly Bear Committee still wrangles over membership and function. Coordination of grizzly management and response after federal withdrawal remains unknown country.

Meanwhile, both humans and nature keep changing the rules of the game. A twentieth century dam-building spree essentially destroyed inland Pacific Northwest salmon habitat, including the connected spawning streams where grizzly bears fed at in the Bitterroot Mountains. Political efforts are afoot calling for restoration of the ecosystem through more effective fish ladders or outright dam removal. Access to a food source such as a salmon migration run can have massive impact on other species. In inland Alaska, places like Denali National Park host between thirty and forty grizzly bears per thousand square kilometers. Along Alaska's major salmon river drainages, that jumps to between three hundred and seven hundred grizzlies per thousand square kilometers.

On the natural side, no one's certain how grizzlies might adapt to increasingly hot and dry climatic conditions, where berry crops shrivel along with the winter denning snows. Arctic Circle biologists have already documented the crossing of paths and interbreeding of polar and grizzly bears as the distinctly white bears lose their ice-shelf seal-hunting habitat and explore the brown bears' pickings, resulting in a hybrid some are calling the "pizzly bear."

And as the example of bears like Ethyl show, grizzlies travel widely and unpredictably from season to season and year to year. The progressively intolerant management zones radiating out from their core recovery areas turn the grizzly's evolutionary-grown landscape use into its biggest survival threat. Bears aren't like migrating salmon, swimming specific rivers at specific times when game wardens can be assigned to ensure unmolested passage and public safety. One grizzly showing up in one wrong driveway could result in legislation affecting all bears in all driveways.

◄ ◄ ◄ · ► ► ►

Public support for the Endangered Species Act remains widespread, but most of those polled live in urban areas where wildlife predators like grizzly bears are safely ensconced in zoos. A 2018 poll and analysis of past ESA opinions led by Ohio State University conservation policy expert Jeremy Bruskotter found about four of every five Americans support the law, while about one in ten oppose it (very few are neutral). That score has stayed stable for the past two decades.

"Every time the ESA is in the news, you hear about how controversial it is," Bruskotter told me. "But the three most recent studies show that, on average, approximately 83 percent of the public supports it, and that's sort of the opposite of controversial."

Burskotter's latest survey found seven of eight interest groups favored the ESA. That included 74 percent of conservatives, 77 percent of moderates, 90 percent of liberals, and at least 68 percent of hunters and property-rights advocates. The margins prevailed throughout various geographical regions of the nation. The most active opposition came from property-rights advocates, 21 percent of whom said they were opposed to the law.

When it comes to the grizzly bear, opposition to ESA efforts tends to manifest most where the bears are within shooting range. Those residents vote, and their votes have disproportionate weight.

This gulf bedevils much more of American life than just ESA debates. Eight of every ten Americans live in an urban area. Forty-three US states have a smaller population than Los Angeles County.

But that's not how Congress works. In the Senate, the will of one-third of the nation living in California, Texas, Florida, and New York gets counterbalanced by the voters (and grizzly bears) of the 1 percent of the US population living in Montana, Idaho, Wyoming, and Alaska. The political power vested in rural states may become a constitutional crisis when the tyranny of the majority faces off against the bottleneck of minority rights. And the Senate controls the choice of federal judges, federal budgets, and international treaties for the rest of the nation. In the 115th Congress, the objection of a single Republican senator from Utah derailed an omnibus public lands bill with support from a filibuster-proof majority of the rest of the chamber. A few sessions before, a single Democratic senator from Montana removed gray wolves from Endangered Species Act protection and judicial review, over the objections of a national majority of wildlife advocates. Economic power may rest in the major cities, but political power remains in flyover country until Americans radically amend the Constitution.

This pattern gets reproduced at state levels like some fractal equation. Rocky Mountain state legislators from rural counties regularly dominate the leadership and purse strings against the interests of their urban colleagues. It goes beyond party politics, to a growing disconnect between urban attitudes and rural experience in the environmental world.

That aggravates yet another duality in the Endangered Species Act: The difference between delisting an animal and recovering it. And here we get to the nub of modern problems with the ESA. Did we really know what we wanted when we passed it back in 1973?

The start of the law reads:

The Congress finds and declares that 1) various species of fish, wildlife and plants in the United States have been rendered extinct as a consequence of economic growth and development untempered by adequate concern and conservation; 2) other species of fish, wildlife and plants have been so depleted in numbers that they are in danger of or threatened with extinction; 3) these species of fish, wildlife and plants are of aesthetic, ecological, educational, historical, recreational and scientific value to the Nation and its people; 4) the United States has pledged itself as a sovereign state in the international community to conserve to the extent practical the various species of fish or wildlife or plants facing extinction; and 5) encouraging the States and other interested parties, through Federal financial assistance and a system of incentives, to develop and maintain conservation programs which meet national and international standards is a key to meeting the Nation's international commitments and to better safeguarding, for the benefit of all citizens, the Nation's heritage in fish, wildlife and plants.

The law calls out human action (*untempered by adequate concern*), rejects simple utilitarian measures (*aesthetic, ecological, educational, historical, recreational and scientific value*), demands a global perspective (*in the international community*) and commits the public to paying its debts (*Federal financial assistance and a system of incentives*) to preserve the *Nation's heritage*.

It's worth mentioning here how universally accepted the Endangered Species Act was at passage. Republican president Richard Nixon signed the Endangered Species Act after it passed the Senate by a vote of 92 to zero, and the House by a vote of 390 to 12. Montana at the time was represented by Democratic senator and Senate majority leader Mike Mansfield, Senator Lee Metcalf (namesake of the wilderness area southwest of Bozeman), Representative John Melcher, and the lone Republican, Representative Dick Shoup. All four voted yea on the ESA.

In Idaho, Democratic senator Frank Church (another future wilderness namesake) and Republican senator Jim McClure both voted yes, while Republican representative Steve Symms made up one-twelfth of the national opposition to the law. Republican representative Orval Hansen did not vote. Wyoming's entire delegation, Republican senator Clifford Hanson and Democratic senator Gale McGee along with Democratic representative Teno Roncalio, all voted yea.

The key action words in that preamble are "to conserve to the extent practical." A couple paragraphs down, Congress defines "conserve": "the use of all methods and procedures which are necessary to bring any endangered species or threatened species to the point at which the measures provided pursuant to this Act are no longer necessary."

What does "no longer necessary" mean? It sounds like after a species gets out of the hospital of recovery efforts, it can go back to its natural life. But what if there is no such place? What if human interests and environmental degradation have reached the point that historical characteristics can only be maintained by intervention in perpetuity? Is that a failure of the law, or a realization of its obligation?

⊰ ⊰ ⊰ · ⊱ ⊱ ⊱

Americans have experience with large-scale environmental remediation. Just east of Missoula, one of Montana's nineteenth-century copper kings built a small dam in 1908. It impounded a shallow reservoir at the confluence of the Clark Fork and Blackfoot Rivers, and turned generators that produced just enough electricity to power a lumber mill and propel a streetcar line bringing workers to their jobs in Milltown.

The year it was finished, the biggest flood on record hit. Spring runoff tore through gigantic piles of mine tailings in Butte and Anaconda, transporting sludge full of arsenic, copper, and other heavy metals a hundred miles downstream. Little Milltown Dam was a run-of-the-river dam, so any high water simply spilled right over it. But it slowed the flood down enough to settle millions of tons of toxic sediment in its reservoir.

Where does the grizzly bear come into all this? In 2006, the same year the US Fish and Wildlife Service first tried to declare grizzlies around Yellowstone Park recovered, engineers at Milltown Reservoir started turning a man-made ecological disaster into a rewilded, free-flowing river.

To remove the sediment, contractors first built a new channel for the Clark Fork and drained its reservoir. Then bulldozers started shoving away the ninety million tons of muck. Thanks to ground-penetrating radar and laser-guided survey probes, the bulldozers were able to scrape exactly to the 1908 riverbed and no farther. The calculation was so precise, the following spring cottonwood seeds that had laid dormant under several meters of mine tailings felt sunlight for the first time in a century and sprouted. That wasn't a lucky accident. It was a planned bit of landscape engineering. We didn't just replace an old riverside forest. We revived it.

The repaired Clark Fork River through Missoula has gone on to kill eight times as many humans (by drowning) since the dam was removed as did all the grizzly bears in the Northern Continental Divide together in the same period. The river's restoration cost more than $200 million to accomplish. People raised a lot of objections to the dam removal, but the increased potential of people dying in faster-flowing water wasn't one.

Yet in the federal court hearing on the second attempt to delist Yellowstone grizzlies, Idaho state attorney Cathleen Trevor's defense of delisting evoked the 1967 killings of two campers from *Night of the Grizzlies* as the driving concern for returning bears to state management. Why should Idahoans keep putting up with restrictions on campgrounds, food, and backcountry fun for the sake of the grizzlies, if they weren't eventually allowed to manage them locally? And that meant the ability to "reduce grizzly concentrations in high-human-conflict areas."

The consequences of environmental degradation were everywhere when the Endangered Species Act was passed in 1973. My Millennial children never had to smell the wet-diaper stench that cottoned the Missoula Valley when an upwind pulp mill mixed its emissions into the winter air inversions. To them, the incinerators known as teepee burners are prehistoric oddities, often turned into public sculpture. They have no recollection of the smoke from heaps of slash and bark that couldn't find profitable use in the valley sawmills.

I grew up watching *The Carol Burnett Show* on TV. Introducing it to my children forty years later, I was shocked to hear the ultimate family-friendly comedian close her September 14, 1974, show with the admonition, "The next time you see someone causing pollution, hit him in the mouth."

Historian Paul S. Sutter has written that American environmental ethics swing like a pendulum on a generational arc, fitting social patterns that draw close or repel from the mass of government. Burnett knew she was riding a safe wave when she aimed her audience against air pollution. Her variety show went on the air in 1967, shortly after passage of the Wilderness Act and the Wild and Scenic Rivers Act. In 1969, Ohio's Cuyahoga River caught fire, spurring on the eventual passage of the Clean Water Act. In between Burnett's comedy sketches in 1971, public service commercials showed an Indian, "Iron Eyes Cody" (actually an Italian actor named Oscar Espera), weeping as he paddled a birch-bark canoe up a trash-filled river.

Nixon also created the Environmental Protection Agency and made it a cabinet-level office in 1970. He signed the Clean Air Act and oversaw the Convention on International Trade in Endangered Species. The National Park Service celebrated its centennial in 1972, the year Yellowstone National Park's grizzly bear population nearly cratered in a ranger-led shooting spree.

When the national environmental movement was in full cry, few politicians were willing to get in the way. But as Sutter predicted, that would swing back by the end of the decade. The Republican Party's idea of conservation shifted away from preserving public lands to a Sagebrush Rebellion preserving individual liberty (usually in the form of profiting from those public lands). Federal courts that opened legal pathways for environmental protection in the 1960s tilted toward property rights in the 1980s, as the doctrine of "takings" hobbled federal regulation of private activity.

"In the West, this backlash had its own unique twist," Michael Dax wrote, in his 2015 book, *Grizzly West: A Failed Attempt to Reintroduce Grizzly Bears in the Mountain West*. "The region had long been a bastion of progressive politics, but as extractive industries faced threats from outside influences, the environmental movement became an easy target that extractive land users saddled with much of the blame for their difficulties."

This was a United States at an inflection point. The Organization of Petroleum Exporting Countries was about to show us the illusion of our economic dominance with the 1973 oil embargo. Nixon himself would discover the limits of presidential power when he resigned in disgrace on August 9, 1974, before the House of Representatives could start impeachment proceedings for the criminal coverup of his Watergate burglaries. Just when Americans seemed to have the power to control the planet, other forces humbled their ambitions.

◄ ◄ ◄ · ► ► ►

The Fish and Wildlife Service's 2007 and 2017 delisting rules proposed a way forward that passes grizzly management to state wildlife agencies. State agencies in turn pledged to follow a conservation strategy developed through the Interagency Grizzly Bear Committee which delineated habitat standards, required legal policies, and set thresholds at which federal control might resume if the states fail in their responsibility. Both delisting rules failed judicial review.

The plaintiffs challenging the 2017 rule had an answer: Look beyond delisting. While securing a victory for the government was a definable goal, it forces everyone to think like a light switch: on or off. Is such a binary shift good for grizzlies? Ask any student who presumed working hard for a diploma would make the world change the day after graduation. Milestones matter, but they only mark progress. They don't make progress.

The Center for Biological Diversity wants an even bigger step. At the end of 2019, it reached a court settlement with the Interior Department to produce a new status review on grizzly bear recovery—something the law required the department to do every five years but which had been neglected since 2011. And CBD attorneys further pressed that the 2011 status review was based on a 1993 grizzly recovery plan which, in the department's own admission, no longer contained the best available science or data. Center attorney Andrea Zaccardi told me the larger goal is to force the Fish and Wildlife Service to consider many more possible places for grizzly reintroduction within the bear's traditional range, from the San Juan Mountains of Colorado to Arizona's Grand Canyon National Park and the Sierra Nevada Mountains of California.

But can we do it? Can we recover grizzly bears *"to the point at which the measures provided pursuant to this Act are no longer necessary"*?

If we assume humans must run the world as well as rule it, then the six designated recovery areas for Lower 48 grizzly bears are little more than multi-million-acre zoos, in need of regular cleaning, food stocking,

Montana Fish, Wildlife and Parks director Martha Williams, left, helps move a tranquilized grizzly bear from a culvert trap during a management action near Kalispell. The bear is blindfolded to protect its eyes during handling because the immobilizing drugs prevent it from blinking. Courtesy Montana Fish, Wildlife and Parks Department.

and visitor management. Although they're considered core habitat by the relevant conservation strategies, those mountains and forests certainly aren't historic habitat. The buffalo prairies of the Great Plains are.

That leaves grizzlies in a category biologists call "conservation-reliant." We recognize the species will never recover in some holistic, ecological sense, but it may avoid extinction with the right amount of help from us. Unfortunately, a 2010 study of the Fish and Wildlife Service's threatened and endangered species catalog concluded that four of every five were conservation reliant, and "will require continuing, long-term management investments."

⊰ ⊰ ⊰ · ⊱ ⊱ ⊱

The Wilderness Act and related legislation grew out of a conservation movement stretching from the natural philosophies of Henry David Thoreau and John Muir, through the landscape ethics of Aldo Leopold and Wallace Stegner, and into a trend later known as Deep Ecology, first pushed into the general conversation by Norwegian philosopher Arne Naess in 1970. Deep Ecology slowly built the argument that all living beings had inherent worth regardless of their value or connection to human beings. That meant allowing the community of life to flourish for its own sake rather than be considered simply raw materials for human benefit. It meant long-range planning for the preservation of functioning ecological communities. And by preservation, it meant leaving Nature alone.

In *The Rambunctious Garden: Saving Nature in a Post-wild World*, science journalist Emma Marris discounts the existence of unmanaged wilderness, calling it a false ambition. She argues humans have already planted their footprints on every part of the globe, and we must now take responsibility for the results.

"If we fight to preserve only things that look like pristine wilderness, such as those places currently enclosed in national parks and similar refuges, our best efforts can only retard their destruction and delay the day we lose," Marris writes. "If we fight to preserve and enhance nature as we have newly defined it, as living background to human lives, we may be able to win."

So which is it? There's a perverse incentive at the heart of hands-off wilderness. If the land can take care of itself without human intervention, that's a problem we don't have to solve. Conversely, if we've somehow domesticated wild land like a captive bear, dangerous and unruly yet dependent on us for survival, then we've added to a to-do list of staggering proportions. We've got to fix poverty and artificial intelligence and war—and make sure our pet Nature gets fed and watered? Who's in charge of that?

"The idea that acceptable environmental management today involves decision-making that ramps up, rather than withdraws from human interference with nature completely changes the conservation game," University of Montana ethics philosopher Christopher Preston writes of Marris's ideas. "With 'hands off' no longer the preferred option, the idea of protecting nature from human influence so that its sheer independence from us can inspire us becomes moot. We simply have to bite that bullet."

If grizzly bears get delisted from the Endangered Species Act, the United States people turn their interest over to the four states that host grizzly bears: Montana, Wyoming, Idaho, and Washington. Handing grizzly management off to the states just puts the keys in the hands of different zookeepers—ones publicly inclined to consider the bears as huntable, big-game animals.

This is a social choice, not a scientific one. Representatives of all four state wildlife agencies have argued that hunting will teach grizzlies to avoid humans. Yet there is contradictory scientific evidence for this, and a lot of recent record that just the opposite is true. The state of Montana attempted to claim it was only hunting "surplus" grizzlies between 1975 and 1991, but couldn't convince the judge a surplus existed. Despite their protected ESA status, the number of Greater Yellowstone grizzlies shot by hunters has soared in the decade since the Fish and Wildlife Service first tried to declare them recovered in 2007. Grizzlies are mostly solitary animals, and dead grizzlies don't teach.

The states could choose to designate grizzlies a non-game animal, like the bald eagle. That would preserve matters as they were before the 2017 delisting rule, where bears might still be killed in management control actions or in self-defense, but not otherwise. And it would mollify the national majority opposed to adding dozens more grizzlies to a trophy wall.

"[T]he only motivation to delist the bear is so it can be hunted and management of the public lands can go back to business as usual, which is why we came close to losing the bear in the first place," grizzly researcher John Craighead said in 1998. His colleague Dick Knight added "I can imagine people out there with chainsaws and herds of sheep ready to move in when the bear population is delisted, and that scares me. Because I don't know how to protect bear habitat . . . You can write some laws, but hell, we couldn't protect the Targhee from widespread clear-cutting and road building in grizzly habitat, even under the Endangered Species Act. You get an administrator who wants to get around a law, and he'll do it." Knight was referring to the logging of the Targhee National Forest in the 1980s, which obliterated one hundred and sixty-five square miles of prime grizzly bear habitat on the edge of Grand Teton National Park—the equivalent of seven Manhattan Islands.

After all the telemetry data and food-source analysis and growth-trend statistics get dispensed, the argument that always closes the government's delisting case is the need for success. The Endangered Species Act needs a win. The Fish and Wildlife Service needs to show it can recover, not just protect, a threatened species. It needs to budge that 2-percent ceiling.

That isn't simply dedicated goal-chasing. Opponents of the Endangered Species Act have filed dozens of measures to modify it, mainly by stripping its authority to force states or businesses to comply whenever the law becomes inconvenient or expensive. In the 1990s and 2000s, Congressional ESA opponents filed an average of five bills to amend or curtail the law. Between 2011 and 2015, that rose to thirty-three a year. The 115th Congress in 2017 and 2018 produced at least one hundred and fifty amendments and bills to reduce the act's authority.

"Delisting the Yellowstone grizzlies can be an incentive to recovering the bears in other areas," Montana Fish, Wildlife and Parks attorney Bill Schenk said during the 2018 Missoula District Court hearing. "But it can be a disincentive if we don't delist. People are already living with high concentrations of grizzly bears. Folks have bought into that, but they need to know this can be achieved. They need to know there's an end-zone here."

The Property and Environment Research Center has published a white paper offering market-based reforms to the Endangered Species Act. That way, landowners who currently receive no benefit from having endangered species on their property would be more inclined to help out.

"By improving landowners' incentives to participate in conservation efforts with states and conservation groups, the ultimate result could be increased importance of state- and environmentalist-led, market-based conservation," the paper states. "Consequently, this reform would complement ongoing state efforts to promote more collaborative means of protecting species through positive incentives."

That emphasizes the Endangered Species Act's direction to the government to work on incentives, but it forgets the very first declaration of the law: that animals are going extinct *as a consequence of economic growth and development untempered by adequate concern and conservation.* In other words, the people who profited while driving the animals into threatened or endangered status in the first place would like to be paid to tolerate them now.

"The ESA has been weaponized against the West because we have these large, vast open spaces and public lands that we make a living off of that we were given to monitor and maintain, and they've been taken off the inventory for us to actually work with and utilize," Representative Gosar told the *Western Wire*, a newsletter published by the Western Energy Alliance. "It's key [for] energy development and tourism and recreation—to be able to get in and access those areas for everyone to see and enjoy while protecting the environment is very important. But what's been happening is private entities have been excluded . . . and it has restricted access and royalties to the people of the United States to whom those public lands belong to."

Gosar didn't mention his role in cutting the Fish and Wildlife Service budget, which in 2018 had less than a tenth of the amount it needed just to finish evaluating more than two hundred plant and animal candidate species to see if they deserved protection. While the service received about $90 million that year, implementing complete recovery plans for the 1,125 species already listed would cost an estimated $1.2 billion.

Schenk noted in his court testimony that most of the critical linkage areas between ecosystems were river bottoms and valleys filled with private ranches and farms—not public land. State wildlife agencies would get the task of negotiating those crossings.

"That private land has to be viable habitat for bears to make those linkages," Schenk said, "and that can only be if we're out there working with people."

11

Bears of the World

GRIZZLY BEARS CHANGE THEIR SURROUNDINGS WHEREVER THEY occur, whether on the ground or in your head.

Natural history author John McPhee described both impacts after a grizzly encounter recounted in *Coming into the Country*: "This was his [the grizzly's] country, clearly enough. To be there was to be incorporated, in however small a measure, into its substance—his country, and if you wanted to visit it you had better knock."

McPhee used language meticulously, and years after he wrote that book he lamented a great oversight. He never thought to probe the bear's Latin name, *Ursus arctos*, while he was traveling in the Arctic. He later learned it stemmed from "the land under the star Arcturus"—the bear star of the northern sky.

Dig a little deeper, and there's more linguistic gold. Arcturus stems from Arkos, the son of Kalisto, a handmaiden of the Greek hunting goddess Artemis. Zeus desired the virgin handmaiden, and seduced her in the guise of a bear. Artemis found out about the ravishment and banished Kalisto and her new son, making them into the Ursa Major and Ursa Minor constellations. Hera, to show her displeasure at yet another of Zeus's infidelities, banned mother and son from ever taking a bath in Oceanus. So the bear stars never set below the horizon or dip into the sea.

It gets better. Arkos gives us Arcadia, the remote central region of Greece, and Arcadian, the European settlers who came first to northeastern Canada. Some of them slid south, both geographically and linguistically, to Louisiana, becoming Cajuns along the way. One of the immigrant Arcadian leaders, Parisian lawyer Marc Lescarbot, declared Arcadian principles thus: "Farming must be our goal. And it is better worth than the treasures of Atahualpafor. Whoso [sic] has corn, wine, cattle, linen, clothe, leather, iron and lastly, codfish, need have naught to do with treasure." *Geography of Hope* essay author Thomas Berger wrote "It is not surprising that these settlers—who came to be known as the Arcadians— had the most harmonious relations of any European settlers with the aboriginal peoples of North America."

Canadian author Margaret Atwood joked that the United States northern border is the longest one-way mirror in the world: Americans look out and only see themselves. A more penetrating gaze would see things differently, including how people in other places confront grizzly bears.

A recent analysis by Søren Faurby at Sweden's University of Gothenburg has reimagined the world of wildlife as if all the extirpated species still roamed their prehistoric home ranges. Faurby's map of *Ursus arctos* shows the great bear habitat spilling across the northern hemisphere like hot fudge on a sundae. It covers most of North America west of the Mississippi (including half of Mexico as well as the Canadian provinces of Quebec and Newfoundland). Across the oceans, it claims all of Europe, the entire old Soviet Union, the Himalayan quadrants of India and China, Japan, and, surprisingly, North Africa and the northern third of the Arabian Peninsula. Mecca had grizzly bears.

◄ ◄ ◄ · ► ► ►

Preserving these bears of the world may serve some deep human cultural or spiritual need. But biology stakes a claim too. Keeping physically big predators in the mix has huge implications for the rest of the biosphere. And big is the operative word. Predators tend to whoop up on the carnivore just below them. Bears challenge wolves. Wolves fight coyotes. Coyotes fight foxes. But wolves don't put the beat on foxes—too insignificant. After wolves got reintroduced to Yellowstone National Park in the 1990s, foxes rebounded as the coyotes retreated.

This isn't just some law of the jungle hierarchy. Researchers at Pennsylvania State University demonstrated around the world that when the top keystone predator gets eliminated, lower-order predators throw systems out of whack. For example, when wolves and mountain lions were extirpated from the continental United States, coyotes and bobcats became the dominant predators. But those species aren't big enough to limit the region's out-of-control ungulate populations. Ergo, I get a backyard full of urban deer (locally known as hooved rats) eating my tulips.

"The fact that we don't have wolves and cougars means we have more deer, and those deer have overbrowsed the forests," said Penn State wildlife population ecologist David Miller. "And having more coyotes—because they don't tolerate foxes—results in fewer foxes, which means we have more mice in our fields and forests. That is affecting the prevalence of Lyme disease spread by ticks that spend much of their life on certain mice. So you see, the way these carnivores compete and co-occur has implications for all our wildlife communities."

Miller's research found similar patterns throughout North America, South America, Africa, Europe, and Asia. The fossil record reinforces this idea. A California Academy of Sciences team examined South Africa's Karoo Basin strata covering the mass extinction event from 254 million years ago on the supercontinent of Gondwana. They found that new ecosystems repopulating the area with a complex mix of predators and prey did significantly better than did more random assemblages.

"When you have species on the move because of environmental upheaval, or you force species together into communities in which they did not co-evolve, those systems are almost invariably less successful than systems where species have shared histories," Academy curator of geology Peter Roopnarine said. "Today, we can't tinker with ecosystems, have them fall apart functionally, and expect life to carry on and recover in a way that normally takes tens of thousands of years to happen. The fossil record shows this approach isn't sustainable."

To double-check their hypothesis, the team computer-modeled millions of alternate ecosystem setups to test how prone they were to extinction. They couldn't explain why more long-established systems did so significantly better, but they found them definitely superior.

One interpretation is that big predators like lions, crocodiles, tigers, and bears keep landscapes ecologically honest. Their keystone position in the ecosystem keeps all the other levels in balance, to the benefit of the whole. And if Americans are honest with themselves, they can accept examples from around the world that such bear-packed wild lands benefit people too, in body and mind.

⊲ ⊲ ⊲ · ▷ ▷ ▷

Throughout their prehistoric range, grizzly bears have left awed impressions on the people who knew them. Assyrians made stone amulets depicting grizzlies. In Norse mythology, Thor often appears as a bear. The Ainu people of northern Japan call *Ursus arctos* "The Divine One Who Rules the Mountains," while the Yukaghir people of Siberia named it "The Owner of the Earth."

Human self-proclaimed earth-owners nevertheless put bears on a perverse pedestal. Author David Quammen recounts how Romanians hold many benevolent myths about their enormous brown bear population, such as daubing a baby with bear fat to give it magical defenses. Perhaps Soviet-era Romanian dictator Nicolae Ceaușescu sought such protection. He claimed to have personally killed about four hundred brown bears, including twenty-four in a single day of canned hunting from a high-seat blind in 1983.

Political toadies in Romania reportedly had given up on influencing Ceausescu through his zipper or his wallet, since he was too old for sex and too rich for bribery. Instead, they vied for attention by developing *fonduri de vânătoare*, hunting districts managed for bear production. At its peak in 1988, the Romanian mountains supported ten times as many brown bears as Yellowstone National Park does at its current population of seven hundred and fifty grizzlies, in roughly the same space. They reached those numbers through diligent nurturing by game wardens, who would leave up to five kilograms of high-calorie food a day in feeders for especially bulky bears.

The fall of southeastern Europe's communist governments triggered ecological as well as political disarray. Most of its estimated seven thousand brown bears have become highly food-conditioned. The Romanian government banned brown bear hunting in 2016. That's amplified a pro-hunting campaign aimed at overturning the ban. Media reports in 2019 with headlines like "Brown bears terrorize a village in northern Romania" played up the increasing encounters between rural residents and bears raiding garbage dumps and livestock pens. Conservationists in Romania counter-accused the hunting groups of artificially inflating the bear populations to justify increased hunting quotas, noting that bear hunting was a pastime mainly for millionaires conducting business deals from those high-seat shooting blinds placed over bait sites.

Independent wildlife biologist Seth Wilson helped develop an innovative predator management program at the southern edge of Montana's Northern Continental Divide Ecosystem, including the carcass pick-up service used by ranchers like Wayne Slaght. Wilson also spent two years doing similar work in Slovenia, where European brown bears prowl a densely populated mountain region spreading across four nations.

"I'm impressed by the willingness of locals to work across borders there," Wilson said. "I'm hoping we can keep that idea alive in North America."

While the lack of accurate population figures or accountable bear management programs makes it hard to get a clear picture of brown bear conditions in the post-communist Carpathian and Dinaric mountain regions, Wilson said the uncontested reality is that the area has many more big bears and people living in less space than the United States grizzly recovery zone, and it has been that way for centuries.

⊰ ⊰ ⊰ · ⊱ ⊱ ⊱

The European version of the bear debate has its wild side. Animal rights activists there tend to be more aggressive, with one Italian group taking a local mayor hostage briefly after he approved killing a brown bear suspected of mauling a hiker. Conversely, French sheep farmers cut down trees to block roads biologists planned to use for bear transplant programs and painted anti-bear graffiti along the Tour de France bike race route.

That landscape produced the infamous Bruno the Problembär, who went on a border-hopping, livestock-killing rampage in Germany during the 2006 World Cup competition. Wildlife officials in three nations pursued a tragi-comic effort to discourage, relocate, and eventually kill Bruno, including an episode where an elite group of bear hunters from Finland went home in disgrace after their trained dogs couldn't handle the thin air of the Alps.

Bruno's rampage had a peculiar aspect. He played the role of the monster, striking with impunity and invulnerability, leaving bloody carnage and waste as calling cards. But he only attacked domestic livestock. Incident after incident followed the same template: sheep or chickens disemboweled or beheaded, but not consumed. At the same time, people would sight Bruno walking through town streets paying no attention to potential human prey. Despite some close encounters, Bruno declined opportunities to menace his *Homo sapiens* antagonists.

Bruno was the cub of a transplanted brown bear from Slovenia, brought into Italy to augment its shrinking native population in the Alps. An estimated five hundred to seven hundred brown bears live in Slovenia. That's about the same number as grizzly bears in the Greater Yellowstone Ecosystem, which is four times larger.

Another Italian colony of brown bears inhabits Abruzzo National Park. The nation's second-oldest national park holds somewhere between thirty and fifty brown bears. At 123,552 acres, it's a little more than a tenth the size of Glacier National Park. It nestles in the Apennine Mountains an hour east of Rome, although it barely rates a mention in most tourist guidebooks.

"The Abruzzo bears have learned to live alongside humans, and they're still disappearing," said Roger Thompson, a journalist who's extensively studied Italian brown bears. "In a thousand years of records, there's never been a fatal attack on a human there."

Apennines residents credit that to a "nature tax" where farmers leave extra fruit trees or beehives for the bears as a way of discouraging more intrusive food raids. Park managers have also air-lifted supplemental food to the bears as they prepare for hibernation in fall.

Although no Abruzzo bear has been documented attacking cattle, a steady campaign of poisoning and poaching bears has greatly reduced their numbers. At the same time, a lack of priority in the Italian federal government has meant few resources for law enforcement or scientific study of the bear population.

Thompson said the biggest threat to the Abruzzo brown bears comes from cattle ranchers controlled by the Italian Mafia. Italian law allows much more liberal use of federal land for commercial purposes like grazing than in the United States. A tradition dating back to Roman times gives a shepherd the right to graze flocks or herds on any pasture available, including the estates of absentee landlords busily running the republic back in Rome. Mafia organizations have exploited that to graze herds inside national parks like Abruzzo and to intimidate any officials who oppose them.

Thompson titled his latest book *No Word for Wilderness: Italy's Grizzlies and the Race to Save the Rarest Bears on Earth*. It explores the very different way people in Italy see wild places and wildlife compared to what's going on in the United States. Although Italy in the twentieth century increased its federally protected lands from 1 percent to 10 percent of the country, the resulting parks lack the public support or interest that Glacier or Yellowstone National Parks command here.

"Talk about a settled land," Thompson said of the Italian landscape, which packs sixty million people into a peninsula that would fit inside the borders of Montana with thirty thousand square miles to spare. "For many people, the idea that you would go somewhere or preserve something wild just for its wild sake is nonsensical."

For proof, Thompson points to any Italian art museum, and the contents of its landscape painting room. No mountain vista is complete without a ruined tower or distant bridge in the background. That's because, according to Thompson, the long history of art, science, and culture in Italy never included a tradition of revering nature the way Americans like John Muir, Theodore Roosevelt, Aldo Leopold, and Ansel Adams preached. For Italians, and many other Europeans, the wild land was the home of barbarians as well as bears—malevolent forces bent on destroying the cultured fruits of civilization. Swiss guides often blindfolded or cowled their clients to diminish the terrors of the glacial crags they traveled past. Mountain climbing as a sport or pastime didn't exist in most of the Alps until British explorers exported their world-conquering enthusiasm in the mid-1800s.

◂ ◂ ◂ · ▸ ▸ ▸

A couple of uniquely American traits bent the European attitude in a different direction. One was the lingering disgust at the idea of feudalism—the notion that nobility got the best of everything within their fiefs. The Founding Fathers crimped that tradition in the Constitution, declaring that the contents of the government's estate belonged to the people, not to the head of state.

The second was a somewhat schizophrenic interest in untrammeled country as a place to prove oneself worthy. Presidents, and not only Abraham Lincoln, touted their upbringings in log cabins both to show they came from humble beginnings and to suggest that they had wrestled with the wild and survived. In 1840 President William Henry Harrison sent his campaign surrogates around the country in wheel-mounted cabins proclaiming him the "Log Cabin Candidate" even though at the time he lived in a mansion.

This split personality distilled itself into the form of Theodore Roosevelt, who evangelized the value of pristine public land as a place to collect trophies of accomplishment. Roosevelt both "hated a man who skins the land" and skinned more than his share of its beasts, including some of the last plains buffalo still standing outside Yellowstone National Park. Legal scholar Jedediah Purdy goes so far as to link Roosevelt's hunting urge to his fondness for eugenics theorists like Madison Grant: "The nature they loved was the nature that made them feel noble, socially and, in their imaginations, racially."

Those American ideas developed into laws such as the 1897 Organic Act establishing the US Forest Service, the National Park Service Organic Act of 1916, and the Wilderness Act of 1964 that together designated almost half the land west of the Mississippi River for public ownership. That landscape became the place where a properly ambitious and well-armed pioneer could confront God and grizzly bears and become a legend like Daniel Boone or Grizzly Adams.

One amusing similarity between gun rights advocates and wilderness advocates is a tendency for each to carry their founding documents in a hip pocket: The Constitution for quick reference to the grammar-challenged participles of the Second Amendment and the 1964 Wilderness Act for its testament to untrammeled land.

Any wilderness fan worth a sockful of trail dust can discourse on the definition of "untrammeled." In old English, a trammel was a net or other restraint that controlled something. To be untrammeled dovetailed with another archaic definition of wilderness—"self-willed land." In the text of the Wilderness Act, such places are "recognized as an area where the earth and its community of life are untrammeled by man, where man himself is a visitor who does not remain."

That principle has been borrowed by other cultures and nations wishing to replicate the US pattern of national parks and protected wild lands. But it has no antecedent. No other modern government has a tradition of setting aside some of its property to persevere without some human entitlement or manipulation.

"The U.S. has the most strict definition of wilderness—one of the only laws that has a focus and definition with legal criteria backing it up," said Natalie Dawson, director of the University of Montana's Wilderness Institute. "Many of the European national parks were established relatively recently. They were often done with the political leadership at the time. So there's a lot of gray area in other parts of the world about what people are allowed or not allowed to do than there is in the U.S."

Many hope that our self-willed land will take care of itself in perpetuity. The 2015 *Ecomodernist Manifesto* endorsed by an international signatory list of conservationists, biologists, philosophers, and policy makers asserts that technology will rescue humanity from its excesses. Better food production, renewable and pervasive energy sources, and benign leadership will draw people to megacities. With the worst threats to quality of life relieved, the drive to have big families will relent. That will stabilize the globe's human population at between 9.6 billion and 12.3 billion by 2100. Some 80 percent of that population will contract onto 2 percent of the world's landmass, leaving the rest to some robot-tended farms and continental swaths of self-willed land.

This is already underway in China. By the government's own projections made in 2017, about 300 million people will migrate from agricultural areas to cities in the next decade. They won't be needed on farms because adoption of Western-style farming techniques is expected to increase Chinese food production eightfold. The current small-plot farmers dependent on nonmechanized traditions will no longer be required to feed the nation. That's the equivalent of telling the entire US population to stop doing what they're doing now, move to new homes, and do something else. Left unexamined is what happens to a landscape that used to house those hundreds of millions of people. What happens to the roads, water systems, and other infrastructure designed with regular maintenance in mind? What sorts of unintended ecological consequences might get rolling before anyone notices?

◄ ◄ ◄ · ► ► ►

We've had a few experiments in this rewilding vein, some not by choice. One was Chernobyl, where a nuclear reactor meltdown in Ukraine in 1986 forced the evacuation of thousands of square miles. Radiation from the ruined facility triggered a generation of birth defects in newborns and cancers in adults. But it's failed to turn the place into a *Mad Max*–style wasteland. In fact, much of the forest around the city of Chernobyl has recolonized the streetscape. Elderly Ukrainians, unafraid of accelerating their already declining health, have moved back into the hot zone to take advantage of free housing. However, the vote is still out whether they would agree to share their radioactive senior center with Siberian brown bears.

A more benign example of rewilding is the Netherlands' Oostvaardersplassten. This twenty-three-square-mile failure of an industrial park found success instead as an experiment in rewilding, Dutch-style. It got its start almost accidentally, when neighboring bird-watchers noticed flocks of rare geese had set up nesting colonies in the untrammeled grasses. Other wild birds became resident. That inspired the Dutch authorities to consider more elaborate introductions. By 2010, the Oostvaardersplassten had small herds of a nearly extinct Polish horse breed called the Konik and a genetically back-bred version of the actually extinct super-cow known as the auroch.

Seeing the wildlife return to this enclosed area has been a tourist draw for the region. But it's had an unexpected downside too. According to Dutch wilderness philosopher Martin Drenthen, the neighbors were thrilled with the whole project until the hard winter of 2017–18. Prolonged cold took its predictable toll on weaker members of the herds. So did lack of forage, given that without predators, several species had pushed up to the edge of the zone's carrying capacity.

"The result was some people trying to sneak fodder into the animals," Drenthen said. "Others demanded to be allowed to go in and rescue them, to bring them to their homes. They couldn't stand the idea of the animals dying there."

That, however, violates the idea of rewilding. If humans dip in at will, for their own agendas of preserving certain population levels or species mixes, the Oostvaardersplassten becomes nothing more than a really big zoo.

A third example of rewilding is in the Polish forest of Białowieża. Its 11,500-acre core hosts a few dozen wood buffalo, Old World relations to the American bison. It also displays an extensive human influence on the supposedly pristine reserve, from present-day logging and hunting to the occasional discovery of a fifteen-hundred-year-old sickle knife in the grass.

Białowieża pales in comparison to the ambition of the American Prairie Reserve in central Montana. There a similar project has linked more than four hundred thousand acres of former ranches into a new bison home-land. This was the country Lewis and Clark paddled past buffalo herds miles long, and where they frequently encountered grizzly bears.

The American Prairie Reserve isn't alone in the effort. US Highway 2 bounds its northern acres. Known as the Hi-Line, US 2 also strings together the Blackfeet, Rocky Boy's, Fort Belknap, and Fort Peck Indian reservations. Each one has its own bison herd in various stages of development. The Dakota and Lakota Sioux at Fort Peck acquired some of Yellowstone National Park's bison that had passed a brucellosis quarantine. The Blackfeet arranged to adopt the overflow of Alberta's Wood Buffalo National Park herd (which ironically got its start from the Canadian purchase of a Flathead Indian Reservation captive pureblood bison herd after the US government failed to come up with money to buy the herd in 1908).

As far as Indian tribal historians are concerned, the idea that "rewilding" restores landscapes to pre-human condition is ludicrous: these lands have always known human influence. Teepee rings of stone mark campsites that have been in use since the great ice sheets retreated roughly thirteen thousand years ago. The Plains Indian tribes devised ingenious ways to herd the bison to slaughter long before they acquired horses or rifles to hunt them with. They regularly burned the prairie and surrounding mountains to improve forage for game. Did that make the land somehow not pristine?

Historian Dan Flores challenges the whole notion of some "Golden Age" before humanity screwed up the planet. Archaeological evidence shows human impact on virtually every landscape by eleven thousand years ago. Between fifty million and two hundred million people called North America home for five centuries before Europeans arrived.

"And where, one wonders, along the lengthy trail of connect-the-dots that follows tool-making out of the prehuman primate's rocks and sticks to our bulldozers and the World Wide Web, could we have stopped?" Flores writes. "Judged by the human impact on the nonhuman world, the Clovis toolkit that helped push hundreds of megafaunal species to their extinction in the Americas ten thousand years ago was too much technology."

◄ ◄ ◄ · ► ► ►

Scandinavian countries have extensive brown bear populations that offer intriguing comparisons to North American grizzlies. Montana bear biologist Cecily Costello got to do some field work in Sweden, including observing a helicopter capture of a brown bear.

"It made me realize they're a little bit of a different bear than they are here in the Rocky Mountains," Costello said. "They have a different personality."

While taxonomically Swedish brown bears and American grizzly bears are identical, in the woods they're quite different. North American *Ursus arctos horribilis* are known for ferocity and occasionally eating livestock or picnic supplies. Swedish *Ursus arctos arctos* rarely encounter people or raid human food. Thousands of years of persecution by humans has turned them into secretive, highly nocturnal, vegetarian animals the Swedes often call ghost bears. Sweden has recorded forty bear-related injuries and two human deaths in forty years. One notable injury occurred when a teenaged boy was skiing out of bounds and fell into a bear den occupied by a sow brown bear and cubs.

This "ghost bear" behavior would be a welcome import to American grizzly populations. Seth Wilson documents mauling and fatality figures across Europe are far lower than the United States, especially when factoring for the much larger bear and people densities. Some zoologists theorize the long history of European brown bears living around and avoiding humans resulted in a survival trait, with the more aggressive and promiscuous bears selected out of the population long ago. The brown bears of Abruzzo rank as one of the Italian park's top tourist attractions, in large part because of their nonthreatening nature. Some Italian biologists theorize the bears have lived alongside humans for so many centuries, natural selection may have killed off the aggressive ones.

Before anyone scoffs at such a notion, don't doubt the remarkable power of selective breeding. Since the famous Russian silver fox study in 1959, which produced a line of essentially domestic dogs out of a fur farm of wild foxes in fewer than ten generations, we've demonstrated an ability that some biologists refer to as hunter-induced evolution. The brown bears of Eurasia evolved in direct contact with *Homo sapiens* for thousands of years.

Does that mean Americans might somehow manage their grizzlies into a similar docility? The likelihood that such deep behavioral shifts could be imposed on North American grizzlies, who've only dealt with highly aggressive humans for a century, remains controversial. Decades of aversive conditioning efforts in Glacier and Yellowstone National Parks indicate it won't be a quick fix. The routine use of cracker shells, dogs, and hazing hasn't stopped new grizzlies from checking out campgrounds and popular trails every summer.

◄ ◄ ◄ · ► ► ►

Step through America's one-way looking glass into British Columbia, and you fall into a land of perhaps fifteen thousand grizzly bears. But like a lot of Canadian numbers, there's some disproportionality involved. Nearly 90 percent of Canada's population lives within a hundred miles of the US border. About three-quarters of British Columbia's 4.8 million residents live in or around the cities of Vancouver and Victoria (which is on Vancouver Island, with no resident grizzly bears). The province's thousands of grizzly bears, however, inhabit a long arc surrounding the central Thompson-Okanagan region. That interior is known for producing apples and wines but very few grizzlies. This presents a problem for US grizzly recovery efforts in the transnational North Cascades, Selkirk, and Cabinet-Yaak ecosystems, which presume they'll supplement their populations by Canadian grizzly immigration. A 2017 British Columbia review of North Cascades grizzly populations reported its wildlife managers were assuming they'd get bears from the United States.

"But to date, government has made no commitments as to how it will work with its cross-border partners to assist them with recovery," the audit stated. "For the (Canadian) North Cascades population, it may be that recovery actions have been too little, too late. Since 2004, only one grizzly bear (an adult male) has been confirmed as still living in the B.C. portion, which could mean that this sub-population is locally extinct."

Even so, British Columbians have shown they can rearrange themselves with remarkable speed. The province that had a tradition of hunting grizzly bears going back centuries erased the trophy hunt following a two-year social campaign. Before 2017, hunters there killed about 250 grizzlies a year.

In 2015, British Columbia took in $366,400 in grizzly bear hunting license fees. Of that, all but $34,000 went to the government's general revenue. The remainder funded the BC Conservation Trust Foundation's efforts at grizzly bear monitoring and inventory. Tellingly, a 2018 auditor's report noted "We could find no evidence as to how either the allocation of what goes to the foundation, or the fees that are being charged for hunting, were determined."

It did find that while hunting contributed between $6 million and $7.6 million (Canadian dollars) a year to the provincial economy, commercial bear viewing in the Great Bear Rainforest alone brought in $15 million in 2012.

Two of those bear-viewing outfitters, Julius Strauss and Dean Wyatt, started organizing political pressure against the hunt. With the guests' permission they added $100 surcharges to their bills to build a lobbying fund. They tried all the traditional legislative influence tactics, including spending $10,000 on a fundraiser for the premier of British Columbia for a chance to make their case in person. Strauss said that got them a photo-op but little else.

So they switched horses to the premier's political challenger. They flew him up to one of their lodges, showed him the bears and their satisfied clients, and their economic analysis. Six months later, the new man was premier and three months after that, he eliminated trophy hunting of grizzly bears in all areas where it had still been legal.

"It's mostly a social values issue," BC forests minister Doug Donaldson told the Canadian Broadcasting Corporation. "When it comes down to it, this species is seen as an iconic species for B.C., and people just weren't willing to accept the hunting of grizzly bears anymore in this province."

Hunting grizzlies for meat was still allowed, but the hunters had to turn in the skull, hide, and paws (the trophies) to provincial authorities. In late 2018, a coalition of hunting guides and outfitters challenged the ban in Canadian court, claiming the government never consulted with them or fairly polled the public. A reversal in British Columbia political fortunes could see the ban removed as quickly as it was imposed.

Provincial wildlife managers meanwhile have shifted to more adaptive strategies like hazing and electric fencing to deter grizzlies rather than killing them. The practice has been controversial in places like Bella Coola, a small coastal town where there's one grizzly for every thirty-three residents. While some have profited from the boost of tourists who visit to photograph the bears, others fear the growing accustomization to people will make the grizzlies more likely to invade town when the bears are hungry during poor salmon years.

For example, grizzlies had cruised past the twenty-two houses of the Oweekeeno Village on British Columbia's Queen Charlotte Sound as long as anyone could remember, without causing incident. The bears came to feast on a sockeye salmon run that annually sent more than three million fish up the coastal rivers. But by 1990, upland logging had clear-cut most of the headwaters of the streams and ruined the salmon spawning sites. The practice of spraying herbicide on the cut blocks to prevent native shrubs from competing with the timber companies' sapling replants wiped out the elderberry, huckleberry, and salmonberry bushes that bears fed on. That year, fewer than sixty thousand salmon returned to spawn.

In 1999, the salmon run produced just 3,500 fish. And the grizzly bears, which heretofore had never caused a reported conflict with the tiny village, began ransacking it in search of food. In January 2000 the villagers killed fourteen grizzlies as a matter of public safety.

◄ ◄ ◄ · ► ► ►

Asia historically held both black and brown bears. The brown bears share genetic ties to America's grizzlies. Natural historian Douglas Chadwick, among many others, argues that the tales of Yeti, the Abominable Snowman, stem from encounters with mountain brown bears. Several monasteries in the Solu Khumbu claim to have Yeti skulls in their reliquaries, and they ask hefty donations to bring them out for a brief view. None have been submitted for scientific analysis.

Nepal also has twelve-foot crocodiles, elephants, rhinos, cobras, and tigers, all feared by man. Yet all those charismatic man-killers now survive in a couple national parks that could be dropped inside Glacier National Park with plenty of elbow room. And they may not hold on, even there. Between the pressure of poachers seeking lucrative body parts and farmers defending their crops, the big critters require big investments of both protection and tolerance. Their ability to attract tourist dollars forges their main link to survival.

On the eastern side of the Himalayas, a candidate for world's rarest bear inhabits a corner of Mongolia eighteen times as big as Glacier National Park, and counts perhaps forty individuals in its entire population. Mongolians call them *mazaalai*. Chadwick recounts its story with a combination of awe for the sheer cussed chutzpah of its survival and angst for his encounter with something so wonderful and perched on the edge of extinction.

Chadwick spent three years chronicling the fate of the Gobi grizzly population inhabiting the remote deserts. Those brown bears, numbering less than a couple hundred throughout their international range, cling to an existence even a camel would consider deprived. The bear charging out of the cover photo of Chadwick's book, *Tracking Gobi Grizzlies*, looks like Paddington gone feral on Mars.

The ground it gallops across doesn't support a blade of grass. The bear's claws stick out big as pencils, tips blunted by the rocky surface. And the fur: frizzy as a Steiff teddy bear run through the dryer on high for an hour.

"I wanted to know how it's possible for a grizzly bear to make living in such an arid stonescape," Chadwick told me days after his book came off the press. "They've got this wild, thick bed-hair, which serves as a substitute for layers of fat for insulation. They're hibernating in caves exposed to the air, and it will get 40 below."

The Gobi Desert of Mongolia lurks just beyond the reach of the Indian Ocean storms that water the Himalayas to the west, and Pacific weather that supports the forests of China, Korea, and Japan to the east. Its geologically ancient mountains never knew glaciers, shaped instead by shattering freezes and unending winds.

Yet if Mongolia seems otherworldly, consider this. Montanan fishing guides already lead trips to Mongolian trout streams. Montana University System crews have led expeditions for both modern wildlife and fossil dinosaur research. A quarter of the desert dust in the Earth's atmosphere blows off the Gobi and adjacent Taklamakan Deserts of Mongolia and China. The phosphorus, nitrogen, calcium, and iron components of that Gobi dust can be detected enriching forest soils in America's Rocky Mountains.

Chadwick confesses his professional naturalist career really gives respectability to his inner "11-year-old on a treasure hunt" wondering what the heck is that? He combines that with a willingness to spend multiple springs in the Gobi, enduring camel spiders that are sort of scorpions and camel ticks that occasionally dig into places unmentionable in polite company. Also, Bactrian double-humped camels that are almost as endangered as the bears.

As small as the Gobi grizzly population is, the gang of people who fight for them seems smaller. Chadwick's book paints a family tree linking generations of naturalists. Harry Reynolds, the bear biologist who organized the original Gobi research project, got his start as a fifteen-year-old assistant to Frank and John Craighead during their groundbreaking Yellowstone National Park grizzly research in 1959. John Craighead was Chadwick's academic adviser when the author was doing his graduate work at the University of Montana.

Reynolds teamed with Michael Proctor, the leading grizzly biologist in British Columbia who advises the Interagency Grizzly Bear Committee in the United States. They all depended on baseline research completed by biologist George Schaller in the 1970s. That was about the same time author Peter Matthiessen wrote his classic *The Snow Leopard* about Schaller pursuing with equal frustration Himalayan blue sheep, all-but-invisible felids, and Buddhist understanding.

It was while Chadwick was doing his own snow leopard reporting in Mongolia that he met Tserennadmid Mijiddorj, a translator/naturalist who off-handedly alerted Chadwick to the existence of Gobi grizzlies, which weren't even known to science before 1943.

"And now I'm on the board of the Liz Claiborne-Art Ortenberg Foundation with seven other scientists, one of whom is George Schaller," Chadwick said. "I grew up reading about his studies of gorillas and lions of Africa, and now twice a year I'm sitting there discussing how to allocate significant amounts of money to research projects all around the world."

In true Chadwick fashion, the search for Gobi grizzlies rambles from the comic to the surreal. Just getting to the bears' desert involves cranky Russian-built vans loaded with "full gas drums that leaked a little and burlap bags full of fresh goat and sheep parts, making our caravan a sort of combination of a rolling slaughterhouse and incendiary bomb."

Project photographer Joe Riis sacrificed at least five Nikons to captured grizzlies that, as they came out of their drug-addled research stupor, consistently attacked the first thing making a noise—the automatic camera he'd set up to photograph their departure from the trap.

The bears themselves behave like the vegans of the predator class: Undisputedly the strongest critter in the desert, they apparently never hunt anything bigger than a gerbil. They disdain bacon in the trap bait and even avoid the dog food kibbles mixed in with grain pellets in the government-supplied feed bins, put off by the meat byproducts.

The dietary restrictions extend to people as well. Local herders had no reports of bears attacking livestock, although they would raid food pellets.

"There were no rip-snorting grizzly stories like we have over here," Chadwick said. "And not because they're weenies—they're full-on grizzly. They'll charge an eight-foot-tall van loaded with big Mongolians. They don't back off. They have the grizzly attitude."

Virtually every other place that has successfully kept brown bears on the landscape has done so with intensive human intervention. From bear chow dispensers in the Gobi Desert to airlifted fruit baskets in the Italian Alps, most of the world's brown bears live on welfare.

Only in the North American Rocky Mountains are grizzlies and brown bears required to persist by their own devices. And they do so in a geographical area bigger than the entire European Union: five million square kilometers or two million square miles. They share that landscape with a total population of almost fourteen million people, who would fit in the metropolitan confines of Los Angeles or London.

Actually, strip out the roughly seven million city dwellers in and around Seattle-Tacoma, Vancouver, and Spokane, and you have roughly fifty eight thousand grizzly and brown bears living with roughly seven million rural residents. About forty thousand of those grizzly and brown bears mix it up with less than one million Alaskans and Canadian Yukon Territory inhabitants. The estimated two thousand grizzlies living south of the US border cohabitate with about 1.5 million humans in Montana, northern Idaho, and northwestern Wyoming. By comparison, the ICUN 2018 Red List reports about 15,400 brown bears in the European Union, population 513 million.

Two interesting points about the ICUN Red List. Its contributors include Harry Reynolds and Michael Proctor (Chadwick's collaborators), Chris Servheen (former head of grizzly bear recovery for the US Fish and Wildlife Service), and David Mattson (one of Servheen's most strident opponents). Yet another example of the close-knit community of bear science.

And second, it states about one hundred thousand brown bears live in Russia. This may be true. But Jon Swenson and others have lamented the dearth of reliable Russian data, even among Swedish and Finnish colleagues who have good relations right across the frontier. The Russian government's chaotic inattention to its Far Eastern forests—home to tigers that routinely eat brown bears—makes most of its research unpublishable in international journals.

‹ ‹ ‹ · › › ›

The village of Phaplu, once a famous rest stop on the way to Mount Everest, sits on the edge of the Solu Khumbu region of Nepal. The trekker trailhead for Everest now leapfrogs past it to Lukla, with its "most dangerous airport in the world." Phaplu now makes due as the gateway to Thubten Chholing Monastery, a massive Buddhist learning center founded after China forced thousands of Tibetan Buddhists into exile in 1950.

Phaplu too has an airport of daunting circumstances. Lukla's runway slopes straight down the grade of the mountainside before ending abruptly at a near-cliff overlooking a huge glacial chasm. The grade leverages gravity against its short length, with planes taking off at a downhill run to gain lift and landing on an uphill roll.

Phaplu instead terraced its runway, following the contours of the mountainside. Incoming planes must make a hard U-turn before the wall of a mountain (observed by another cliff-perched monastery). The first thing my daughter and I saw on disembarking was a pile of airplane seats jumbled against the retaining wall alongside the runway. Salvage from past failed landings?

We had come to Phaplu to interview Buddhist lamas who shared teachers and traditions with a new Buddhist teaching center back in the States half an hour north of my home in Montana. What connections, I wanted to know, did the lamas feel between their centuries-old ancestral homeland and the new site in mountains literally on the opposite side of the planet?

It took three days to reach Thubten Chholing, where more than a thousand monks and nuns live at the end of a glacial valley. Ania and I returned to Phaplu for a flight to Lukla and further interviews with the Sherpa community of the Solu Khumbu.

At the airport, some assembly was required. A twin-engine Otter sat empty on the runway—stripped to its floorboards—its two pilots chatting with the ground crew and watching the windsock. Nearby was a pile of cement bags, and another pallet stacked with instant Ramen noodles and cases of beer—and the pile of seats. The pilots were gauging the weather and wind, calculating how much cargo they might carry should the breeze shift to a favorable direction. Until it did, the plane couldn't take off at all.

The pilots wandered off to get lunch. Ania and I stood alone by the cargo loads, making hopeful bets that we would join the delivery of bar food so we'd have something to party with if we crashed into a river canyon. That's when the army guards came over.

Nepal's peaceful, tourist-oriented atmosphere notwithstanding, the sight of three armed guards coming to inspect the only foreigners in view was a little unsettling. Our guide, Ang Dawa Sherpa, was talking with someone beyond earshot at the far end of the runway. We'd already passed through what amounted to airport security. Was this an unscheduled baggage check looking for bribable infractions?

The army trio didn't look threatening, but they did walk straight over to us. I palmed my hands to my chest and offered the all-purpose Nepali greeting "Namaste." The lead guard did the same. Then we stood for a long minute, saying nothing.

Having exhausted my Nepali vocabulary, I pointed to Ania and then up the valley toward the faraway monastery and said "Thubten Chholing." The guard nodded and looked at us. "American?" We nodded.

For the monastery visit, I'd prepared a set of photographs of Montana to show the monks the similarities and differences of their new base of operations. Perhaps that might break the runway ice as well. I pulled out my iPad and opened the folder of photos. The guards closed in.

I'd brought pictures of the Garden of One Thousand Buddhas in Arlee, Montana, as well as a collection of shots from nearby Glacier National Park. These included jagged peaks, wildflowers, deer, marmots, mountain goats, and a black bear.

"Baloo!" the guard suddenly cried. It had all been polite nods and hmms until we reached the bear photo. The word fell into place in my mind: Baloo the Bear, *The Jungle Book*. "The Bear Necessities" song suddenly ear-wormed into memory.

The three guards crowded close to see the picture of Baloo. I pointed around the surrounding mountains? Baloo? I asked with a shrug. Any Baloo here?

The lead guard looked wistful. "No," he said in English. "Very rare. No Baloo."

12

No Going Back

WHERE DO WE FIND A TABLE TO RESOLVE MATTERS, LIKE HOW TO live with the grizzly bear, before we wind up on a battlefield? What scale can we share that can balance willing sacrifice against fear?

In thinking about how to answer that, I've looked back at the people whose stories recount our attempt to recover *Ursus arctos horribilis*. Love and fear and awe and reverence and risk and strong emotion and danger mix together like the occult perfume biologists use to lure bears to hair-snares. Grizzlies attract some people and repel others. We tend to congeal those elements into a story that locks us into one corner or another, unwilling to perceive another configuration.

Near the beginning of this book, I described the culvert trap used to capture grizzly bears and how something so unnatural could be so enticing to bears. There's another kind of bear trap, possibly apocryphal but worth mentioning for its relation to human nature. It was a cone-shaped bucket with an opening at the narrow end and the wide bottom welded to a stout chain looped around a tree. A piece of meat was put inside, and when the grizzly grabbed it, its clinched paw was too large to pull out of the opening. The bear would trap itself by its refusal to let go of the bait. Bear stories can have the same effect. Here are two to consider.

◄ ◄ ◄ · ► ► ►

It takes endurance, logistics, and courage to complete the 3,100-mile Continental Divide Trail (CDT). Dave Murray did it barefoot.

Along the way, he ran into grizzly bears four times. The biggest bear he'd ever encountered in the Lower 48 states stepped on the strap of his backpack, which lay five feet away from where Murray was resting on a fallen log. His can of bear spray was attached to the pack. The grizzly walked away.

"I was just amazed at the people who don't pack bear spray on that trail," Murray told me the day after he completed the CDT. "They would start the trail in New Mexico or Colorado, get in the middle of Wyoming, and realize *there's grizzlies on the trail*."

By tradition, CDT hikers give themselves trail names. Murray's was "Barefoot." A bear was involved there too.

"I quit wearing shoes after I got chased across Camus Creek by a bear that tore up our camp," Murray said of a summer he spent dynamiting an old mining operation for salvage scrap on Idaho's Salmon River when he was 14. "I had a pair of those 1970s high-top Vasque boots. I tried to dry them out by the fire, and they shrunk about two sizes. The tops turned hard as rocks. I cut the backs out of them so I could slip my feet into them, using socks to hold them together. But they just cut into my legs. It took about three weeks, but it got to the point where I could walk barefoot without anything bothering me."

Forty years later in the Wind River Range just south of Yellowstone National Park, Barefoot ran into Charge and Zorro.

"Zorro was from Spain, and he had rocks in his face," Murray told me. "His nose was bleeding. Charge says, Zorro, tell Barefoot what happened to you."

Zorro had been on the same path as Charge and Barefoot, when he felt something watching him. He looked to his right, saw a flash of movement, and suddenly a grizzly bear was on top of him, knocking his face into the trail.

"It was doing pushups on his back," Murray said of Zorro's account. "Then it moved twenty feet away and sat down, staring at him. Zorro opened his eyes and when it wasn't there, he got up and ran. I don't know if he went back to Spain or finished the trail."

Obviously, people like Murray verge into the charismatic megafauna category of human performance. Even his wife Connie—although she completed much of the CDT with him—admits she can't walk from the front door to the truck barefoot. Murray dedicates huge amounts of time and resources doing things that put him at risk of encountering grizzly bears. From Wyoming to the Canadian border, Murray packed not only his bear spray but a .44-caliber pistol. He drew both on at least one grizzly encounter. Those encounters were the highlights of his adventure. But do they justify imposing that kind of fear on people who would rather not test their courage the same way?

◄ ◄ ◄ · ► ► ►

Maggie Nutter ranches in the Sweet Grass Hills east of Glacier National Park. She represents many in Montana's ranching community who consider grizzlies as brucellosis with fur. And the furry threats were way too close.

In 2018, Nutter became a regular face at the IGBC meetings as delisting of grizzly bears in the Northern Continental Divide Ecosystem seemed imminent. The meetings took place in poorly lit hotel conference rooms, where two dozen uniformed government agents and researchers spoke around a cumbersome U-shaped forum while audience members strained to hear. The officials presented on grizzly population trends, conflict incidents and responses, and the types of education efforts most successful at earning public acceptance of grizzly management.

Nutter would drive at least four hours each way and spend a day and a half away from her chores to claim her three minutes of public comment time. A small-framed woman often appearing in the same work shirt and jeans she'd wear on the ranch, she sounded like a combination of business owner and school teacher. Although she claimed to personally like grizzly bears, she represented the Marias River Livestock Association in north-central Montana, and she let the bear policy people know the limits of her social tolerance.

"Educating people on what to do if you meet a bear and how to use bear spray—that does not increase tolerance," Nutter testified. "I think of it as forced compliance. If there wasn't a big old fine for shooting a grizzly bear, I don't think there would be any tolerance. Those are not my goals, not my values and not my culture."

Nutter backed up her opinions with photos showing a grizzly bear napping next to a child's backyard trampoline near Valier, Montana. She spoke of a neighbor whose daughter wanted boards nailed across her bedroom window because she was afraid grizzlies might get in.

"I don't want to keep my grandkids as prisoners in my home," Nutter told the members of the IGBC. "You can secure livestock and chickens with electric fences, but that won't keep my family safe as they work on the ranch."

Then she put the issue in rancher terms. Nutter had recently attended a workshop on preventing hoof-and-mouth disease in cattle. She passed on the new information at gatherings with fellow ranchers.

"I'm doing education, but that doesn't mean there's increased tolerance for hoof-and-mouth disease among the livestock community," she told the IGBC. "Education does not increase tolerance."

Nutter saw grizzly bears approaching her land as an imposition on her "freedom of the use of that land as we see fit." She questioned why Glacier National Park had a no-tolerance policy for grizzlies in campgrounds, but she was expected to allow them in her driveway.

During the previous hundred years Nutter's family had raised cattle and sheep on Montana's prairies, grizzly bears were a pest and predator to be dispatched, not accommodated. Nutter confronts bad weather and broken trucks and fickle markets every day in order to put food on others' tables. Does she deserve to be outvoted by the majority of her fellow Americans who want to see the grizzly recovered in her backyard? While doing research on this book at Boston's Harvard University, I encountered several urban Americans who couldn't believe Nutter was literally referring to grizzlies in her driveway. "Are they in danger on their property?" one asked me. "Hard to believe a government agency would allow that."

Dozens of stuffed bears decorate a fence along Montana's Rocky Mountain Front. As grizzly bears have started coming out of the remote wilderness areas to explore the farms and ranches of the Montana prairie, the people who now occupy those lands have reacted with a mixture of anger and acceptance colored by widely different assumptions of what the bear means. Photograph by the author.

Like the old playground con—"He hit me back first!"—starting points and motives matter. I have a significant number of Montana ranchers, farmers, and loggers in my family tree. They struggled and bled to earn a living that allowed successive generations to live easier, to the point I can make my career writing about other people's sweat and effort.

So I know those ancestors may find it disrespectful when I observe they cut trees in places where they will never grow back, to sell in markets that will never compete with trees grown in wetter, flatter landscapes like Alabama; and when I note they chased cattle that will never fill as many hamburger buns as the feedlot-fattened herds of Oklahoma, in an industry where four companies control 85 percent of the American beef production. When we talk about highest and best use of land in a purely capitalist sense, money doesn't care much about your grandpa's homestead.

And they'll be downright insulted when they're reminded that they cut those trees and ran those cows on land that used to be dominated by someone else, someone deprived of their rights and possessions by a greater military and legal force. Nutter puts her century of hard work against the Blackfeet Indians' multiple millennia of culture and practice, not to mention their very different traditions about living with grizzly bears.

Agriculture remains a dominant social and political force in grizzly country—specifically Montana, Idaho, and Wyoming. Yet the American Farm Bureau Federation acknowledges that less than 2 percent of the United States population still farm or ranch, and that fraction is falling. They make up just over a tenth of Montana's half-million workers. Arguing that grizzly bears cause fear and impinge on freedom is legitimate. But if you're worried about your way of life as a rancher, I'd be far more frightened about getting mauled by market forces than a grizzly bear.

In other words, we can't pretend to do things the way we always did them, because *always* has never existed in the context of American landscape management. In the space of two generations, we nearly eradicated the grizzly bear from the Lower 48 states. We've spent about one generation actively trying to restore them, using methods that run counter to the grizzly's thousands of years of evolution and adaptation to a plains habitat that we insist on using for other purposes.

So this is a test and there is a time limit. Satellite maps of the planet show we've radically transformed a fifth of the earth's habitable surface between 1992 and 2015, increasing the size of the Sahara Desert, shrinking wetlands in the southeastern US, and urbanizing vast populations in China and India. The number of chronically undernourished people in the world grew from 777 million in 2015 to 820 million in 2019. Migration crises like North Africans moving to Europe or Rohingya moving to India or Central Americans moving to the United States aren't simply the effect of political or social disputes. Each refugee upheaval can be traced to an environmental factor, frequently droughts degrading food and water supplies.

Meanwhile, just twenty nations oversee 94 percent of the remaining wild land on the planet. The United States is among five countries with dominion over nearly three-quarters of that supply, along with Russia, Canada, Australia, and Brazil. The biggest swath of the continental US portion overlays the grizzly bear recovery areas of Montana, Idaho, Wyoming, and Washington.

To preserve the wild grizzly bear, we must preserve those wild places. But we could make other choices. If you were Noah standing at the ark in the rain with room left for one more creature, would you let in the unicorn or the leviathan? Would you make room for a symbol of tranquility and beauty, or the one the Bible called "the king over all the children of pride"?

We *Homo sapiens* have positioned ourselves as the judges of *Ursus arctos horribilis*' fate. We must decide why it matters. To determine the fate of the grizzly bear, it must have a worth to weigh. Safari Club International has filed friend-of-the-court briefs valuing the grizzly by the desire its members have to kill one as a trophy. Illicit medical markets put steep price tags on grizzly gall bladders, paws, and other body parts. Photography schools sell expensive workshops focused on commuting a grizzly into pixels. Advocacy groups propel fundraising campaigns with posters of grizzlies, especially sows with cubs. Wyoming artist Thomas Mangelsen has built a career around selling grizzly coffee table books, and Canadian hunting outfitters earn $25,000 per client whether they shoot a grizzly or not. Shortly after the grizzly was declared a threatened species in 1975, Montana schoolchildren overwhelmed a reluctant state legislature to make the bear Montana's state mammal. But when the US Fish and Wildlife Service proposed reintroducing grizzlies to the North Cascades National Park area, an Idaho legislator called the idea "nothing but a polite form of genocide" for the human residents. Do the two thousand grizzly bears lurking in the northern Rocky Mountain West reflect either vision—child's mascot or vicious threat? Does it matter what a real grizzly bear is before we play God with its future?

◄ ◄ ◄ · ► ► ►

Several analyses by both supporters and opponents of the Endangered Species Act show that some critters will never recover, no matter what effort we put in. Glacier National Park is home to a tiny stonefly that depends on meltwater from ice fields which in a few decades may no longer exist due to increased summer temperatures and shrinking snowfall. While industrial activity and urban pollution triggered those climactic disruptions, humans haven't found a solution to reverse them in time to save the stonefly. Will they be any better at resisting the forces of markets, recreation, and greed that impinge on the needs of grizzly bears?

This plays into a trait woven deep into the American character of the Frontier as a source of personal renewal, recreation, and unlimited resources. Despite warnings going all the way back to Frederick Jackson Turner that the Frontier's geographic and mythical edges had been reached by the end of the nineteenth century, we continue to presume that if we push a little further, we can leave our old mistakes behind; that with enough technology, we can fix whatever we put our mind and laws to. Clinging to this belief stifles the need to find answers in a limited world, bounded by competing interests and finite possibilities.

Murray and Nutter each define large parts of their lives through the act of living with grizzly bears. Both speak from experience, having looked grizzlies eyeball to eyeball, breathing the same air. That gives their testimonies weight. While I doubt they'd agree on the particulars, I'll bet both would say the encounters helped them describe what makes their lives matter.

Yet both stories have a common problem. They describe individual responses to specific animals in the wild. For the rest of the urbanized world lacking such personal observation, forming opinions about a creature that lives mostly in the mind depends as much on myth as method. Absorbing either Murray's or Nutter's story as your own reveals your values and wishes about where you fit in creation. Someone who resonates to Nutter's recollection will likely disagree with someone who is more partial to Murray's. Each thinks they are discussing the same species, but they each imagine very different beasts.

That matters because the fate of the grizzly bear will not be settled by rugged individualists who've lived on the frontier. It will resolve in a rule promulgated by a federal bureaucracy guided by influential vested interests and representing the will of the United States at large. The grizzlies that Murray and Nutter met did not belong to them (although they faced the possibility they might have become the possession of the bears, body and soul). Legally, those bears belong to all Americans. So does most of the landscape those bears depend on. That landscape and its community of life face unprecedented change and disruption just at the moment Americans hope to create some sort of permanent "normal" for the apex predator living there. The choice they make will affect every other plant and animal down the trophic cascade, from the elk and the wolves to the huckleberries and the sucker fish. It will affect the experience of every human who enters those wild places as a backpacker, hunter, bird-watcher, or prospector. It will make it easier or harder for those with aims to profit from the trees, crops, minerals, energy, or homesites available for harvest on those lands. Whether you've met a grizzly or not, you have a stake in its fate.

We all seek proof of our existence. Nineteenth-century writer Stephen Crane pinned it with his line: "A man said to the Universe: Sir, I exist. This is true, the universe replied. But that has not incurred in me any sense of obligation."

Overcoming that universal indifference is the point of existence. We all seek evidence of when we made the decision, took the action, felt the pain, witnessed the event, savored the joy. When we did something worth making a song about when we're gone.

And so we scrounge. We wear the jerseys of the sports teams we root for, vicariously sharing the victories and humiliations of our avatars who actually handle the ball. We buy tickets to the festivals, tour the battlefields, bronze the baby shoes, frame the diplomas, and otherwise signify our passage through life. We want to leave a mark. Some of us have created ways to experience intense existence without ever getting off the couch. Through video games, we negotiate life-and-death situations by the flexing of our thumbs, sometimes with 3-D goggles to complete the sensory plunge. Karaoke mic in hand, we soak up the applause of imaginary fans.

But does self-justification justify dominance? Ranchers and military veterans band together over shared sacrifices and shed blood, but their means can't automatically justify their ends. Because you saw a comrade die on the battlefield or pulled a calf out of its mother in a February blizzard does not mean your opinions on war or agricultural policy outweigh all contenders. Nor do your miles of backpacking or files of grizzly photos entitle you to determine wildlife management. Sweating is not a political act.

◄ ◄ ◄ · ► ► ►

When British colonists were debating the future shape of a revolutionary American government, they saw the world as a progression from a state of nature to a state of civil society. Nature was to be outgrown, evolved beyond, in favor of a more humanistic order. Political philosopher John Locke argued "God gave the world to men in common (but) it can not be supposed he meant it should always remain common and uncultivated. He gave it to the use of the Industrious and Rational (and Labour was to be his title to it)." Historian Jill Lepore points out the stunning irony in Locke's formulation, where he defines the rights of life, liberty, and property of white men as a God-given natural state, separate from "Negro slavery" which he excuses as a relationship between "a lawful conqueror and a captive."

I see two crucial elements in this foundational vision of American culture. One is the cramped value put on landscape, where if it does not display a brand or a boundary it must be going to unacceptable waste. It underpinned the presumption of anthropologist W. J. McGee, who in 1894 declared Americans showed virtue by "transforming the face of Nature, by making all things better than they were before, by aiding the good and destroying the bad among animals and plants and by protecting the aging earth from the ravages of time and failing strength." It allowed white settlers to praise the park-like forests of the Rocky Mountains without recognizing the effort Indian tribes expended regularly burning away the underbrush. That was cultivation on a decadal timeframe, outside the reference of farmers who only looked from spring to fall. And it never considers the possibility that wildlife communities might have their own systems of productivity with a value separate from a human price tag.

The second, more philosophical observation is the American tendency to define what's intolerable for us in terms of what we find acceptable for someone (or something) that's not us. Historian Lepore marvels at how Locke drafted the constitution for the colony of Carolina illuminating the rights of free citizens by contrast to the "vile and miserable estate" of slaves. He had to squirm through some logical contortions to establish how one form of human could be so separate from another.

As we become more aware of the interconnected state of the planet's ecology, might not the same be asked of human's relations with other creatures? American society does not hold that children or the intellectually disabled may be enslaved or killed for convenience, even as it does withhold some civil or legal privileges such as driving a car. Yet that's not the respect we offer to the grizzly bear, the only other creature that uses the landscape with the same impunity and violence we consider acceptable only amongst ourselves. Until the 1970s, Americans killed grizzly bears by government order, by state policy, and by personal whim. State and private interests argue that after federal delisting, such loosely justified killings of grizzly bears may resume, so long as we don't cross some arbitrary population threshold. And that legal argument holds that any grizzly bear which frightens a human or takes from a human's possessions deserves to be executed. Could we humans justify the same capital sentence on our own behavior?

Whether the grizzly bear gets granted legal standing or agency in American society, or more simply gets recognized as a ward of the nation deserving consideration of interests beyond the tiny minority of property owners directly in contact with them, the value of their lives deserves an honest and accurate accounting.

I don't propose some quasi-religious return to authentic nature. In *Uncommon Ground: Toward Reinventing Nature*, William Cronon joked about that false presumption: If nature dies because we enter it, then the only way to save nature is to kill ourselves. Neither do I presume we can invent some solution that sustains wild things without infringing on our convenience. Just because we have powerful tools to manipulate the global environment doesn't mean the planet won't push back. Any human believing that wasn't paying attention during the Covid-19 pandemic of 2020.

The viral nature of *Facebookii* grizzly bears has spread stories of their power and value far beyond the mapped boundaries of their Rocky

Mountain recovery zones. While that's created some unrealistic, even destructive impressions of the species, it has also given millions of Americans a visceral stake in the grizzly's survival. The avalanching pace of technology in our lives aggravates an understandable anxiety. But it also expands our awareness. And once you see and hear a grizzly bear, even on social media, you can no longer say you don't know or care about their existence.

In 2019, the United Nations Intergovernmental Science Policy Platform on Biodiversity and Ecosystem Services announced that one million plant and animal species stood on the verge of extinction, and "grave impacts on people around the world are now likely." Some of my ecologist friends took the news like their parents might have if told the nuclear missiles of the Cold War had launched. Game over. We lost. Terminal.

The Reverend Donald Guthrie, who made me rethink my understanding of "fear," also confounded me with the meaning of "terminal." It commonly defines an end or closing. But Guthrie poked a little further. In the world of travel, a terminal is also the place where one boards their bus or train or plane—the place where journeys begin as well as end. Its Indo-European root, *ter*, implies both a boundary and the act of crossing or going beyond.

I drive by some of those nuclear missile silos every time I go to the east side of Glacier National Park. We did not blow up the world then. We found other ways of settling disputes, by raising standards of living rather than resorting to standards of war. I believe our species' best chance of surviving the coming global disruption requires doing things differently, rather than doing the same things harder.

The challenge, then, is where to start. I offer the grizzly bear. Making life better for grizzlies requires humans to rethink their acceptance of risk, their tolerance for inconvenience, and their responsibility for the long-term consequences of actions they've avoided in the past. It might require envisioning the management of landscapes less for short-term gain, and for more than just human benefit. We may have to hunt grizzly bears but leave their trophies in the woods. The people who want to see wild places managed for wildness will need to pay for conserving those wild qualities the same way hunters have long paid taxes to support the wildlife they like to kill.

All this will require progress, rather than stasis. Because of the grizzly bear's keystone ecological status, choices affecting it will amplify our efforts for thousands of other plants and animals and landscapes. Those choices matter. Whether we lean toward free-ranging co-existence or to artificial containment, our actions will have impact on a global scale. That may seem miraculous, but to quote St. Augustine, "Miracles are not contrary to nature, but only contrary to what we know about nature."

We have to make that choice, without benefit of some artificial intelligence algorithm. In a single life form, the grizzly bear contains all the elements of nature we can't control: its beauty, its indifference, its complexity, its terror and wonder, and its vulnerability. Keeping the grizzly commits us to limiting our influence over the planet, to letting some places retain the resources and processes they've depended upon for eons longer than we've controlled fire and wheels. That takes humility.

Still, grizzlies eat humans. They pose a threat to our survival, however disproportionate. We could eliminate them at any time. We nearly did so once, and can easily do so again.

That action carries a price. Yet we handle the tools we'd use with all the responsibility of a toddler carrying a crystal goblet: He's using both hands, but you can't say he's really in control.

My Norwegian grandmother Nell gave me my first book about grizzly bears in 1974, the year before *Ursus arctos horribilis* landed on the Endangered Species list. She loved adventure, telling me stories about the Vikings who would send their dead kings out to sea in a flaming ship loaded with the kingdom's treasure. But she also told me about the explorers who, upon sailing to a new land, would burn their ships on the beach. That focused the crew on seeking solutions ahead—because there was no going back.

ACKNOWLEDGMENTS

I am grateful for interviews with tribal members and elders including John Murray, Jimmy St. Goddard, Joe Durglo, Johnny Arlee, Patrick Weasel Head, and Jack Gladstone; as well as written accounts by George Bird Grinnell, Frank Linderman, and James Willard Schultz.

For guidance on the evolution of human technology, I am especially indebted to American Computer Museum director George Keremedjiev. I also received advice and resources from Christopher Preston, author of *The Synthetic Age*. Emma Marris and E. O. Wilson both personally gave great interviews that helped structure my thoughts.

University of Montana Bolle Center director Martin Nie was a valuable sounding board for explaining Endangered Species Act policy debates. David Mattson was also essential in personal interviews.

None of this would be possible without the patience and accessibility of the research community orbiting grizzly bears in the Rocky Mountains. They include Kate Kendall, Michael Proctor, Rick Mace, Joel Berger, Mark Hebblewhite, Wayne Kasworm, Sandra Zellmer, Frank van Manan, Cecily Costello, Louisa Willcox, Keriy Gunderson, and Hilary Cooley. A Nieman fellowship at Harvard University gave me access to the intellects of Ian Miller and Michael Jackson, who opened great vistas into the nature of environmental history and storytelling.

But most of all I appreciate the contributions of Jamie Jonkel of the Montana Department of Fish, Wildlife and Parks for leading me through grizzly country, and Chris Servheen of the US Fish and Wildlife Service for guiding me through the maze of grizzly policy.

SELECTED REFERENCES

PREFACE. FEAR THE BEAR

Edwards, J. Gordon. *A Climber's Guide to Glacier National Park.* Oakland, CA: Sierra Club, 1966.

Goff, Paepin, and David R. Butler. "James Dyson (1948) Shrinkage of Sperry and Grinnell Glaciers, Glacier National Park, Montana." *Geographical Review* 38, no. 1: 95–103; *Progress in Physical Geography* 40, no. 4 (2016): 616–21.

McKibben, Bill. *The End of Nature.* New York: Random House, 1989.

Olsen, Jack. *Night of the Grizzlies.* New York: Putnam Publishing Group, 1969.

CHAPTER 1. ENTERING GRIZZLY COUNTRY

Burke, Monte. "America's Largest Landowners." *Forbes Magazine,* November 2015.

Dood, Arnold R., Robert D. Brannon, Richard D. Mace, and Montana Department of Fish, Wildlife and Parks. *Final Programmatic Environmental Impact Statement: The Grizzly Bear in Northwestern Montana, Summary.* Helena: Montana Department of Fish, Wildlife and Parks, 1986.

Servheen, Christopher, and US Fish and Wildlife Service. *Grizzly Bear Recovery Plan.* Missoula, MT: US Fish and Wildlife Service, 1982.

CHAPTER 2. *Ursus horribilis Facebookii*

Clark, Susan G., and Murray B. Rutherford. *Large Carnivore Conservation: Integrating Science and Policy in the North American West.* Chicago: University of Chicago Press, 2014.

Farese, Nancy. Shorenstein Center on Media, personal interview, 2019.

Forrester, J. A., C. P. Holstege, and J. D. Forrester. "Fatalities from Venomous and Nonvenomous Animals in the United States (1999–2007)." *Wilderness and Environmental Medicine* 23, no. 2 (2012): 146–52.

Leclerc, M., S. C. Frank, A. Zedrosser, J. E. Swenson, and F. Pelletier. "Hunting Promotes Spatial Reorganization and Sexually Selected Infanticide." *Scientific Reports* 7, no. 1 (2017): 45222.

McMillion, Scott. *Mark of the Grizzly.* 2nd ed. Guilford, CT: Lyons Press, 2012. 1st ed. 1998.

Mikkelson, David. "Did Disney Fake Lemming Deaths for the Nature Documentary 'White Wilderness'?" *Snopes.com*, February 1996.

Press, Gil. "A Very Short History of Digitization." *Forbes Magazine*, December 2015.

Primm, Steve. "The Drone That Stalked a Bear Cub and Nearly Pushed It Over the Edge." *Mountain Journal*, November 2018.

Servheen, Chris. *Board of Review Report: Fatality of Mr. Lance Crosby from a Bear Attack on Elephant Back Mountain in Yellowstone National Park on August 6, 2015.* US Fish and Wildlife Service, 2016.

Wright, William H. *The Grizzly Bear.* Lincoln: University of Nebraska Press, 1909.

CHAPTER 3. THE ONLY GOOD BEAR

Allendorf, F. "No Separation between Present and Future." In *Moral Ground: Ethical Action for a Planet in Peril*, edited by Kathleen Dean Moore and Michael P. Nelson. San Antonio, TX: Trinity University Press, 2010.

Black, Megan. *The Global Interior.* Cambridge, MA: Harvard University Press, 2018.

Hemingway, Ernest. *Under Kilimanjaro.* Edited by Robert W. Lewis and Robert F. Fleming. Kent, OH: Kent State University Press, 2005.

Hemingway, Ernest, and Seán A. Hemingway. *Hemingway on Hunting.* New York: Scribner, 2003.

Jackson, Michael. *The Politics of Storytelling: Variations on a Theme by Hannah Arendt.* Copenhagen: Museum Tusculanum Press, 2013.

Knibb, David. *Grizzly Wars: The Public Fight over the Great Bear.* Spokane: Eastern Washington University Press, 2008.

Lapinski, Mike. *Grizzlies and Grizzled Old Men: A Tribute to Those Who Fought to Save the Great Bear.* Guilford, CT: Falcon, 2006.

Latour, Bruno. "Agency at the Time of the Anthropocene." *New Literary History* 45, no. 1 (2014): 1–18.

Murie, Adolph. "Cattle on Grizzly Bear Range." *Journal of Wildlife Management* 12, no. 1 (1948): 57–72.

Posewitz, J. *Beyond Fair Chase: The Ethic and Tradition of Hunting*. Guilford, CT: Falcon Guides, 2002.

Prodgers, Jeanette. *The Only Good Bear Is a Dead Bear*. Helena, MT: TwoDot, 1986.

Quammen, David. *Monster of God: The Man-Eating Predator in the Jungles of History and the Mind*. New York: W. W. Norton, 2003.

CHAPTER 4. SPIRIT ANIMAL

Berry, Wendell. *The World-Ending Fire*. London: Penguin Books, 2017.

Christensen, Chief District Judge Dana. Order Vacating Final Rule of the US Fish and Wildlife Service Delisting the Greater Yellowstone Ecosystem Population of Grizzly Bears. Case CV 17-89-M-DLC. Filed September 24, 2018, US District Court for the District of Montana.

Cronon, William. *Uncommon Ground: Toward Reinventing Nature*. New York: W. W. Norton, 1995.

Crow Indian Tribe et al. vs. United States of America and Ryan Zinke. Case 9:17-cv-00089-DLC-JCL, Petition for Permanent Injunction and Declaratory Relief. Filed June 30, 2017, US District Court for the District of Montana.

Flores, Dan. *American Serengeti: The Last Big Animals of the Great Plains*. Lawrence: University Press of Kansas, 2016.

———. *The Natural West: Environmental History in the Great Plains and Rocky Mountains*. Norman: University of Oklahoma Press, 2001.

Gaston, K. Healan. *Imagining Judeo-Christian America: Religion, Secularism, and the Redefinition of Democracy*. Chicago: University of Chicago Press, 2019.

Hatley, James. "The Uncanny Goodness of Being Edible to Bears." In *Rethinking Nature: Essays in Environmental Philosophy*, edited by Bruce Foltz and Robert Frodeman. Bloomington: Indiana University Press, 2004.

Kimmerer, Robin Wall. *Braiding Sweetgrass: Indigenous Wisdom, Scientific Knowledge, and the Teachings of Plants*. Minneapolis, MN: Milkweed Editions, 2013.

Marris, Emma. *Rambunctious Garden: Saving Nature in a Post-wild World*. New York: Bloomsbury USA, 2011.

Nelson, Richard. *Make Prayers to the Raven: A Koyukon View of the Northern Forest*. Chicago: University of Chicago Press, 1983.

Pope Francis. *On Care for Our Common Home: Laudato Si'; The Encyclical of Pope Francis on the Environment*. With commentary by Sean McDonagh. Maryknoll, NY: Orbis Books, 2016.

Rockwell, David. *Giving Voice to Bear: North American Indian Myths, Rituals, and Images of the Bear*. Lanham, MD: Roberts Rinehart, 2003.

Tetlock, Barbara. *The Woman in the Shaman's Body: Reclaiming the Feminine in Religion and Medicine*. New York: Bantam Books, 2005.

White, Richard. *The Organic Machine: The Remaking of the Columbia River*. New York: Hill and Wang, 1995.

CHAPTER 5. FROM A SINGLE HAIR

Benson, Etienne. *Wired Wilderness: Technologies of Tracking and the Making of Modern Wildlife*. Baltimore, MD: John Hopkins University Press, 2010.

Berger, Joel. *The Better to Eat You With: Fear in the Animal World*. Chicago: University of Chicago Press, 2008.

Boulanger, J., K. Kendall, J. Stetz, D. Roon, L. Waits, and D. Paetkau. "Multiple Data Sources Improve DNA-Based Mark-Recapture Population Estimates of Grizzly Bears." *Ecological Applications* 18, no. 3 (2008): 577–89.

Chase, Alston. *Playing God in Yellowstone: The Destruction of America's First National Park*. San Diego: Harcourt Brace Jovanovich, 1987.

Craighead, Frank C., and John J. Craighead. "Grizzly Bear Prehibernation and Denning Activities as Determined by Radiotracking." *Wildlife Monographs* 32 (1972): 3–35.

Craighead, John J., and Frank C. Craighead. "Grizzly Bear–Man Relationships in Yellowstone National Park." *BioScience* 21, no. 16 (1971): 845–57.

Craighead, John J., Jay S. Sumner, and John A. Mitchell. *The Grizzly Bears of Yellowstone: Their Ecology in the Yellowstone Ecosystem, 1959–1992*. Washington, DC: Island Press, 1995.

Craighead, John J., Jay S. Sumner, and Gordon B. Scaggs. *A Definitive System for Analysis of Grizzly Bear Habitat and Other Wilderness Resources, Utilizing LANDSAT Multispectral Imagery and Computer Technology*. Wildlife-Wildlands Institute Monograph, no. 1. Missoula: University of Montana, 1982.

Kendall, Katherine C., Amy C. Macleod, Kristina L. Boyd, John Boulanger, J. Andrew Royle, Wayne F. Kasworm, David Paetkau, et al. "Density, Distribution, and Genetic Structure of Grizzly Bears in the Cabinet-Yaak Ecosystem." *Journal of Wildlife Management* 80, no. 2 (2016): 314–31.

Kendall, Katherine C., Jeffrey B. Stetz, David A. Roon, Lisette P. Waits, John B. Boulanger, and David Paetkau. "Grizzly Bear Density in Glacier National Park, Montana." *Journal of Wildlife Management* 72, no. 8 (2008): 1693–1705.

Leopold, Aldo. *A Sand County Almanac: With Essays on Conservation*. New York: Oxford University Press, 2001.

Long, Ben. *Great Montana Bear Stories*. Helena, MT: Riverbend Publishing, 2002.

McKelvey, Kevin S., Michael K. Young, Taylor M. Wilcox, Daniel M. Bing-ham, Kristine L. Pilgrim, and Michael K. Schwartz. "Patterns of Hybrid-ization among Cutthroat Trout and Rainbow Trout in Northern Rocky Mountain Streams." *Ecology and Evolution* 6 (2016): 688–706.

Quammen, David. *The Tangled Tree: A Radical New History of Life.* New York: Simon & Schuster, 2018.

Smith, Jordan Fisher. *Engineering Eden: The True Story of a Violent Death, a Trial, and the Fight over Controlling Nature.* New York: Crown Publishing, 2016.

White, Don, Jr., Katherine C. Kendall, and Harold D. Picton. "Grizzly Bear Feeding Activity at Alpine Army Cutworm Moth Aggregation Sites in North-west Montana." *Canadian Journal of Zoology/Revue Canadien de Zoologie* 76, no. 2 (1998): 221–27.

Wilcox, Taylor M., Kevin S. McKelvey, Michael K. Young, Adam J. Sepulveda, Bradley B. Shepard, Stephen F. Jane, Andrew R. Whiteley, Winsor H. Lowe, and Michael K. Schwartz. "Understanding Environmental DNA Detection Probabilities: A Case Study Using a Stream-Dwelling Char Salvelinus fonti-nalis." *Biological Conservation* 194 (2016): 209–16.

Wilson, E. O. *Half-Earth: Our Planet's Fight for Life.* New York: Liveright, 2016.

CHAPTER 6. ETHYL'S RAMBLE

Allendorf, F., and C. Servheen. "Genetics and the Conservation of Grizzly Bears." *Trends in Ecology and Evolution* 1, no. 4 (1986): 88–89.

Bruskotter, Jeremy T., Sherry A. Enzler, and Adrian Treves. "Rescuing Wolves from Politics: Wildlife as a Public Trust Resource." *Science* 333, no. 6051 (2011): 1828–29.

Bruskotter, Jeremy T., John A. Vucetich, Kristina M. Slagle, Ramiro Berardo, Ajay S. Singh, and Robyn S. Wilson. "Support for the U.S. Endangered Species Act over Time and Space: Controversial Species Do Not Weaken Public Support for Protective Legislation." *Conservation Letters* 11, no. 6 (2018).

Chaney, Robert. "Grizzly's 2800-Mile Montana, Idaho Ramble Intrigues Experts." *Missoulian*, December 10, 2014.

———. "Grizzly Conference Precedes Delisting Decisions." *Missoulian*, Octo-ber 15, 2017.

Cubaynes, Sarah, Daniel R. MacNulty, Daniel R. Stahler, Kira A. Quimby, Douglas W. Smith, and Tim Coulson. "Density-Dependent Intraspecific

Aggression Regulates Survival in Northern Yellowstone Wolves (*Canis lupus*)." *Journal of Animal Ecology* 83, 6 (2014): 1344–56.

Dax, Michael J. *Grizzly West: A Failed Attempt to Reintroduce Grizzly Bears in the Mountain West.* Lincoln: University of Nebraska Press, 2015.

Mattson, David. Personal interview, 2019.

———. "Use of Ungulates by Yellowstone Grizzly Bears *Ursus arctos.*" *Biological Conservation* 8, no. 1–2 (1997): 161–77.

Pease, Craig, and David Mattson. "Demography of the Yellowstone Grizzly Bears." *Ecology* 80, no. 3 (1999): 957–75.

Savage, C. "The Ripple Effect: When 31 Canadian Wolves Were Relocated to Yellowstone National Park, the Impact Was Swift and Surprising." *Canadian Geographic* 123, no. 5 (2003): 66–76.

US Fish and Wildlife Service. *Grizzly Bear Recovery Plan, Supplement: Habitat-Based Criteria for the Northern Continental Ecosystem.* Missoula, MT: US Fish and Wildlife Service, 2018. 20180516_SignedFinal_HBRC_NCDE _Grizz.pdf.

CHAPTER 7. THE BEAR ON THE BICYCLE

Flathead National Forest, Montana. *Revision of the Land Management Plan for the Flathead National Forest and an Amendment of the Helena, Kootenai, Lewis and Clark, and Lolo National Forest Plans to Incorporate Relevant Direction from the Northern Continental Divide Ecosystem Grizzly Bear Conservation.* Washington, DC: USDA Forest Service, 2015.

Headwaters Economics. "Montana Losing Open Space." April 2018. https:// headwaterseconomics.org/economic-development/local-studies/montana -home-construction.

Naylor, Leslie M., Michael J. Wisdom, and Robert G. Anthony. "Behavioral Responses of North American Elk to Recreational Activity." *Journal of Wildlife Management* 73, no. 3 (2009): 328–38.

Proctor, Michael F., Wayne F. Kasworm, Kimberly M. Annis, A. Grant Machutchon, Justin E. Teisberg, Thomas G. Radandt, and Chris Servheen. "Conservation of Threatened Canada-USA Trans-border Grizzly Bears Linked to Comprehensive Conflict Reduction." *Human–Wildlife Interactions* 12, no. 3 (2018): 348–72.

Servheen, Chris. *Board of Review Report: The Death of Mr. Brad Treat due to a Grizzly Bear Attack June 29, 2016, on the Flathead National Forest.* Prepared for Interagency Grizzly Bear Committee, March 3, 2017.

Sinnott, Rick. "When Cyclists Collide with Bears." *Anchorage Daily News,* December 2, 2017.

CHAPTER 8. ROADKILL

Barker, Rocky. *Saving All the Parts: Reconciling Economics and the Endangered Species Act*. Washington, DC: Island Press, 1993.

Bellringer, Carol. *An Independent Audit of Grizzly Bear Management*. Victoria: Office of the Auditor General of British Columbia, October 2017.

Chaney, Robert. "Grizzly Roadmap: Studies Show Grizzlies Finding Their Way around People." *Missoulian*, October 30, 2017.

Costello, Cecily, Richard D. Mace, and Lori Roberts. *Grizzly Bear Demographics in the Northern Continental Divide Ecosystem 2004–2014: Research Results and Techniques for Management of Mortality*. Helena: Montana Department of Fish, Wildlife and Parks, 2016.

Gailus, Jeff. *Failing B.C.'s Grizzlies: Report Card and Recommendations for Ensuring a Future for British Columbia's Grizzly Bears*. Vancouver, BC: David Suzuki Foundation, 2014.

Proctor, Michael F., Bruce McLellan, Gordon B. Stenhouse, Garth Mowat, Clayton T. Lamb, and Mark S. Boyce. *Resource Roads and Grizzly Bears in British Columbia and Alberta, Canada*. Canadian Grizzly Bear Management Series. 2018. https://doi.org/10.13140/RG.2.2.11780.83846.

van Manan, Frank T., Mark A. Haroldson, Daniel D. Bjornlie, Michael R. Ebinger, Daniel J. Thompson, Cecily M. Costello, and Gary C. White. "Density Dependence, Whitebark Pine, and Vital Rates of Grizzly Bears." *Journal of Wildlife Management* 80, no. 2 (2016): 300–13.

CHAPTER 9. GRISLY HUNTING

Brinkley, Douglas. *The Wilderness Warrior: Theodore Roosevelt and the Crusade for America*. New York: Harper Perennial, 2010.

Chaney, Robert. "Forest Service Tried to Quash Paper Debunking Montana Wildlife Authority." *Missoulian*, September 24, 2017.

———. "Wilderness Institute Looks to Future with New Leader." *Missoulian*, February 1, 2019.

Emlen, Douglas J. *Animal Weapons: The Evolution of Battle*. New York: Henry Holt, 2014.

Frank, Shane C., Andrés Ordiz, Jacinthe Gosselin, Anne Hertel, Jonas Kindberg, Martin Leclerc, Fanie Pelletier, et al. "Indirect Effects of Bear Hunting: A Review from Scandinavia." *Ursus* 28, no. 2 (2007): 150–64.

Herrero, Stephen. *Bear Attacks: Their Causes and Avoidance*. Piscataway, NJ: Winchester Press, 1985.

Hertel, Anne G., Andreas Zedrosser, Atle Mysterud, Ole-Gunnar Støen, Sam M. J. G. Steyaert, and Jon E. Swenson. "Temporal Effects of Hunting on

Foraging Behavior of an Apex Predator: Do Bears Forego Foraging When Risk Is High?" *Oecologia* 182, no. 4 (2016): 1–11.

Kindberg, Jonas, Jon E. Swenson, Göran Ericsson, Eva Bellemain, Christian Miquel, and Pierre Taberlet. "Estimating Population Size and Trends of the Swedish Brown Bear *Ursus arctos* Population." *Wildlife Biology* 17, no. 2 (2011): 114–23.

Marcus, W. Andrew, James Meacham, Ann Rodman, and Alethea Steingisser. *Atlas of Yellowstone.* Berkeley: University of California Press, 2012.

Miller, Sterling D. "Trends in Brown Bear Reduction Efforts in Alaska, 1980–2017." *Ursus* 28, no. 2 (2017): 135–49.

Nie, Martin. "State Wildlife Policy and Management: The Scope and Bias of Political Conflict." *Public Administration Review* 64, no. 2 (2004): 221–33.

Pollan, Michael. *The Omnivore's Dilemma: A Natural History of Four Meals.* New York: Penguin Press, 2006.

Ripple, William J., Sterling D. Miller, John W. Schoen, and Sanford P. Rabinowitch. "Large Carnivores under Assault in Alaska." *PLOS Biology* 17, no. 1 (2019): e3000090.

Roosevelt, Theodore. *The Wilderness Hunter: An Account of the Big Game of the United States and Its Chase with Horse, Hound, and Rifle.* Birmingham, AL: Palladium Press, 1999.

Smith, Tom S., and Stephen, Herrero. "Human-Bear Conflict in Alaska: 1880–2015." *Wildlife Society Bulletin* 42, no. 2 (2018): 254–63.

Treves, Adrian, Guillaume Chapron, Jose V. López-Bao, Chase Shoemaker, Apollonia R. Goeckner, and Jeremy T. Bruskotter. "Predators and the Public Trust." *Biological Reviews* 92, no. 1 (2017): 248–70.

US Department of the Interior, US Fish and Wildlife Service, and US Department of Commerce, US Census Bureau. *2016 National Survey of Fishing, Hunting, and Wildlife-Associated Recreation.* Washington, DC, April 2018. (Addenda published 2019.)

Van de Walle, Joanie, Gabriel Pigeon, Andreas Zedrosser, Jon E. Swenson, and Fanie Pelletier. "Hunting Regulation Favors Slow Life Histories in a Large Carnivore." *Nature Communications* 9, no. 1100 (2018). https://doi.org/10.1038/s41467-018-03506-3.

CHAPTER 10. GRIZZLY AT LAW

Filaroski, Curtis. "Single-Minded Determination: The Problems with the Endangered Species Act and the Consensus on Fixing Species Conservation Law through a Focus on Ecosystems and Biodiversity." *Journal of Environmental Law and Litigation* 30 (2015): 57–341.

Schwartz, Charles, Jon Swenson, and Sterling Miller. "Large Carnivores, Moose and Humans: A Changing Paradigm of Predator Management in the 21st Century." *Alces* 39 (2003): 41–63.

Sutter, Paul. *Driven Wild: How the Fight against Automobiles Launched the Modern Wilderness Movement.* Seattle: University of Washington Press, 2002.

Wood, Jonathan. *The Road to Recovery: How Restoring the Endangered Species Act's Two-Step Process Can Prevent Extinction and Promote Recovery.* PERC Policy Report. Bozeman, MT: Property and Environment Research Center, April 2018.

CHAPTER II. BEARS OF THE WORLD

Asafu-Adjaye, John, Linus Blomqvist, Stewart Brand, Barry Brook, Ruth DeFries, Erle Ellis, Christopher Foreman, et al. *An Ecomodernist Manifesto.* April 2015, www.ecomodernism.org.

Clark, Susan G., and Murray S. Rutherford, eds. *Large Carnivore Conservation: Integrating Science and Policy in the North American West.* Chicago: University of Chicago Press, 2014.

Faurby, Søren, Matt Davis, Rasmus Ø. Pedersen, Simon D. Schowanek, Alexandre Antonelli, and Jens-Christian Svenning. "PHYLACINE 1.2: The Phylogenetic Atlas of Mammal Macroecology." *Ecology* 99, no. 11 (2018): 2626.

McPhee, John. *Coming into the Country.* New York: Farrar, Straus and Giroux, 1976.

Miller, David, et al. *Surviving Large Carnivores Have Far-Reaching Impact.* Pennsylvania State University, College of Agricultural Sciences, August 2018.

Preston, Christopher. *The Synthetic Age: Outdesigning Evolution, Resurrecting Species and Reengineering Our World.* Cambridge, MA: MIT Press, 2018.

Purdy, Jedediah. *This Land Is Our Land.* Princeton, NJ: Princeton University Press, 2019.

Roopnarine, Peter D., Kenneth D. Angielczyk, Savannah L. Olroyd, Sterling J. Nesbitt, Jennifer Botha-brink, Brandon R. Peecook, Michael O. Day, and Roger M. H. Smith. "Comparative Ecological Dynamics of Permian-Triassic Communities from the Karoo, Luangwa, and Ruhuhu Basins of Southern Africa." *Journal of Vertebrate Paleontology* 37 (2017): 254–72.

Thompson, Roger. *No Word for Wilderness: Italy's Grizzlies and the Race to Save the Rarest Bears on Earth.* Ashland, OR: Ashland Creek Press, 2018.

Wilson, Seth. *A Guidebook to Human–Carnivore Conflict: Strategies and Tips for Effective Communication and Collaboration with Communities.* Ljubljana, Slovenia: LIFE DINALP BEAR Project, 2016.

Douglas, William O. *The Three Hundred Year War: A Chronicle of Ecological Disaster*. New York: Random House, 1972.

Lepore, Jill. *These Truths: A History of the United States*. New York: W. W. Norton, 2018.

Pearce, Fred. "How Big Water Projects Helped Trigger Africa's Migrant Crisis." *Yale Environment 360*, October 17, 2017.

United Nations. "UN Report: Nature's Dangerous Decline 'Unprecedented'; Species Extinction Rates 'Accelerating.'" *Sustainable Development Goals* (blog), May 6, 2019. https://www.un.org/sustainabledevelopment/blog /2019/05/nature-decline-unprecedented-report.

GENERAL REFERENCES

Abbey, Edward. *Desert Solitaire: A Season in the Wilderness*. Tucson: University of Arizona Press, 1988.

———. *The Monkey Wrench Gang*. Salt Lake City: Dream Garden Press, 1999.

Ambrose, Stephen. *Undaunted Courage: Meriwether Lewis, Thomas Jefferson, and the Opening of the American West*. New York: Simon & Schuster, 1996.

Bass, Rick. *The Lost Grizzlies: A Search for Survivors in the Wilderness of Colorado*. Boston: Houghton Mifflin, 1995.

Campbell, Joseph. *The Power of Myth*. In collaboration with Bill Moyers. New York: Anchor Books, 1991.

Chadwick, Douglas H. *Tracking Gobi Grizzlies: Surviving beyond the Back of Beyond*. Ventura, CA: Patagonia, 2016.

———. *The Wolverine Way*. Ventura, CA: Patagonia, 2010.

Cheek, Roland. *Learning to Talk Bear: So Bears Can Listen*. Columbia Falls, MT: Skyline Publishing, 2000.

Clarke, James F. *Man Is the Prey*. New York: Stein and Day, 1969.

Cole, David, and Laurie Young, eds. *Beyond Naturalness: Rethinking Park and Wilderness Stewardship*. Washington, DC: Island Press, 2010.

Craighead, Frank C., Jr. *Track of the Grizzly*. San Francisco: Sierra Club Books, 1982.

Craighead, John J., Jay Sumner, and John A. Michell. *The Grizzly Bears of Yellowstone: Their Ecology in the Yellowstone Ecosystem, 1959–1992*. Washington, DC: Island Press, 1995.

Eisenberg, Cristina. *The Carnivore Way: Coexisting with and Conserving North America's Predators*. Washington, DC: Island Press, 2014.

———. *The Wolf's Tooth: Keystone Predators, Trophic Cascades, and Biodiversity*. Washington, DC: Island Press, 2010.

Gertner, Jon. *The Idea Factory: Bell Labs and the Great Age of American Innovation.* New York: Penguin Books, 2013.

Gleick, James. *The Information: A History, a Theory, a Flood.* New York: Pantheon Books, 2011.

Long, Ben. *Backtracking: By Foot, Canoe, and Subaru along the Lewis and Clark Trail.* Seattle: Sasquatch Books, 2000.

———. *Great Montana Bear Stories.* Helena, MT: Riverbend Publishing, 2002.

Lyon, Ted B., and Will N. Graves. *The Real Wolf: Science, Politics and Economics of Co-existing with Wolves in Modern Times.* Self-published, 2014.

McNamee, Thomas. *The Grizzly Bear.* New York: Knopf, 1984.

Nie, Martin A. *Beyond Wolves: The Politics of Wolf Recovery and Management.* Minneapolis: University of Minnesota Press, 2003.

Peacock, Doug, and Andrea Peacock. *The Essential Grizzly: The Mingled Fates of Men and Bears.* Guilford, CT: Lyons Press, 2006.

———. *Grizzly Years: In Search of the American Wilderness.* New York: H. Holt, 1990.

Pozewitz, Jim. *My Best Shot: Discovering and Living the Montana Conservation Ethic.* Helena, MT: Riverbend Publishing, 2018.

Quammen, David. *Monster of God: The Man-Eating Predator in the Jungles of History and the Mind.* New York: W. W. Norton, 2003.

Robisch, S. K. *Wolves and the Wolf Myth in American Literature.* Reno: University of Nevada Press, 2009.

Russell, Andy. *Grizzly Country.* New York: Knopf, 1967.

Salish–Pend d'Oreille Cultural Committee and Elders Advisory Council, Confederated Salish and Kootenai Tribes. *The Salish People and the Lewis and Clark Expedition.* Lincoln: University of Nebraska Press, 2005.

Shivik, John. *The Predator Paradox: Ending the War with Wolves, Bears, Cougars, and Coyotes.* Boston: Beacon Press, 2014.

Storl, Wolf D. *Bear: Myth, Animal, Icon.* Berkeley: North Atlantic Books, 2018.

Urbigkit, Cat. *Return of the Grizzly: Sharing the Range with Yellowstone's Top Predator.* New York: Skyhorse Publishing, 2018.

INDEX

Indigenous traditions and, 72–73; radio collars and, 94–95

highway crossing structure: for wildlife, 161

Holocene era, 72

Homo sapiens, 71; fate of grizzly and, 237; fire and, 140; phobias of, 37

honeyroll, 49

House of the Sun, 75

huckleberry, 127, 138, 145, 224

Hudson Bay Company, 45

human performance, 154–55

Hungry Horse News, 40, 62

Hunt, Carrie, 60, 67

hunter safety, 181

hunting: in British Columbia, 223; of grizzly bear, 56–59, 163, 169–91; of Montana grizzly, 62, 177; North American Model of Wildlife Conservation and, 185–86; safety of, 181–82

Hutterite: as colony, 125–26; farming by, 84–86

hyperphagia, 145

ID mark, 93

IGBC. *See* Interagency Grizzly Bear Committee (IGBC)

Iglulik seance, 77

inbreeding, 124

India: Chris Servheen and, 122, 132, 138; Facebook and, 44; Gir lions in, 124; sacred cows in, 84; satellite maps and, 236; *Ursus arctos* habitat in, 210

infanticide, 25

Innuit community, 75

Interagency Grizzly Bear Committee (IGBC): anthropomorphic content and, 34; Bitterroot Subcommittee of, 157; Chip Weber report to, 138; competing values and, 82–83; composition of, 11–15; Gregg Losinski and, 128; grizzly delisting and, 122;

Jack Gladstone and, 78–79; Kate Kendall and, 102, 120, 187–88; Maggie Nutter and, 233–34; Mike Bader and, 132, 167; purpose of, 70; review of Treat incident and, 135; Standing Grizzly Bear and, 67–68; state conservation strategy and, 203

Interagency Grizzly Bear Study Team, 107, 118, 120, 162

Interior Appropriations Subcommittee, 105

International Human-Bear Conflict Workshop, 61

International Mountain Bicycling Association (IMBA), 148

International Union for Conservation of Nature (IUCN): 2018 Red List, 228

International Wildlife Film Festival, 3

Internet Age, 38–39; bear presence in, 23–26

IUCN. *See* International Union for Conservation of Nature (IUCN)

Ivan the Terrible (bear), 92

Jackson, Andrew, 49

Jefferson, Thomas, 46

Jersey barrier, 159

Jobs, Steve, 100

Jonkel, Chuck: Border Grizzly Project and, 18; career of, 3–6; differential calculus and, 11; Joe Durglo and, 67–68

Jonkel, Jamie, 5; bear tracking and, 11; Bitterroot golf course grizzly and, 156–57; grizzly mortality and, 159; Mike Bader and, 130

Kant, Immanuel, 72, 83

Kasworm, Wayne, 95, 137

Kellert, Stephen, 79–84

Kelsey, Henry, 45

Kendall, Kate, 101–7; conservation strategy and, 167

transplanting: of grizzlies, 25–26, 132, 139, 157, 214
transport, mechanized, 141
trap, cone, 231–32
trap, culvert, 22
travel corridor: computerized mapping of, 157–59
Treadwell, Timothy, 41–42
Treat, Brad, 134, 139–43
Treat, Somer, 143–44
Trevor, Cathleen, 201
trout. *See* bull trout; cutthroat trout; lake trout
Truman, Harry, 17
Tso'Ai, 75
Turner, Frederick Jackson, 238
Turner, Leo, 62–65
Tyer, Dan, 145–46

Uighur ethnic group, 112
United Nations Intergovernmental Science Policy Platform on Biodeversity and Ecosystem Service, 242
Uptain, Mark, 181
Ursa Major, 209
Ursa Minor, 209
Ursus americanus. See black bear (*Ursus americanus*)
Ursus arctos, 209, 210, ix
Ursus arctos arctos, 221
Ursus arctos horribilis. See grizzly bear (*Ursus arctos horribilis*)
Ursus horribilis Facebookii, 25, 43, 241–42
US Department of Agriculture, 49
US Department of Interior: Advisory Board on Wildlife Management in National Parks of, 97; Center for Biological Diversity and, 203; delisting rule and, 121; hunters and, 191; National Biological Survey by, 102
US Department of Justice, 194
US Fish and Wildlife Service (USFWS): Center for Biological

Diversity and, 203; Chris Servheen and, 12–14; critical habitat and, 129; delisting rules of, 203; grizzly delisting and, 176–77; grizzly recovery and, 122; lions and, 191; Wayne Slaght and, 53
US Fish and Wildlife Service Bear Recovery Coordinator, 51
US Forest Service (USFS): bicycle use and, 140; Leopold center and, 189; responsibilities of, 184
utilitarianism: wildlife management and, 80

value decisions: Stephen Kellert and, 79–84
van Manan, Frank, 162, 166
Varney, Joel, 94
Viral Hog, 38
Vital Ground, 43; road crossings and, 161
Voyage of Discovery. *See also* Lewis and Clark: as grizzly bear history, 45; open grassland and, 119

Waller, John, 29
Warren, Nancy, 163; Flathead Forest bear policy and, 163–64
Watson, James, 99–100
Wauer, Roland, 12
Weber, Chip: bear population and, 165; as Flathead National Forest Supervisor, 29; land use legislation and, 151; Servheen's report and, 137–38
Western Energy Alliance, 208
westward expansion, 48
wheels: regulation of in wilderness, 140–42
whitebark pine nuts, 122
Whitefish Ultra Marathon, 137–38
wilderness: definition of, 217
Wilderness Act of 1964, 9, 140, 205, 216
Wilderness Institute, University of Montana, 217

ABOUT THE AUTHOR

Photograph by Lisa Krantz

Robert Chaney grew up in western Montana and has spent most of his journalism career writing about the Rocky Mountain West, its people, and their environment. His reporting has also taken him from Jamaica and Brazil to Japan and Nepal. He studied political science at Macalester College and has won numerous awards for his writing and photography, including fellowships at the Nieman Foundation for Journalism at Harvard University and the National Evolutionary Science Center at Duke University.